DIGITAL PREPRESS *for* COMIC BOOKS

THE DEFINITIVE DESKTOP PRODUCTION GUIDE

by Kevin Tinsley

STICKMAN GRAPHICS, New York, NY

All brand names and product names used in this book are trademarks, registered trademarks, or trade names of their respective holders. In all instances where Stickman Graphics is aware of a claim, the product names appear in Initial Capital letters. Readers, however, should contact the appropriate companies for more complete information regarding trademarks and registration.

This publication is designed to provide accurate and authoritve information in regard to the subject matter covered. It is sold with the understanding that neither the publisher nor the author are engaged in rendering legal, accounting, or other professional services. If legal advice or other expert assistance is required, the services of a competent professional person should be sought. Every effort has been made to make this manual as complete and accurate as possible. However, there may be mistakes both typographical and in content. The author and publisher shall have neither liability nor responsibility to any person or entity with respect to any loss or damage caused, or alleged to be caused, directly or indirectly by the information contained in this book.

Copyright © 1999 by Kevin M. Tinsley. All Rights reserved. No part of this book may be reproduced by any means, electronic or mechanical, without written permission from the author, except for the inclusion of brief quotations in a review. Published by Stickman Graphics. Generic Comics, Wolf-Girl, Majestic Seven, and Homebrew (including all prominent characters featured in this book and the distinctive likenesses thereof) are trademarks of Stickman Graphics.

Published by: Stickman Graphics
141 16th Street
Brooklyn, NY 11215-5302
www.stickmangraphics.com
stickmangraphics@stickmangraphics.com

Library of Congress Card Number: 99-091203
Tinsley, Kevin
Digital prepress for comic books: the definitive production guide / by Kevin Tinsley
p. cm.
Includes glossary and index.
ISBN 0-9675423-0-8 (pbk.)
1. Desktop Publishing–Computer Publishing etc. I. Title.
2. Graphic Arts–comic books, cartoon illustration
3. Self-publishing– United States
4. Printing, Practical–Handbooks, manuals, etc.

Printed in the United States of America
10 9 8 7 6 5 4 3 2 1

CONTENTS

INTRODUCTION **9**

PREFACE **11**

CHAPTER 1
BEFORE YOU BEGIN **15**
*Formats•Binding Techniques•
Trapping•Trapping Guidelines •
Coordinate With Contractors•
Terminology•Page Diagram•
Dimensions•Cover Dimensions*

CHAPTER 2
SCANNING **27**
*Determining Resolution•
Variable Resolution• Line Screen•
Dot Gain• Scanning• Threshold•
Bit Depth•Scanning and Halftoning*

CHAPTER 3
PAGE SET UPS **39**
*Set Ups for Digital Lettering•
Quark Bleed Dimensions•
Proportion Constant•1/4 Resampling•
Set Ups for Color Separations•
Color Overlays and Hand Lettering•
Double-Page Spreads •Cutting Art in
Front of Balloons•Naming Conventions
and File Info*

CHAPTER 4
DIGITAL LETTERING **53**
*Resolution Free Vectors•
The Page Template•Font Creation•
Bounding Box•Lettering•Creating
Balloons•Balloon Shapes•
Sound Effects•Cutting Art in Front of
Lettering• Double-Page Spreads•
Pre-Flighting Documents•
Trapping in Illustrator*

CHAPTER 5
COLOR SEPARATIONS **77**
*CMYK vs. RGB• Monitor Colors and
Printing Codes •Channels and Layers•
K-Tones• Flesh Tones• Resampling•
Modeling and Gradations•
Secondary Light Source•
Conversions and Underprinting•
Adding Special Effects• Applying
Textures• More on Textures•
Lens Flare• Color Holds vs. Overlays•
Saving Formats• Photoshop & Memory*

CHAPTER 6
QUARK COMPOSITING **99**
*Quark Template •Assembling Pages •
Double-Page Spreads • Separate TIFF
Plates•Designing and Trapping•
Text Pages•Title Pages•Letter Pages*

CHAPTER 7
COVER LAYOUT & LOGO PREP 111
Logo Design• Digital Logos• Compound Paths•Tradedress• Creating the Quark Cover Template • Cover Template• Template with Spine• Layout• Simple Quark Covers • Gatefold Template•Simple Quark Cover• Clipping Paths •Clipping Path Do's and Dont's• Multiple Cover Art

CHAPTER 8
PHOTOSHOP COMPOSITING 127
Trapping Modes •Dropping in Illustrator Logos•Paste-Up and Trapping Logos in Photoshop• Black in Logos / Separate Black Plate • Colored Outlines Logos / Separate Black Plate•Combined Plates• K-Tones and Combined Plates• Special Effects

CHAPTER 9
SPECIALTY COVERS & COLOR CORRECTION 141
Fifth Colors•Choosing Pantone Colors• Foils and Die-Cuts •Embossing• Color Corrections•Scanning Color• Gamut Warning•Heavy Blacks

CHAPTER 10
FINAL WRAP UP 157
Legalese •Disk Copy •Printouts • Reports •Afterword

APPENDIX A
IMAGESETTING AND HALFTONES 163

APPENDIX B
TRAPPING 169
Trapping Colors • General Guidelines• Trapping in Illustrator•Digital Logos • Compound Paths •Gradation Traps• Trapping in Photoshop•CMYK vs. RGB• Conversions and Underprinting Trapping Modes •Dropping in Illustrator Logos •Paste-Up and Trapping Logos in Photoshop•Trapping in Quark

GLOSSARY 185

RESOURCES 196

INDEX 198

CONTRIBUTOR BIO's 201

Acknowledgements

This book is a compilation of knowledge and experience I've accumulated in over 15 years as a graphic artist. Many people have been helpful, and I hope that the many names that will go unmentioned will forgive the omission. First off, I would like to thank my family and friends for their support and encouragement. I would like to thank my editor, Deborah S. Creighton, who made a valiant effort to make me appear somewhat literate.

A special thanks to the Marvel Bullpen for their input and advice throughout the entire process of writing and designing this book. They include: Dan Carr production manager; Johnny Greene, assistant production manager; cover coordinators Thomas Velasquez, Tim Smith, and Lorretta Krohl; digital compositors Susan Crespi, Chris Giarrusso, Jerry Kalinowski, and Steve Bunche; letterers David Sharpe and Paul Tutrone; scan master Robbie Carosella; color guru George Roussos; my apologies to scanning technician Julio Herrera for my constant interruptions and abuse; and an extra special thanks to Flo Steinberg for proofreading above and beyond the call of duty. And lest I forget the Art Department: Michael Golden, Darren Auck, and the lone raider Scott 'Pondscum' Elmer.

Most importantly, let me thank the illustrious crew listed below, without whom this book would have never so good. Thanks to all.

Illustration Credits:

Homebrew
pencils by Timothy Smith III
inks by Scott Koblish

Majestic Seven
pencils by Fred Haynes
inks by Keith Williams

Wolf-Girl
pencils by Gregg Schigiel
inks by Scott Koblish

Lettering Layouts
pencils by Dave Sharpe
inks by Pondscum

Neon Shoulder
by Timothy Smith III

Lettering by Dave Sharpe
colors by stickman

Editor: Deborah S. Creighton

INTRODUCTION

Welcome to the digital age, where knowledge is power. And that is exactly what this book is: knowledge! The knowledge of experience and expertise.

Sure, there are plenty of books on how to draw comics, or how to ink comics. Dozens of books on anatomy and story telling. But none of these books will have been of any use if your art doesn't print well. This is the only book specifically designed to teach you the individualized knowledge you need to get your pages off of the drawing board and onto a computer disk.

Comics are a unique and specialized form of publishing that require unique and individual techniques during prepress production. And don't expect your printer to have all the answers. There are NO classes on this subject. But there is now a book devoted to just this area: ***Digital Prepress Production for Comic Books.***

This book can guide you over the unexpected problems and complications that arise when producing a comic. Learn what it takes to print your art at its best quality. Avoid the mistakes that even the major companies are still making, despite years of experience.

Technology has advanced so rapidly, that many of the techniques covered in this book are only known to a handful of individuals. Until now. This book will help you be two steps ahead of most working 'professionals' already making money in the field.

Today, with the help of computers, anyone can be a publisher, not just a select few conglomerates. This includes you, my friend.

ENERIC
COMICS
DEC '99
1

PREFACE

Art hath an enemy called Ignorance.
-John Donne, 1599

In the past few years, computers and desktop publishing technologies have brought about some of the most sweeping and profound changes to take place in the comic book industry in decades. These technologies have also brought along a great deal of confusion, misconceptions, and paranoia. Companies and creative artists alike have been faced with the very real possibilities of being unable to print their product, or obtain work, without shifting their production process from analog 'cut and paste' to digital 'drag and drop.'

This atmosphere has caused a mad dash to learn the latest tricks of the trade, and hop on the 'cool new special effect' bandwagon. Amidst all the rush, however, there has been a complete disregard for the basics of printing and publishing.

During the early '90s, Marvel Comics was informed that its printers and separators could no longer accept or handle jobs that were a combination of digital design elements (such as computer generated three-dimensional logos) and physical paste-up (such as photostats or overlays). This type of work included ALL of Marvels covers. The choice was clear, either the editors had to give up all their eye catching new logos, or the production department would have to computerize.

In 1994, I was shouldered with the responsibility of helping in this conversion process. I quickly learned how many computer 'experts' did not have a clue as to what was involved in producing, and more important, printing a comic magazine. I was forced into a position of not only learning the basics of desktop publishing, but in many cases, creating new techniques geared specifically towards comic books.

Now, that the conversion process at Marvel is complete, I find myself explaining the same basic principles over and over again. Principles that, despite the computer revolution, have not changed much over the last three to four decades. We still print ink on paper. If the computer artists truly want more control of the final outcome, then they need to take the responsibility, and the time, to do it right.

It basically comes down to 'all flash and no substance.' Anyone with enough RAM can make anything look great on a computer screen, but it takes a sound knowledge of the basics to make it look just as good coming off a four-color printing press. (And direct-to-press technology will not change that fact!)

Which brings us to the nature of this book. This book will ***not*** tell you how to create great art, but it will tell you how to get it off the drawing table and into the hands of a printer. This book will ***not*** teach you any snazzy new art techniques, but it may explain why some techniques reproduce better than others. This book will ***not*** teach you how to be a great designer, but it can prevent your designs from turning into mud on the press.

The writing of this book assumes a certain amount of knowledge about the computer programs and hardware involved in the production process. It is not intended to teach you how to use Quark Express or Photoshop. If you are not familiar with specific software, there are a multitude of books that cover each individual program in depth. Instead, this book covers the specific features and preferences of these programs that directly apply to the subject at hand.

This book is about basic production techniques, and more important, ***why*** you need to know the basics. It is about the essential technical details that must be taken into account in order to take your product to completion. The goal of this book is to teach you what you need to know to get your digital files to print correctly on a four-color press.

In this age of affordable, powerful personal computers, the phrase *'knowledge is power'* has never been more true. If you have a firm grasp of the basics and the ability to adapt and extrapolate, there is no one who will be able to stop you from accomplishing your goals.

ALL BLEED ART MUST EXTEND TO SOLID LINE
WOLF-GIRL
ILLUSTRATION QUALITY PAPER FOR NON-BLEED COMIC PAGES
PRINTS AT 60%
ALL BLEED ART MUST EXTEND TO SOLID LINE
KEEP ALL LETTERING INSIDE BROKEN-LINE BOX
ILLUSTRATION QUALITY PAPER FOR NON-BLEED COMIC PAGES
PRINTS AT 60%

OHHH! I JUST CAN'T GET A BREAK! IF IT'S NOT ONE THING IT'S ANOTHER.
IT'S A COMMON MISCONCEPTION THAT MOST TEENAGERS ARE OBLIVIOUS TO THEIR SURROUNDINGS.

OR THAT THEY DON'T CARE ABOUT THE PLIGHT OF OTHERS.
THEY ARE SELFISH, AND RUN AWAY FROM THEIR RESPONSIBILITIES.

THEIR ACTIONS AND MIS-ADVENTURES CAN DRIVE THEIR PARENTS AND TEACHERS UP A WALL!
QUITE LITERALLY, IN FACT.
THEY ALLEGEDLY HAVE NO INHIBITIONS.

MAD DOGS & Englishmen
TALKING TO SOME PARENTS...
...YOU WOULD EXPECT TO SEE MOST TEENAGERS RUNNING ACROSS THE ROOFTOPS...
...BAYING AT THE MOON.
LUCIENDA ISN'T MOST TEENAGERS.
WRITER- KEVIN TINSLEY
PENCILLER- GREGG SCHIGIEL
INKER- SCOTT KOBLISH
LETTERS- DAVE SHARPE
COLORS- STICKMAN
EDITOR- DEBORAH S CREIGHTON

CHAPTER 1 BEFORE YOU BEGIN

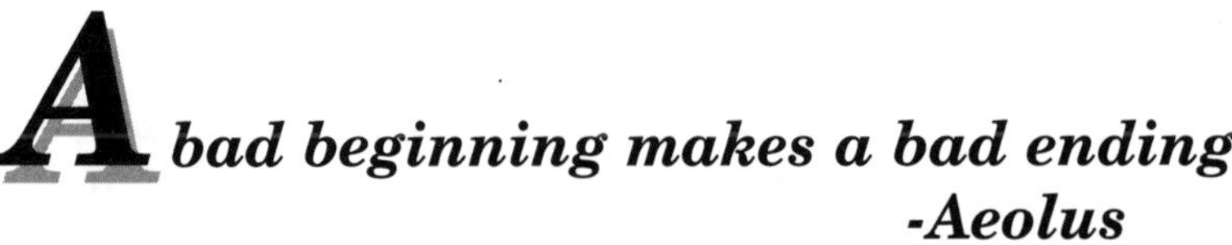

A bad beginning makes a bad ending.
-Aeolus

So, you want to be a comic book publisher? Well you are going to need more than good luck and a lot of talent. A plan is most definitely in order. If you sit down and start drawing and inking first, worrying about all the other details as they arise, you are asking for trouble with a capital **T**! Oddly enough, the best place to begin is at the end, or more precisely, the end product.

Generally, the most logical approach to any project of this type is to plan backwards. Before you ever put pen to paper, you need to have a good idea of what you want your book to look like after it has been printed. How a book is printed will affect how it should be drawn. Size, proportions, reduction ratio, and cropping must all be taken into account before hand. The original art must be the correct dimensions in relation to the final product.

This is why many major comic publishers have three or four standardized formats for their books. These companies will print art board to correspond to their formats, and try to insist that freelance artists use this preprinted stock when working on their books. A freelancer who uses another company's boards may be creating unforeseen headaches for the production department. An artist who mixes several types of board into one project is risking death–to his career.

Formats

The dimensions on most comics are roughly the same, about 6 ⅝" by 10" or 10 ⅛." Precise size varies from printer to printer, but the general size is fixed as an industry standard.

The most obvious format issue is black and white versus four-color. Black and white comics are less expensive to produce than color comics. A small print shop can print a one-color job just as easily as a large printing company. There are no registration problems to contend with, and you only have to pay for one specific ink.

However, with the advent of computer coloring, separating a comic can, theoretically, be brought in-house. Be forewarned: this prospect can be seductive and dangerous. Computer coloring is both tedious and time consuming. The availability of this technology can be advantageous, even if an outside separator is used.

In the past, there were only a few companies that separated color comics. They normally charged by the hour or by the page, and there was a set cost no matter which company did the work. Now there are many small computer coloring studios popping up all over the country. All though they are far from being inexpensive, you are afforded the luxury of shopping around. Other advantages may include that they will be willing to work for one fixed price to color an entire book, as opposed to an hourly rate. Also, many of these studios act as colorist for the books they separate. So not only do you get one price for two jobs, but invariably you get better quality work because their names are going in the credits next to yours.

Next on our format list is how the book is bound. The vast majority of comics are ***saddle-stitched***. Saddle-stitched binding involves inserting folded impositions, or signatures, inside one another to form a common spine. They are then 'stitched' together with metal staples.

More expensive books may be ***perfect bound*** with a spine. Perfect binding involves gathering signatures together in a stack. The back of the signatures are ground to create a rough surface end then glued to the spine of the cover. This requires additional cost for a heavier stock of paper on the cover. Do not assume any single printer is able to do one or the other–or even both–of these binding techniques. You should always talk to your printer to find out what they can or can not do.

Binding Techniques

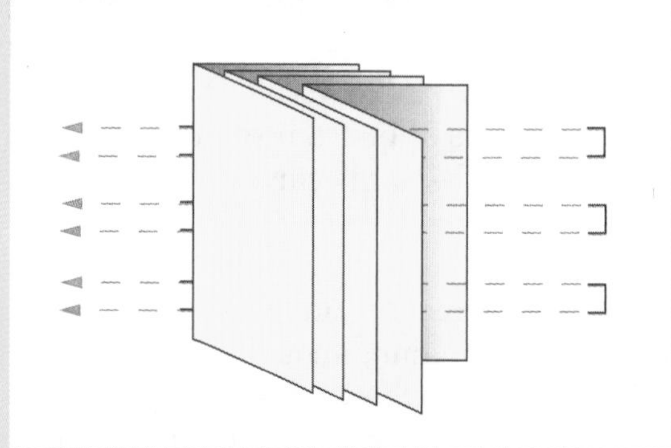

figure 1-01: saddle-stitched binding

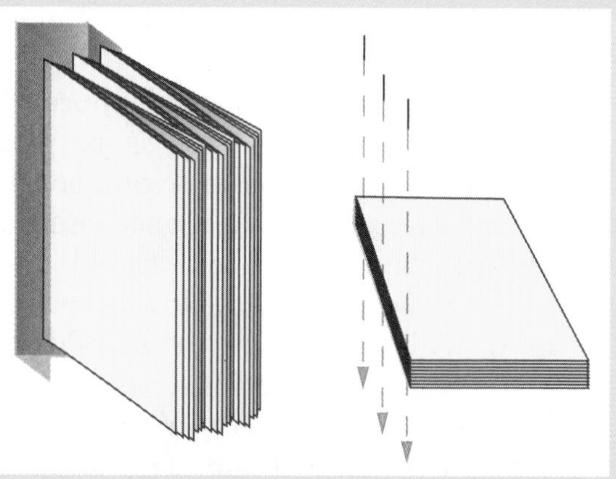

figure 1-02: perfect binding

figure 1-03: Examples of penciled pages on pre-printed non-bleed and bleed boards. Note that this example of non-bleed art is reduced 40% (prints at 60%), whereas the bleed art is reduced 31% (prints at 69%), requiring a different scale of drawing.

The final format issue is not only the most overlooked, but also has the most impact on the size and proportions of the original art. Will the artwork bleed off the edge of the page? A bleed book allows art to be printed beyond where the comic trims. In a non bleed book the art is constrained to the center of the page by a white gutter. Bleed books use more paper, and therefore cost more money. Non-bleed books use less paper, because they can be butted closer together on a single printing plate.

Once the final product is clearly visualized, prioritize which aspects of the format are most important. This will allow for the opportunity to compromise later if prices dictate. You do not want to appear inflexible when dealing with printers, but you must be happy with the final product or it will not be worth the effort. It is never too early to begin speaking with any printers, separators, and service bureaus that may be used, for there are a great many details to work out before the process can begin.

Trapping

Trapping is the intentional overlapping of colors along common boundaries to prevent unprinted paper from showing in the event of misregistration during the printing process. As paper runs through a printing press at high speed, a certain amount of shifting occurs from page to page. Slivers of white paper sandwiched between two colored inks are particularly distracting to the human eye. Therefore trapping strives to prevent this from occurring.

The following terms are used in relation to trapping:

choke: creating a trap using the background color.

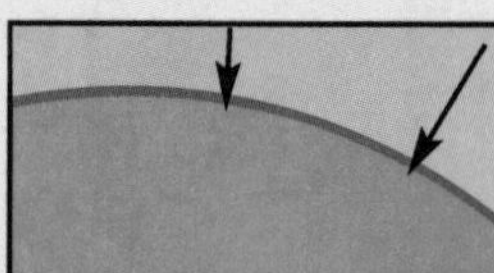

spread: creating a trap using the color of the object in the foreground.

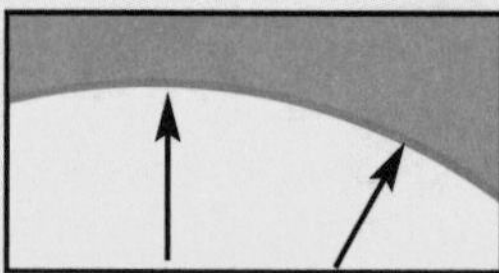

overprint: When colors or inks are printed one on top of another. For instance magenta overprints blue to create purple.

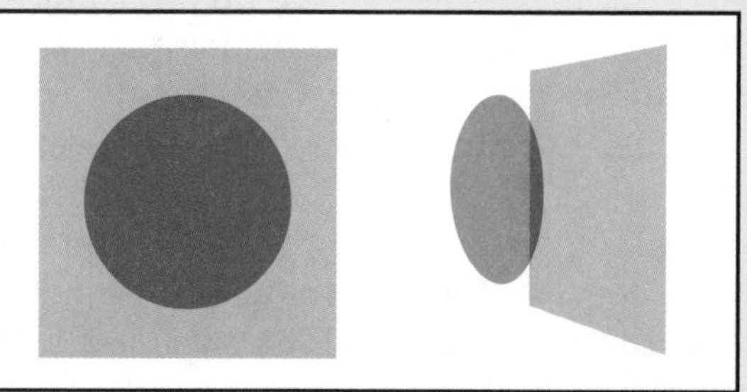

knockout: The opposite of overprint, knockouts create a hole in background colors to accommodate objects or colors in the foreground. Unless properly trapped, knockouts will create a 'kiss-fit' where two colors butt together without overlapping.

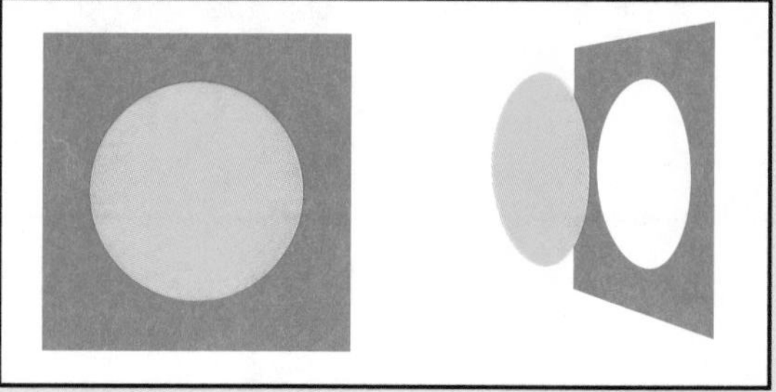

path: In Adobe Illustrator, it is the vector lines that defines the shape of an entire object and falls exactly in the center of a stroke.

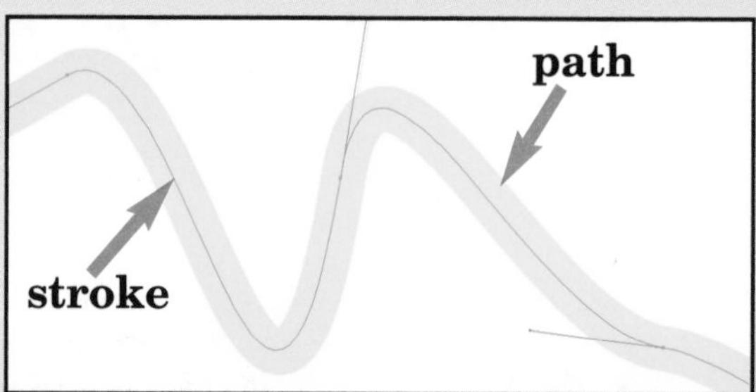

stroke: In Illustrator, it is a colored line that can be created on top of a path that can be used to trap an object.

General Guidelines to trapping colors:

Rule #1: In general always use the lighter of two colors as a trap. If there is a question as to which color is lighter use the following steps:

1) Determine the RGB values of the colors in question.

2) Use the following formula: (30% x R)+(59% x G)+(11% x B)

3) The higher the outcome the lighter the color.

If the colors in question are both dark or the combination of both colors will create a noticeable third color or a distracting trap, then you may wish to trap with tints of one or both colors. However, never set any CMYK values in a trap color to less than 15%, the Postscript language will knockout any value less than 15%.

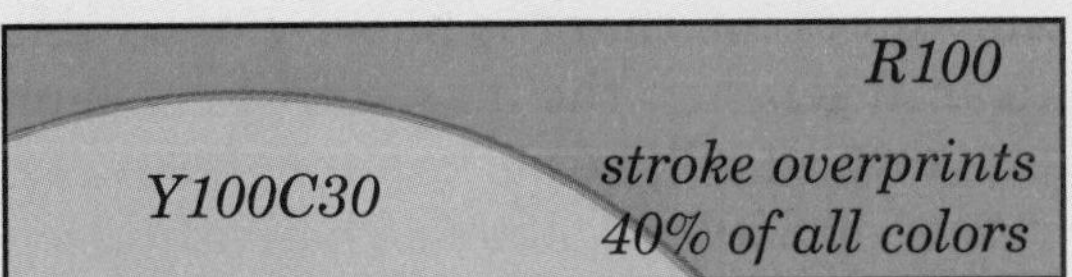

Rule #2: You do not have to trap colors that trap naturally. Objects that have at least one color in common will not leave any paper unprinted if the plates are misregistered. Examples are: green object on yellow background or yellow on red.

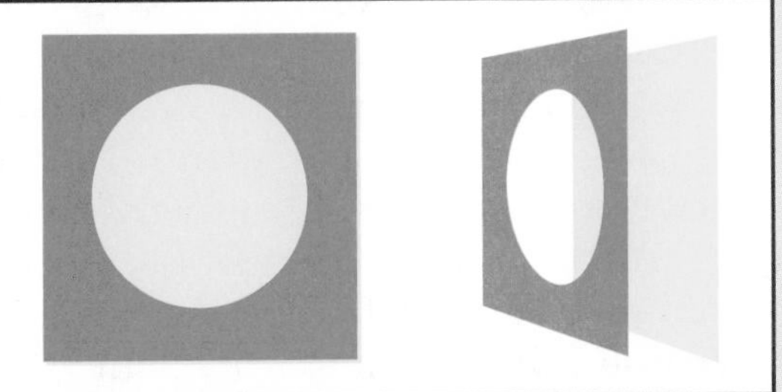

Rule #3: Illustrator documents must be trapped to the Photoshop and Quark documents that they are placed upon. This is done with the use of an overprinting stroke.

Rule #4: All Illustrator documents must be brought into Quark at 100%. Scaling Illustrator documents in Quark will scale the size of the trap as well, and this is incorrect.

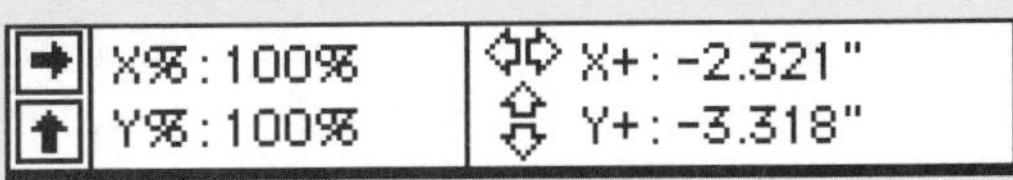

Rule #5: A Quark document can be corrupted or damaged if trapped wrong. If Quark tells you that a document is damaged when you try to open or save it, this is what you should look for in the trapping palette (in order of likely cause):

a) Items labeled MULTIPLE: change them to a single setting where applicable.

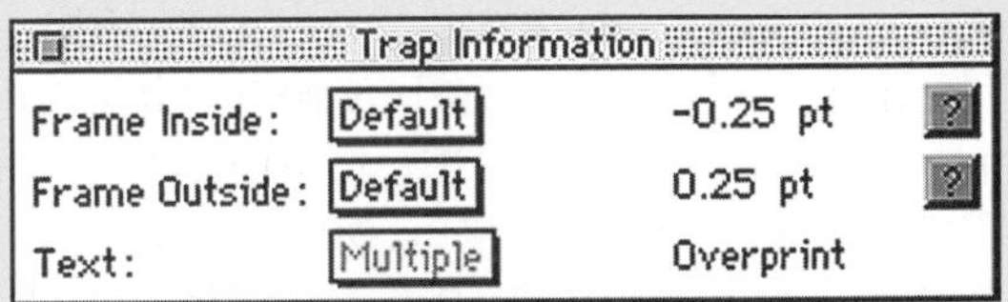

b) Items labeled DEFAULT: change them to an applicable single setting. Default settings can vary from computer to computer, therefore it is incorrect to leave an item at default.

Color files must be trapped in their program of origan, where as, bitmap files will be trapped in Quark. As a result trapping a job containing multiple files may appear more difficult than it actually is in reality. Since each software program traps differently, more specific instructions will be covered in later chapters.

An example of an untrapped misregistered Photoshop file.

Coordinate With Contractors

The first issue will be price. How much will it cost to print the book? How much lead time will the printer need to schedule the book? What kind of paper will be used? Always have the printer supply the paper. Printers can usually get a discount on paper because they can buy it in bulk. Also, if something is wrong with the paper that causes printing errors, it is the printers' problem to fix. You do not want to eat the cost of a bad print run.

After cost has been worked out, you need to determine how the work will be supplied to the printer. Generally, the three choices are disk, boards, or film. The best solution is to have the printer produce the film, so that adjustments that need to be made can be done at any stage in the printing process with minimal delays.

Most printers are capable of outputting their own film from computer files supplied on disk. If they cannot, arrangements will have to be made with the separator or with a service bureau. It is important to find out from the printer what film format (one-up, two-up, or four-up) is required before the film is output.

When supplying computer disks to the film outputter–whether that is the printer or a service bureau–make sure that all files are present and that the software and hardware used on the project are compatible with the contractors. Find out in what format your computer files need to be supplied (file formats will be discussed in later chapters).

There are certain factors that only the printer can determine which are crucial to you and the separators. The ***line screen***, sometimes referred to as ***screen frequencies***, that the job will print at, is crucial for making accurate scans of artwork. You cannot determine the resolution of your scans until you know the lines per inch at which the job will print.Screen frequencies for comics vary from 85 lpi to 133 lpi depending on paper quality and dot gain–how much the ink spreads when it is absorbed by the paper.

Ink saturation is another factor when printing in color. This is the amount of ink that the paper will be able to absorb before the inks start to pick up or smear. It will be a percent value in the range of 230% to 300%. The saturation level needs to be passed along to the separators to insure that they do not accidentally over saturate the coloring. Keep in mind that if a different stock of paper is used for the covers, there may be a different set of values for both ink saturation and screen frequency.

One of the most important issues that needs to be worked out with the contractors is: *who will be responsible for trapping color files*. This should be a key issue in discussions with ALL contractors, and who will be responsible for the trapping what, should be clearly resolved beforehand. (Trapping will be discussed in depth throughout this entire book.)

Finally, exact specifications for the dimensions of the printed page will be needed. This not only includes the size of the magazine itself, but also bleed allowances and safe copy areas. You will need these measurements to determine the final proportions of your original art.

The basic idea here is to open lines of

communication between yourself and the contractors early in the process. Treat these people as partners in this project and listen to their advice. Understand that this job cannot be complete without them,so iron out who is responsible for what, and what to expect from each other. If this simple advice is followed, you will avoid many unforeseen problems.

Terminology

Now that the specifications have been worked out with the printers, it is time to rule out art boards. The size of the original art is usually 143% of print size for non-bleed books, and 145% for bleed books. This is the largest size the art can be and fit on an 11" x 17" board, and include an outside gutter.

The art boards printed by comic companies contain guides for bleeds, trims, safe copy areas, and gutters. A light cyan ink is used because its value is somewhat lighter than the average pencil lead. Therefore, the guides are less likely to show up during scanning. The cost of printing boards should be worth the time it saves ruling individual boards, and will prevent inconsistent image sizes and proportions.

Also, the following terms must be understood before we continue:

art size: The size and dimensions of the original hand drawn artwork.

bleed: The area on the outside of a page that will be cut off when the final comic book is cut down to size. In a bleed comic, art is drawn into this area and 'lost' so that the printed art will extend beyond the trim. Non-bleed art also have a bleed, but no art is allowed to be drawn in this area so that pages can be butted closer together on the printing plates.

gatefold: Additional paper added to a page, usually a cover, which folds out from the book.

gutter: The space left between panel boarders, which, in non bleed books includes the outside white area between the art and the trim.

print size: The size and dimensions of the printed magazine. Examples in this book will be using standard measurements for an 6 5/8" x 10" comic book, with a 3/8" bleed at print size.

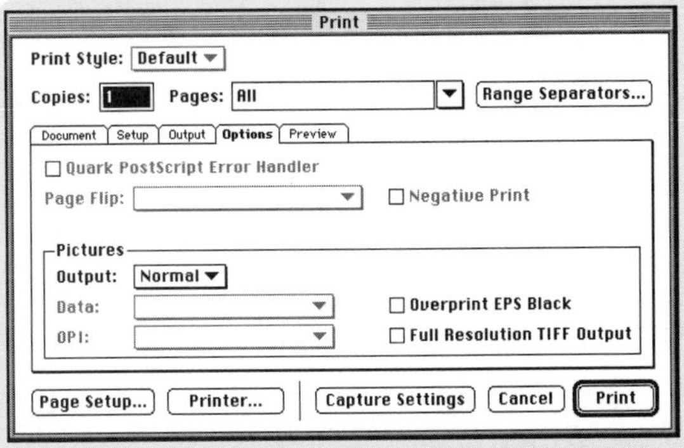

figure 1-05: A recent addition to the list of printing discussions is the print options for Quark 4. Many people are unaware that the new version of Quark will–by default–resample TIFF files in relation to the outputting device it is printing to. This is a bad idea for line art such as comics. The 'Full Resolution TIFF Output' box should be checked. If digital lettering or clipping paths are being used, 'Overprint EPS Black' should also be checked. Since this is a printing preference, it can not be saved with the file, and must be set by the imagesetter before he outputs film.

proportion constant: Documents created by different software applications must be created with identical dimensions in order to properly align when printed. This size is determined by the trim for non-bleed books, and the bleed for bleed books and covers. This proportion constant is used to create all templates, and to set-up all Photoshop documents.

safe area: Also called **safe copy area**. Since there is a certain amount of movement on the printing press, binders, and cutters the exact location were each individual comic will trim varies slightly. The area of the page in which the cutter will *never* intrude upon is called the safe area. It is important that you keep all copy and word balloons inside this area so they don't accidentally trim off.

trim: The 'line' where a comic will be cut when printed. Any art that goes outside this line will 'bleed' off the page.

Page Diagram

TRIM LINE

This line indicates where the comic should be cut when printed.

SAFE COPY AREA

The area within the inside dotted line is known as the safe area. Any copy or art that falls outside of this area runs the risk of being trimmed.

BLEED

The area of the page that falls between the trim and the outside border of the art. This area will be cut off when the comic is printed.

GUTTER

The negative space left between panel boarders, which may includes the outside white area between the art and the trim.

INDICIA GUIDES

This board has pre-printed guides for the indicia area. The indicia is a legal statement of ownership which appears within the first five pages of a magazine.

CROP MARKS

Production marks used to indicate trims, folds, and safe copy area.

Dimensions

The following charts give the dimensions for art and print size pages for a 6 5/8" x 10" magazine. Measurements are listed in picas and inches. Fractions are given at art size for ruler measurements. Decimals are given at print size for computer files.

Bleed Book	Art Size (inches)	Art Size (picas)	Print Size (inches)	Print Size (picas)
Dimensions	10 1/8 x 15	60.75p x 90p	7 x 10.375	42p x 62.25p
Trim Boundaries	9 37/64 x 14 15/32	57.5p x 86.83p	6.625 x 10	39.75p x 60p
Bleed Allowance	1/4	1.5p	.1875 (3/16)	1.17p
Safe Area	9 x 13 27/32	54p x 83p	6.1875 x 9.5625	37.17p x 57.42p

Non-Bleed Book	Art Size (inches)	Art Size (picas)	Print Size (inches)	Print Size (picas)
Dimensions	10 x 15 29/64	60p x 92.75p	6.1875 x 9.5625	37.17p x 57.42p
Trim Boundaries	n/a	n/a	6.625 x 10	39.75p x 60p
Bleed Area	n/a	n/a	7 x 10.375	42p x 62.25p
Safe Area	10 x 15 29/64	60p x 92.75p	6.1875 x 9.5625	37.17p x 57.42p

Note that the dimensions of non-bleed art correspond exactly with the safe copy area. Also, it is fairly safe to break an outside panel border on a non-bleed book by about 1/4" at art size without it interfering with the bleed area. But remember that this is beyond the safe area, and may interfere with later attempts to center the art within a document.

Interior gutters, those that fall inside the safe area, on both bleed and non-bleed pages are usually 1/4" at art size and 3/16" at print.

Double-page spreads need to be scanned in two separate halves to accommodate an 11" x 17" scanner. To create art that will fit into a single scan will require smaller dimensions. However, this not only requires drawing smaller, but also calculating a different scanning resolution. Dimensions for double-page spreads are as follows:

Double-Page Spread	Art Size (inches)	Art Size (picas)	Print Size (inches)	Print Size (picas)
Double-Scan Bleed	19 3/4 x 11	118.5p x 90p	13.625 x 10.375	81.76p x 62.25p
Double-Scan Non-Bleed	20 7/8 x 15 29/64	125.22p x 92.75p	12.922 x 9.5625	77.51p x 57.42p
	Maximum Art Size		Minimum Art Size	
Single-Scan Bleed	15 x 11 27/64	90p x 68.64p	13 5/8 x 10 3/8	81.76p x 62.25p
Single-Scan Non-Bleed	15 x 11 7/64	90p x 66.64p	12 59/64 x 9 9/16	77.51p x 57.42p

It is important to note that the widths for the double-page spreads do not exactly double. Bleed books are slightly less than double because you want the art to butt at the fold, therefore eliminating the center bleed on both pages. The butting effect is also true for non-bleed books, however, you are extending art beyond the safe area to reach the fold line.

Cover Dimensions

All covers are considered bleed. The width of a gatefold cover is 18 9/16" at art size. This will accommodate a fold inside the trim area, and for the gatefold itself tucking neatly inside the cover without interfering with the interior fold. Gatefolds will be covered more in depth later in this book.

Remember, all of the measurements given here are examples based on a 6 5/8" x 10" comic book. The dimensions that you use should be based on the specifications worked out with the printer. Once you have those specifications, it would be a good idea to rule out an art size template and start drawing.

figure 1-07: To create a double-page spread with bleed art board, cut the boards at the center trim lines, and tape the back of the boards together. The bleed must be eliminated so that the art will butt properly at the fold line.

Note how much smaller the bleed spread is compared to the non-bleed at art size proportions.

figure 1-08: For non-bleed boards, no cutting is required. Simply butt two boards together, and tape them together along the back. This is necessary in order to create the additional art necessary to butt properly at the fold line.

figure 1-09: To create a wrap-around cover, cut the art boards at the center trim lines, as would be done with interior bleed pages.

To create a gatefold cover, cut the left art board at the center (right-hand) **copy** *line, and cut the right art board at the left-hand trim line. The right-hand copy line becomes the trim and the trim becomes the outside bleed boundary.*

The front cover of a gatefold is smaller than the back cover, and the gatefold itself is smaller than the front cover. This allows the gatefold to fit snugly inside the front cover and not interfere with the interior fold. Furthermore, the folded covers need to fall inside the safe area so that the exterior fold is not cut off when the magazine is trimmed.

CHAPTER 2
SCANNING

For many men that stumble at the threshold
Are well foretold that danger lurks within.
King Henry the Sixth, Part I
William Shakespeare, 1591

Perhaps the most important task in the production process of any line art for print is the art of scanning. A bad scan can adversely affect every aspect of the job that follows, and the only correction is usually to start over from scratch. A scanner is an extremely precise reproduction tool; but beware, that same precision can prove to be a double edged sword.

Before scanning can even begin, it is imperative that you know not only how the book will be printed, but also what production steps will be taken to get to print. This is especially true when creating a four-color comic. How a book is separated can determine the single most important issue when scanning: ***resolution***.

Resolution is one of the most confusing and misused word in desktop publishing. The word has different meanings in different areas of the prepress industry. It can mean something entirely different when discussing computers. When these two fields are combined, which is the case with this book, the confusion increases exponentially!

For the sake of expedience–and the sanity of all–this book will not focus on the more obscure aspects of resolution, such as bit depth, unless to point out where they can be misleading, such as monitor resolutions. Instead we will focus on the two most important areas of resolution to publishing. These are ***image size*** and ***film output***.

Film output is the *fixed* resolution of the imagesetter used to output the film used to create printing plates. Knowing the imagesetter's resolution is key to determining ***line screen***, or **LPI** (lines per inch). The line screen is used to define both the halftone **DPI** 'resolution' (dots per inch), and the appropriate scanning (image size) resolution.

Image size is the *variable* resolution most closely associated with computer files, and is defined as pixels per inch or **PPI**. This is often inaccurately referred to as dpi. The two, although related, are quite different. This difference is discussed in depth in Appendix A.

The resolution associated with image size is variable because it is dependent on the proportions of the image as well as the number of pixels in the image. Therefore, a stated resolution of 300 ppi is meaningless unless associated with a height and width proportion. The proportions of the pixels can change with the proportions of the art without losing data. In other words, a scanned image with a resolution of 300 ppi at 10.375" x 15.75", is identical to the same scan at 445 ppi at 7" x 10.375". To determine this relationship, the following formula applies:

(print size/art size) x resolution @ print size = resolution @ art size

Unfortunately, this does not answer the question of what is the proper resolution to use at print size.

Determining Resolution

If you ask most printers what resolution to use the standard response will be: twice the line screen of the imagesetter. This formula will give a final resolution of 266 ppi for a line screen of 133 lpi.

On the other hand, most computer experts, including both Adobe and Agfa, will recommend half the resolution (dpi) of the output device, up to 1200 ppi. Imagesetters today range from 1800 dpi

Variable Resolution

figure 2-01: The resolution of a scan includes height, width, and pixels per inch. Scans A and B below are the same dimensions but have different pixel resolutions. However, B and C are identical scans despite being different sizes, because their height/width/ppi ratio is the same.

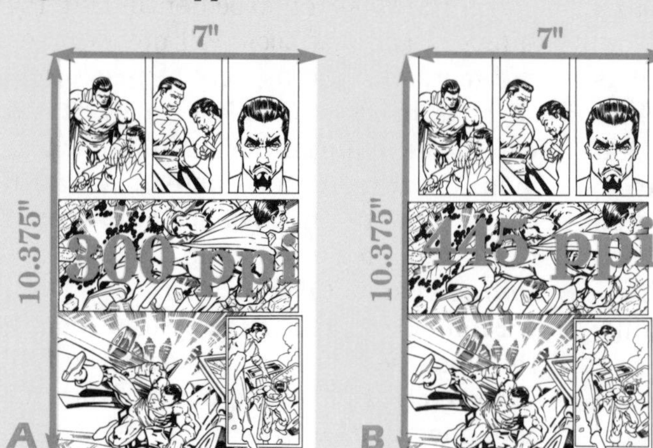

Dot Gain

figure 2-02: Dot gain occurs when the spots of ink that make up a color linescreen spread upon contact with the paper. A 20% dot gain means that a 50% linescreen will reproduce as 70%. Dot gain effects mid-tone values more than lighter or darker tones and can be plotted on a graph similar to the one below. Therefore, both 25% and 75% will only increase by about 15%.

50% dots (left) spread to 70% (right)

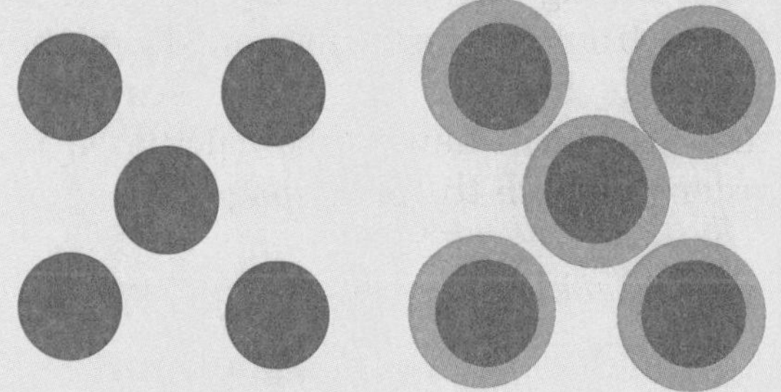

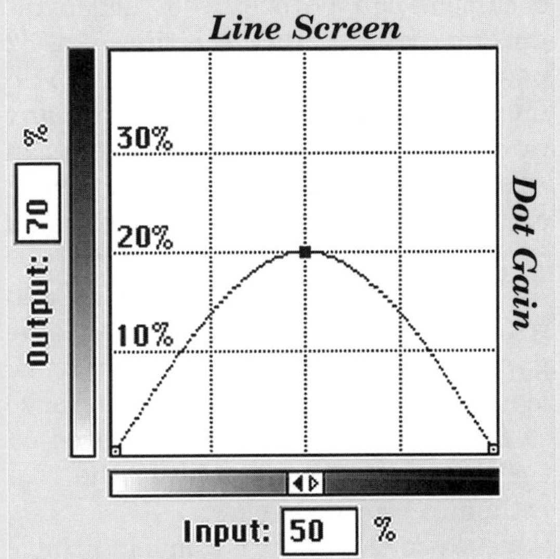

to 2400 dpi, which suggests a printing resolution between 900 ppi to 1200 ppi. That is a far cry from the printers recommendation of a 266 ppi maximum.

Both of the recommendations are invaluable, and should be committed to memory by any publishing professional. Unfortunately, they are also both inappropriate for the task at hand. Namely producing a comic book.

The printers '2 x line screen' calculation is an important rule of thumb to remember if you are printing photographs. Printing photos at a high resolution can adversely affect the quality of the image. The opposite is true when dealing with line art. As a general rule of thumb, the lowest resolution recommendation for art is 400 ppi, although some comic companies do go as low as 300 ppi.

On the other hand, the computer experts' '½ dpi' recommendation can be overkill. More is not necessarily better. Usually they are not considering paper quality or the memory requirements of color separated documents.

The interior pages of a comic are usually printed on relatively cheap quality paper, just a few steps up from newsprint. This type of paper is more absorbent than higher quality paper, causing the ink to spread a small amount. This is called ***dot gain***, and is not as bad as it may sound. In fact, *all paper* experiences some amount of dot gain, and it is normally only a small concern. However, at some point dot gain will obliterate any noticeable difference between resolutions higher than 600 or 700 ppi for black and white printing, and even less for four-color printing.

Another consideration, especial for four-color work, is the amount of memory space high resolution documents use. Black and white bitmap art take up very little space, no matter how high the resolution. On the other hand, a single 700 ppi color document can be over 100 megabytes uncompressed. Imagesetting 22-32 pages at this resolution could tie up an imagesetter for far longer than any printer is willing to invest. And you can rest assured you will be charged accordingly. This is far more grief than a negligible quality increase is worth.

Unless, you are printing black and white on high-quality art magazine paper stock, there is no reason to go overboard with resolution. You will have to make an educated decision based on the material on hand, and on the best estimates provided below.

Based on the average comic in print:

•Black and white art printed on interior paper stock: no higher than 600-700 ppi

•Black and white art printed on cover (glossy) stock: 700–800 ppi

•Four-color line art printed on interior paper stock: no lower than 300; recommend between 400-500 ppi

•Four-color line art printed on cover (glossy) stock: no lower than 400; recommend between 400–520 ppi

The estimates for the four-color line art listed above are assuming the black line art is an integral part of the color document. In later chapters using lower resolution color files with a separate high resolution black line plate will be discussed.

Scanning

The key to an efficient production work flow is consistency. When scanning a series of pages over several different days this becomes all the more important.

The scanner technician attempts to place each page in the same position on the scanner bed, squaring up each page in a corner using the small lip surrounding the glass. Any page that varies from the rest will slow down the process, because a new scanning resolution will have to be calculated in order to match the other pages.

figure 2-03: Most scanners have a small lip around the glass that can be used to square off pages when scanning.

This is the main reason why major companies print their own art board, and why they complain so bitterly when freelancers use the wrong paper. Another complaint often raised is mixing bleed and non-bleed boards on the same project. If a project utilizes this combination, separate the pages by type, and scan them at their proper resolution.

As an example, assume a resolution of 584 ppi at print size. The scanning resolution at art size for a bleed page would be 392 ppi, and 352 ppi for a non-bleed page.

Scanning double-page spreads (art that prints on two facing pages of the magazine) can also present problems. Since the largest flatbed scanners can only accommodate an 11" x 17" work area, the art will have to be scanned in sections or drawn to scale. When scanning in sections, it is advisable to include art that 'overlaps' on both scans. This will allow for more precise alignment during set ups.

Drawing to scale requires a recalculation of scanning resolutions, so be consistent if multiple spreads are necessary. The problem that arises with this method is that there will be a noticeable difference in line quality between the scaled spread and the individual pages drawn at normal art size. Reproducing ink lines at 64%-67% of their original size makes them appear cleaner or crisp. The art that is drawn to scale loses this advantage, and may appear sloppy or rushed. This difference is especially noticeable in a book where some pages are drawn full size, and others are drawn to scale. This being the case, it is usually preferable to have spreads drawn at full art size and scanned in sections.

figure 2-04: Note how reducing a scan by 50% can have an effect on fine line work and hatching.

Threshold

All scanners come with their own unique software, which is usually in compatible with any other type of scanner. It would be impossible to cover all the different varieties of software, but they all have the same basic features. Occasionally, some software will use different terminology for these features, but they should still function the same.

The most important feature when scanning line art is ***threshold***. When scanning in bitmap mode, each individual pixel will either be 100% black or 100% white. When the scanner encounters a pixel area that is either gray or is partially divided into black and white, it must decide if that pixel will be 100% black or 100% white. The scanner will rely on the threshold preference to make this decision.

The scanning technician can alter the threshold preference for each scan. This preference is usually given as a percentage scale (occasionally it may be given as a value between 1 and 256 shades of gray). If the tech sets the threshold at 60%–or the equivalent value of 154 out of 256–any pixel that has 60% or more of its area covered by black (or is a 60% shade of gray, like a pencil line) will become 100% black. Conversely, any pixel that has 59% or less of its area covered by black–or is a 59% shade of gray–will be 100% white.

The result of changing the threshold on a scan is to alter the thickness of the

figure 2-05: The examples above demonstrate the effect that threshold can have upon a scan. Too high a threshold can cause hatching to close up and may pick up pencil lines (top). Too low and fine lines may start to break up (middle). A good medium value must be found to maintain line quality (bottom).

black lines that are present. Too high a threshold can cause hatching to close up; too low can cause thin lines to break up or disappear. This may be particularly obvious on hand lettering. However, if the original art contains lines which are broken up, incomplete, or gray (including pencil lines), ***NO*** threshold will make them complete.

Keeping this in mind, it is important to remember to erase pencil lines from original art. Scanning art that has not been thoroughly erased can be extremely difficult. Setting a threshold that will eliminate gray pencil while maintaining fine ink lines is nearly impossible. Pencil lines will also contribute to the number of artifacts, or black dots, that need to be erased during the set up process.

Using non-reproductive blue pencils will not solve this problem. Traditionally, these pencils were used because stat cameras, used to create film before scanners came along, would not reproduce the blue color. Scanners operate under different scientific principles, and will pick up blue pencils just as easily as gray. Also keep in mind, non-repro lead contains a fair amount of wax. This may result in a drawing that will resist water based ink, and is far more difficult to erase.

Of equal importance is the use of black ink. That may sound obvious, but look carefully at the inked page *after* it has been erased. Some erasers can pick up a small amount of ink, turning areas of black into areas of gray. Also, some artists water down their ink, or use magic markers that do not give an even tone of black. This can create a mottled, damaged look to the art.

Pay careful attention to fine thin lines. Mechanical pens are notorious for skipping, or creating a dotted, incomplete line. The finer the line, the more likely the human eye will 'connect the dots,' especially if the skipped ink line is on top of a pencil line. The human eye may connect the dots, but a scanner will not; resulting in broken, jagged lines. This problem will be accentuated if the lines are diagonal, creating a 'stair step' look. Add gray ink into the equation, and you have ***big*** problems.

Bit Depth

A **bitmap** is a grid upon which the location of individual pixels are mapped. Pixels have two attributes: size and depth. The size is the actual height and width of the square shaped pixel. The depth is measured in bits.

A **bit** is the smallest form of computer information, a binary number. A bit can only be one of two things. It can either be a 1 or a 0, on or off, black or white, yes or no. Generally, the term bitmap refers to an image that contains one bit of information per pixel. The pixels in such an image are either black (1) or white (0), with no possible shades of gray.

However, pixels can be assigned more than one bit of information. The number of bits assigned to pixels is referred to as bit depth. A one-bit image is the bitmap referred to in the preceding paragraph. A two-bit image will have pixels that can be black, white, plus two additional shades of gray, because there are now four possible binary combinations: 00, 01,10, and 11. With each additional bit of information, the number of binary combinations increase exponentially.

An 8-bit image will create 256 (that is 2^8) shades of gray, including black and white. This type of image is usually referred to as a gray scale document, because the 256 shades can create a gradation from white to black without a noticeable jump in between gray scale values.

RGB color has a bit depth of 24-bits per pixel, and can create over 16 million possible colors (2^{24}). These colors are created using three 8-bit channels, one each for red, green, and blue. CMYK is a 32-bit color space, having four channels of 8-bit each. Although the computer generated CMYK color space has billions of colors in theory, in actuality it has far less colors than RGB.

There are two reasons for this. The first is that computer monitors display colors in RGB, and are limited to the 16 million colors (if there is enough memory) generated by this color space. The second reason is that the CMYK color space simulates the four-color inks in the printing process. These inks are combinations of pigments that contain impurities. The combinations of these inks will generate a limited number of colors and values.

Certainly, bit depth is not limited to these combinations. Many scanners are capable of producing up to 16-bits per channel. Although rarely used, this super sampling can be quite useful for drawing out detail in extremely light or dark images.

Also, the information carried in the bit depth of a channel can be redefined. The **HSL** color space has three 8-bit channels of information. One channel defines all the hues or colors present, the second defines the saturation or intensity of the colors, and the last contains the tonal values or lightness of the colors. **LAB** color space has two channels that define colors and one that defines tonal value.

However, as bit depth increases, so does file size. An 8 bit image uses eight times the memory as a similar 1-bit image. A 24-bit image is 24 times larger and so on. When working in Photoshop, adding a channel mask increases the file size by eight bits per pixel. Adding a layer in CMYK is in actuality adding an additional 32 bits of information per pixel.

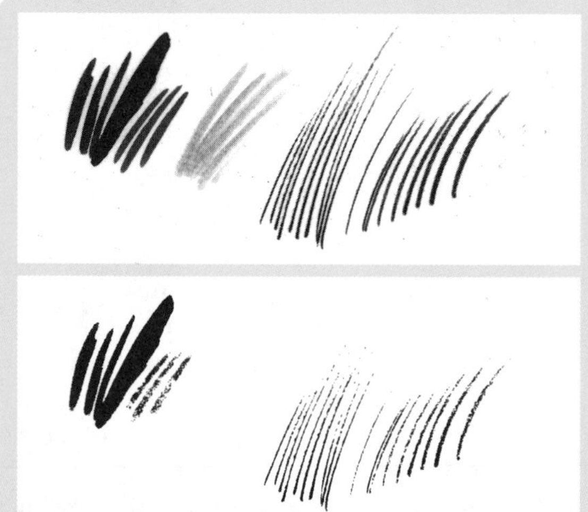

figure 2-06: The examples above demonstrate how grey ink and broken lines (top) will reproduced when scanned as bitmap line art (bottom). Increasing the threshold will may not improve the quality, but could make it far worse.

Scanning and Halftoning Gray Scale

Scanning artwork that is intended to reproduce as gray, such as pencil drawings and ink washes, tends to be easier than one would expect–although it may take three to four times longer for the scanner to complete the task. The information needed from the printer are the following: imagesetter dpi resolution and line screen, screen angle of black plate, and the estimated dot gain.

Gray scale images take up approximately eight times more storage space than bitmap images. Ultimately, imagesetter software converts the various shades of gray into screens of various sized black dots which gives the illusion of being gray. This is called a ***halftone***, and is a task that can be completed long before the image ever reaches the imagesetter. This will save on storage space and speed up processing time.

Threshold is replaced by selecting white points and black points (also called ***dmin*** and ***dmax*** by some software). For each individual scan, the scanner technician selects a point on the image that will be 100% white or the lightest shade of gray in some cases. The process is repeated for the darkest shade of gray or black. The software then calculates the various shades of gray using these two points as a guide.

The initial gray scale scan may be a little dark, but this may be advantageous when correcting values. Bring the scanned image down to print size before making any corrections. The original art should be on hand when making corrections, and you should predetermine areas that you want to print at 25%, 50%, 75%, and 100% black. At this point, you may have to take dot gain into account when making these determinations.

Most printers may give a better estimate for dot gain for fear of looking

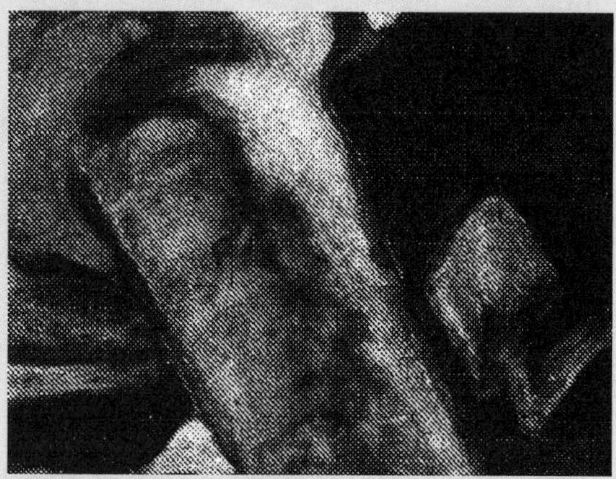

figure 2-07: A detail of how a halftone breaks up shades of grey into a line screen of black and white dots.

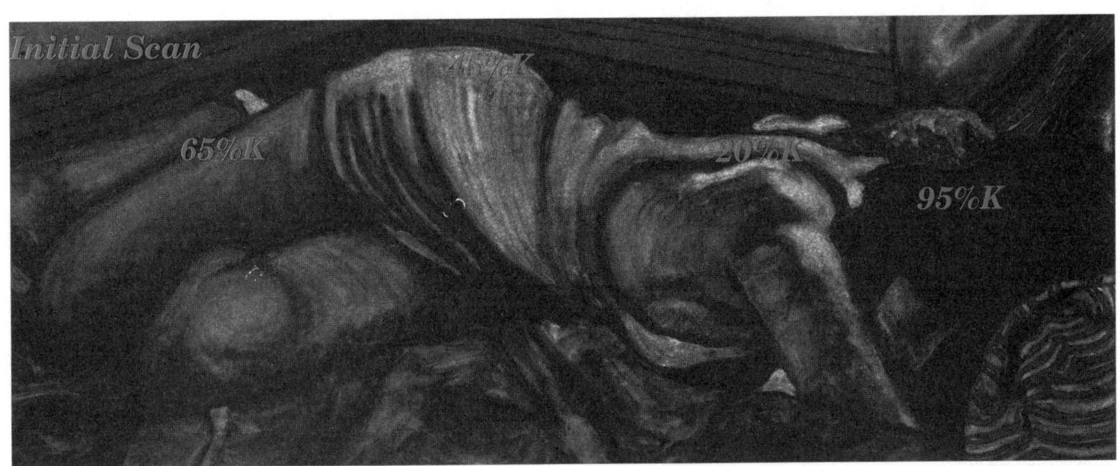

inferior to their competition. In fact, dot gain happens to be a fact of life that printers have very little control over. A good estimate to use for uncoated paper printing on sheet-fed offset presses will be a range falling between 10%-20%. For web offset presses: a range falling between 15%-25%. Subtract 3%-5% for coated cover stock paper.

Dot gain has more impact on mid-tone values than values closer to the white or black extreme. Therefore, if the dot gain is 15%, a 50% gray will print closer 65% gray. However, a 20% gray may only print 5% or 6% darker, because smaller dots contain less ink, spreading less. It is also safe to assume that any gray value above 85% will print 100% black under any circumstance. Even though you should take dot gain into account, do not get carried away worrying about it. Ultimately, it boils down to guess work and hoping for the best.

When correcting an image, the info palette should be visible on your desktop, and should be set to view gray scale values as percentages of black (K). Then using IMAGE>ADJUST> CURVES, alter your pre-selected tones of gray to their appropriate values. An area destined to print at 50%K may have an original scan value of 65%K, and be altered to approximately 43%K.

The image can be halftoned once it

has been value corrected. However, it is important to keep a copy of the raw scan in case future corrections are required. Halftone the image by changing the mode from gray scale to bitmap. At this point a window will appear giving threshold options. Also make sure the resolution input and output match.

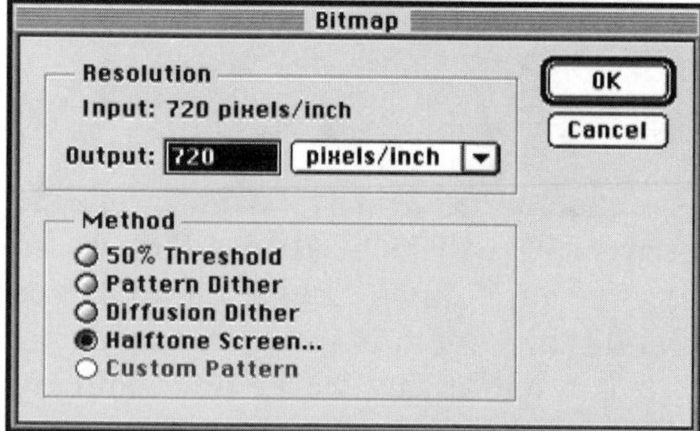

Choosing the halftone option will bring up a second window. In this window enter the appropriate line screen and screen angle. The shape of the dots should either be ellipses or dots (unless you want a weird special effect).

The halftone document is now a bitmap and is much smaller than the original gray scale document. Don't be surprised if the image looks terrible on the monitor, computer screens do not display halftones well. This is also true for desktop printers. Even high-quality desktop printers have problems printing halftone images properly. However, if these instructions are followed carefully, the images should print as well as the examples shown.

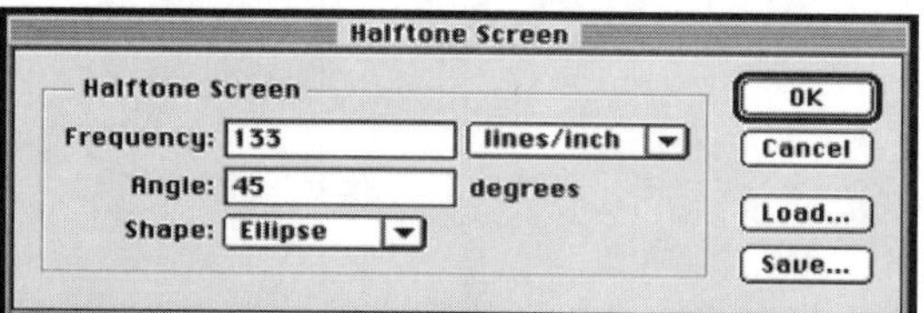

One last note about gray scale scans: If the gray scale image is ultimately destined to be colored in Photoshop, it should NOT be halftoned. Follow the directions for creating a CMYK document as any other line art. CMYK documents are made up of four separate gray scale channels. This explains why color documents are four times larger than gray scale documents, and 32 times larger than bitmaps.

Finally, the information in this chapter also applies to scanning full color art, such as paintings and hand-colored art. However, the issues that result from scanning and color correcting such art will be covered in detail in Chapter Nine.

figure 2-11: Compare the halftoned image at left with the 'grayscale' image at left.

Technically speaking, the gray scale image was halftoned by the imagesetter when the film for this book was produced, however it takes up approximately eight times more memory than the image that was halftoned before imagesetting.

figure 2-12: Occasionally, pencil drawings need to be reproduced from photocopies. Since these copies generally reproduce the gray lines as black (bottom left), it is best to scan them as gray scale images. Then reduce the value from 100%K down to 60%K in curves, and halftone the image (bottom center). Even though this will work as a last resort, it is always better to scan from the original pencils (bottom right).

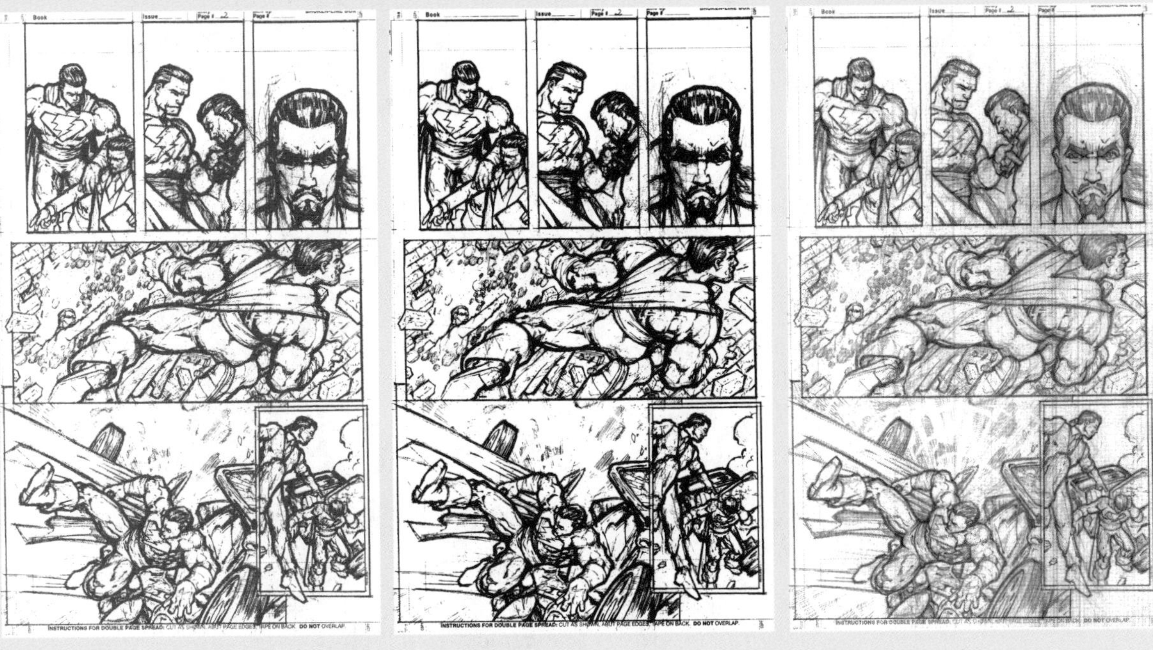

BAD LUCK! YOU CROOKS REALLY ARE A SUPERSTITIOUS LOT.
I'LL POINT OUT A COUPLE OF DOOZIES YOU MAY HAVE MISSED!
WHAT THE...!?
STEP ON A CRACK, BREAK A MUGGER'S BACK!
AND WHEN A WOLF-GIRL CROSSES YOUR PATH... FURGEDDABOUTIT!
SOMEBODY GET THAT FURBALL!
WHO YOU CALLIN' FURBALL?
SSHRIIIPP!!

CHAPTER 3
PAGE SET UPS

What has once been settled by a precedent will not be unsettled overnight, for certainty and uniformity are gains not lightly to be sacrificed.

Benjamin Nathan Cardozo, 1928

It is now time to set up the pages for all the different work that needs to be done. If the comic is going to be four-color, the pages need to be set up for color. If the job is going to be lettered on the computer, a low-res document must be created. If the end product is a hand lettered black and white comic, the job is almost done. The pages still need to be set up for the printer.

Open the raw scan in Photoshop and go to IMAGE>IMAGE SIZE. In the window that appears, make sure constrain proportion is on and resample image is off. Then change the resolution number, which should be the art size scanning resolution, to the proper print size resolution. As the resolution number changes, so too will the height and width. Click OK to apply this change.

Crop the scan fairly close to the art without trimming any of the image. In the case of bleed art, the crop can actually touch the edge of the image. The image will have to be rotated if it appears to be crooked.

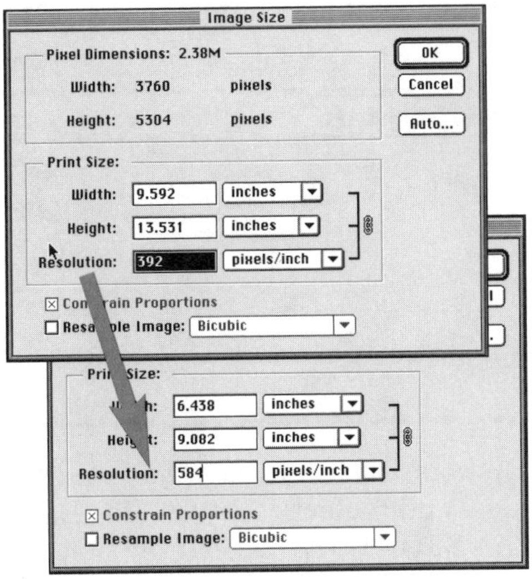

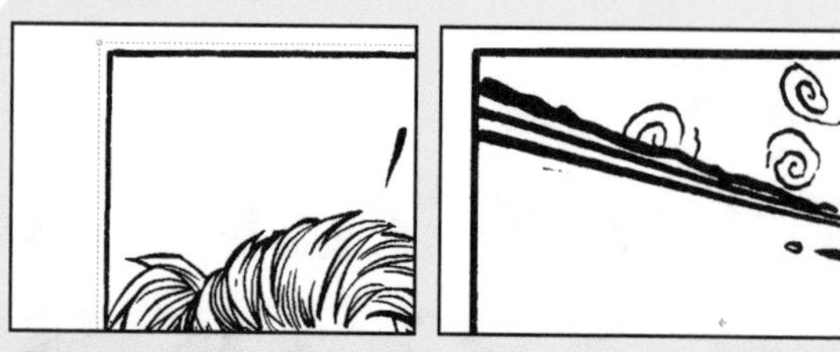

figure 3-01: Crop as close as possible to the art. The crop may actually touch art that is destined to bleed.

Earlier versions of Photoshop required a lot of guess work and manual rotation to get the job done. Photoshop 5, however, provides a more precise means to that end.

Make sure the Info palette is visible on the desktop. Then select the ruler tool and find a straight horizontal line. This line should cross the entire width of the page, and the bottom of two or three panel borders is usually perfect. Starting on the left endpoint of this ink line, and moving to the right, create a ruler line that lines up at the same angle. This angle will appear in the info palette, and may be a positive or negative number. ***Do not*** deselect the ruler tool. If the ruler tool has been deselected, the Numeric window will not correspond with the info palette.

Options Info
K :
A : 0.5°
D : 15.256
X : 0.149
Y : 7.949
W : 15.256
H : -0.131

Change the image mode to gray scale, and select all. Go to EDIT> TRANSFORM>NUMERIC. A more precise angle is listed under rotate than appears in the Info palette, which only goes to one decimal.. Change only the positive/negative aspect of this number, making positive numbers negative, and negatives to positives. Apply this change, and the image will rotate into a level position. Change the image mode back to bitmap with a 50% threshold.

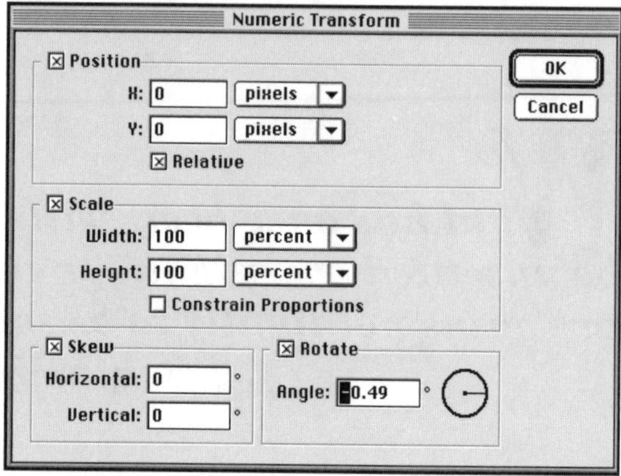

Now take the opportunity to erase any unwanted artifacts, spots, or scratches from the art. This entire process will be done on every single scan no matter what the format.

It is crucial at this point to know what the proportions of the final product will be. All documents use these dimensions as a proportion constant in order to guarantee alignment of separate documents, as well as positioning on the printed page. For example purposes this chapter will assume a printed book at 6 ⅝" x 10" with a 3⁄16" bleed when necessary.

The simplest set up will be the job destined to be printed in black and white, with hand lettering already on the board. In some cases, the printer will take the cropped images and center them on the printed page. If this is the case, be cautious of how open-panel borders may affect how an image is centered on a page.

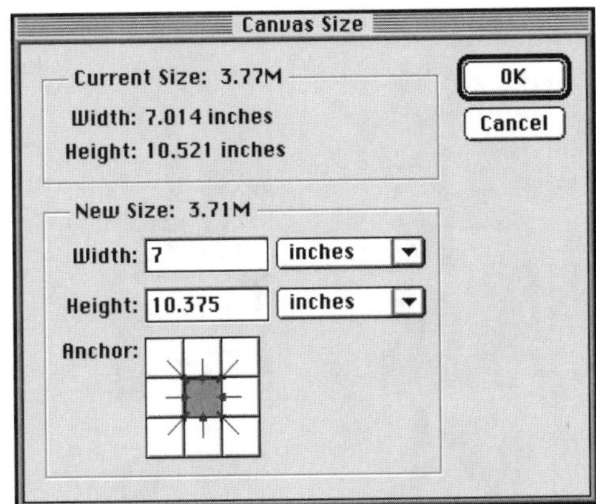

If more precise control over the positioning of the art on the page is required, canvas size the image up to the proportions of the printed book. If the art bleeds this may trim the outside edges of the art. Now position the art to its proper place on the page. It may be wise to set up an action in Photoshop to lay down guides for the 'safe area' of the printed page. This will assist in placement and save time.

As long as there are no digital lettering files, or color separations there is no need to place these files in Quark. Simply save the files as TIFFs and send them off to the printer.

Set Ups for Digital Lettering

Now is the time to emphasize ***consistency, consistency, consistency!***

This is absolutely necessary when dealing with combinations of digital lettering, color separations, and art files. All digital files must be exactly the same proportions to insure accurate alignment in the page layout.

For non-bleed books, this ***proportion constant*** is equal to the dimensions of the printed product. Bleed book proportions must include a bleed allowance on all four sides, even if the art itself does not bleed. The documents for books that contain both bleed and non-bleed art must ***all*** conform to ***bleed*** proportions. **DO NOT** mix proportions on a single job!

The proportion constant will be identical in all of the programs used

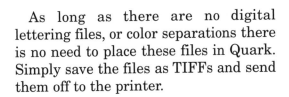

figure 3-02: It is a good idea to create actions to place guides for crops and safe-copy areas in Photoshop. They will assist in more precise placement of art.

Non-bleed art (left) will fall inside the safe copy area. Bleed art (right) may be more tricky. Note that the left side of panel four may trim, while the right side remains in the copy area. Keep the original art close by to check placement.

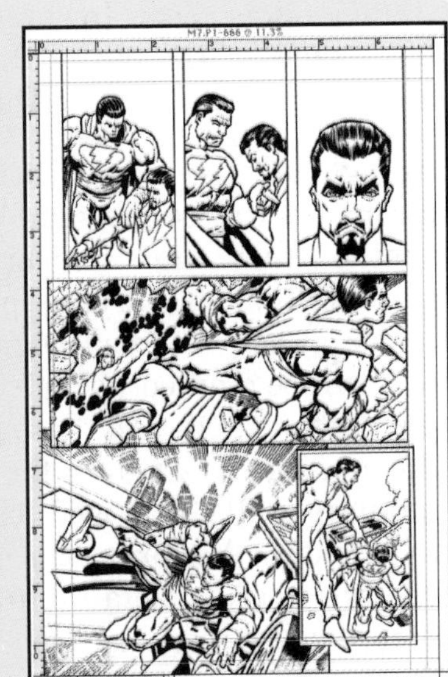

Proportion Constant

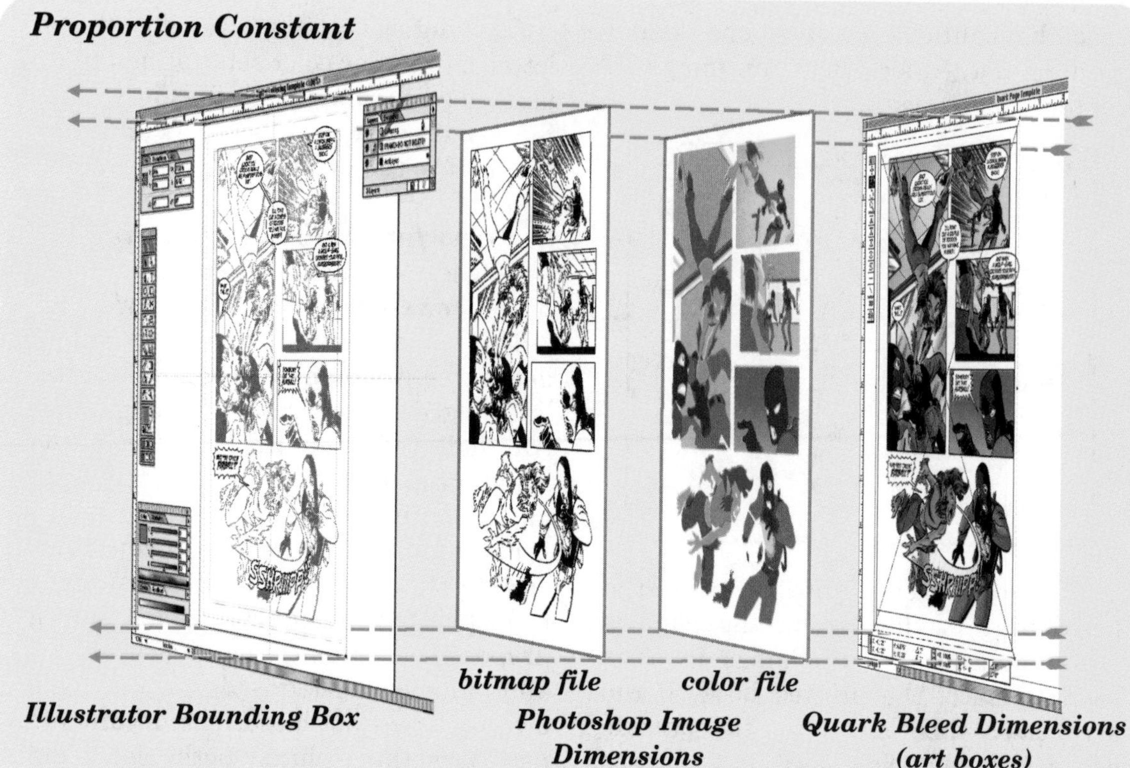

A proportion constant is required in order for multiple files to align properly when assembled together. Each file ***must*** have the identical dimensions.

In Illustrator, it is the dimensions of the bounding box. In Photoshop, the dimensions of the entire document (no matter the resolution). In Quark it is the dimensions of the bleed sized art box. (Quark's document size corresponds to the trim.)

As long as this proportion constant is maintained, the files should fall into place no matter how they are aligned by the imagesetter.

throughout the project. *all* Photoshop documents will be the same proportions, whether they are color or black and white (although varying pixel resolutions may be called for). Digital lettering files will be created using an Illustrator template created with these proportions. The document settings for the Quark template will be based on the trim proportions. All programs must work together in order to fall into place.

Once a raw scan has been set up to its proper placement on the printed page , which will now be referred to as the ***black line art***, Photoshop documents must be set up for the digital letterer, and color separator. These documents will be created from the black line art after set up.

The digital letterer will require a low resolution version of the black line art to place in the Illustrator template. To maintain *precise* proportions, this low res file should be exactly a quarter of the

1/4 Resampling

When resampling images, it is best to change pixel resolution by a factor of four. The reason for this is simple: pixels are square. When resing down by a factor of four, four individual pixels will be combined to form a single pixel. When resing up, each individual pixel is divided into four.

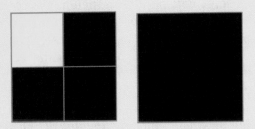

Four pixels convert smoothly into one, and vice-versa.

If a factor of four is not used, new pixels have to be generated from scratch when resing up. These new pixels are generated by averaging the values of the pixels that will surround it.

Resing down means some pixels have to be thrown away because they do not fit into the new grid. This type of resampling can blur edges making them softer. In bitmap images, edges may appear more stair stepped.

60% C	60% C	100 Y
100 Y	100 Y	60% C
100 Y	60% C	60% C
100 Y	60% C	60% C

67% C 33% Y	33% C 67% Y
33% C 67% Y	60% C

Uneven pixel conversion will utilize color averaging which in turn leads to the blurring of edges.

At first glance, this distinction appears to be merely an aesthetic dilemma. However, there is a serious production issue involved. The height and width of a Photoshop image is actually defined by pixels. When changing the number of pixels unevenly, the physical dimensions may change slightly. That means the image no longer matches the proportion constant of the project.

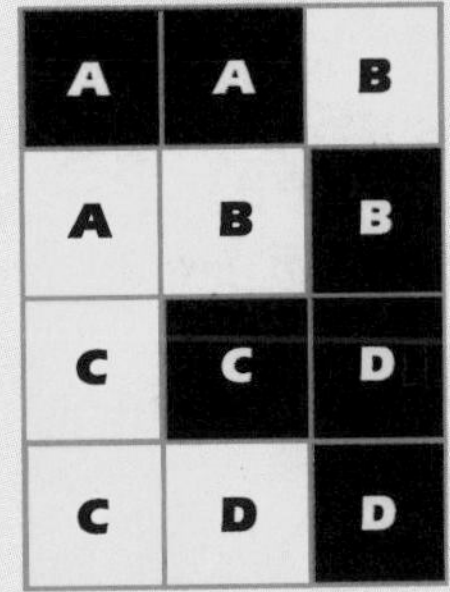

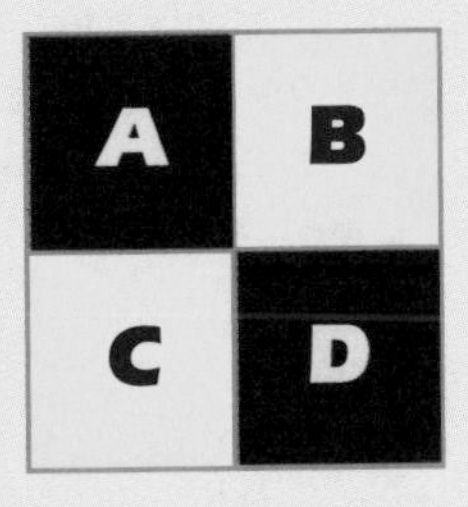

In bitmap images, stair stepping can occur. Also note how the overall dimensions were forced to change.

A small change in the dimensions may not be noticeable. However, we know from experience that creating a 72 ppi lettering document from a 500 dpi original creates a major problem with placement. The lettering created to align perfectly with the 72 ppi document is noticeably mis aligned when placed on the high res file. Lettering created over a one quarter resampled document should align with very few problems.

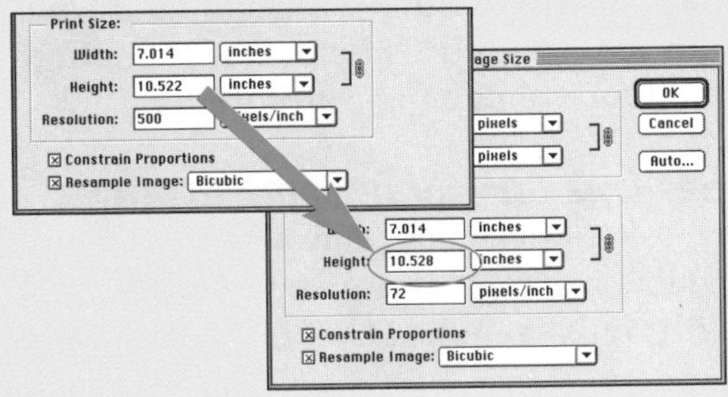

pixel resolution of the high res black line art. It is recommended that the line art be converted to gray scale before any resampling (changing pixel resolution) is done. Furthermore, pixel resolution should **NEVER** be increased on any *line art*.

To create the low-res lettering file, convert the black line art to gray scale. Then go to IMAGE SIZE, and activate RESAMPLE IMAGE: BICUBIC. This allows pixel resolution alterations to be made without affecting the height and width of the document. Reduce the resolution to one quarter of its original size. For example, a 500 ppi resolution would be changed to 125 ppi. If a reduction percentage other than one quarter is use, there may be a minuscule change in the proportions. This can lead to the lettering being positioned out of alignment in the Illustrator template.

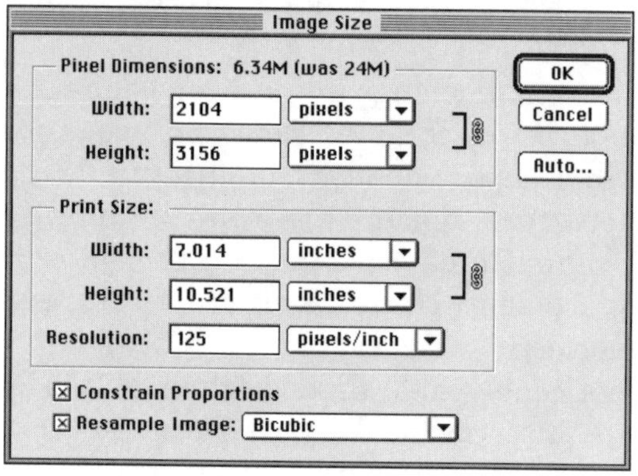

Image Size
Pixel Dimensions: 6.34M (was 24M)
Width: 2104 pixels
Height: 3156 pixels
Print Size:
Width: 7.014 inches
Height: 10.521 inches
Resolution: 125 pixels/inch
☒ Constrain Proportions
☒ Resample Image: Bicubic
OK
Cancel
Auto...

Change the image mode back to bitmap with a 50% threshold, and save the file as a **TIFF**. Remember to follow appropriate naming conventions.

Set Ups for Color Separations

Color separators may want to create their own color document set ups, and will only require the black line art document. In some rare cases, separation companies need a specific art proportion to work with their systems. However, most freelance computer colorists can work with whatever is sent to them. Just make sure that everyone involved is working with identical proportions.

If the separations are being done in house, it will be more efficient to create the color documents at the same time as the black line art. The only question that arises is one of resolution. Some color separations contain no black and have a relatively low-pixel resolution. The higher resolution black line art is then added to the coloring in Quark. Other separations begin at a low res, but the resolution is increased to equal the original set up so that the black line art and subsequent special effects can be added to the color files. This is done to increase speed and efficiency of both separator and computer.

These types of resolution changes do not have to follow the one-quarter rule. In the first instance, the black line art and proper trapping will cover any slight misalignment. In the second case, the file is returned to its proper proportion, although special attention should be given to make sure the digital

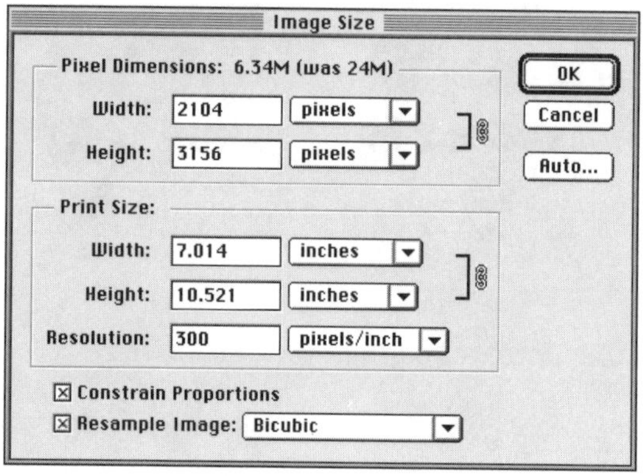

Image Size
Pixel Dimensions: 6.34M (was 24M)
Width: 2104 pixels
Height: 3156 pixels
Print Size:
Width: 7.014 inches
Height: 10.521 inches
Resolution: 300 pixels/inch
☒ Constrain Proportions
☒ Resample Image: Bicubic
OK
Cancel
Auto...

lettering file will properly align.

Before creating a color document, make sure all art corrections have been done, and any separate hand lettering or color overlays have been added to the black line art (as indicated later in this chapter). Convert the art to gray scale, and make any necessary resolution changes with *resample image* activated.

Select all and 'cut' the art (EDIT>CUT). The art will vanish leaving a white page. In the channels palette, create a new channel named 'LINE' that is 100% opaque black with 'selected areas' checked. Paste the art into this new channel (EDIT>PASTE).

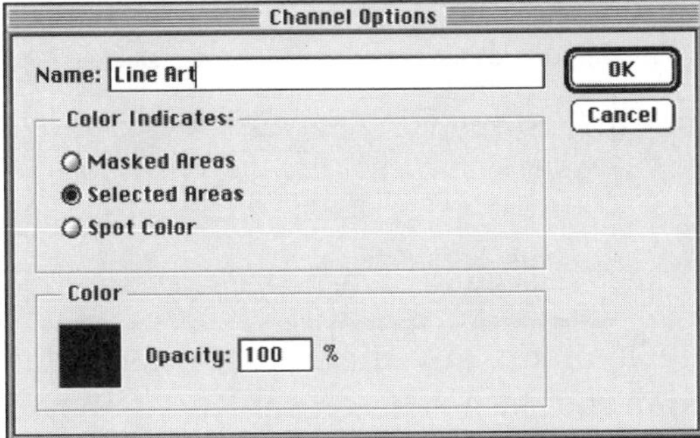

Now convert the mode to CMYK, and save the file as a Photoshop document using the appropriate naming conventions. The file is now ready to be colored, but that will be dealt with later.

Color Overlays and Hand Lettering

Occasionally additional art must be added to the black line art to complete the set up process. These additions are usually created as overlays to the original art, and are scanned separately. Usually these overlays are used to create special effects in the coloring file–ergo; a color overlay.

After the line art has been completely set up, convert its mode to gray scale. Open the raw scan of the overlay and change its *constrained* resolution to the proper printing resolution. Select and copy the overlay art. There is no need to select all if the overlay is significantly smaller than the black line art.

Return to your gray scale art and create a new channel using the channels palette. Name the channel 'overlay' and make sure that 'selected areas' is checked. The color of the new channel should be bright, such as red or neon green. It does not matter what color this overlay will be in the finished product, for now it just needs to stand out and be obvious. The opacity for overlays should be set between 50%-70% for a more precise visual placement.

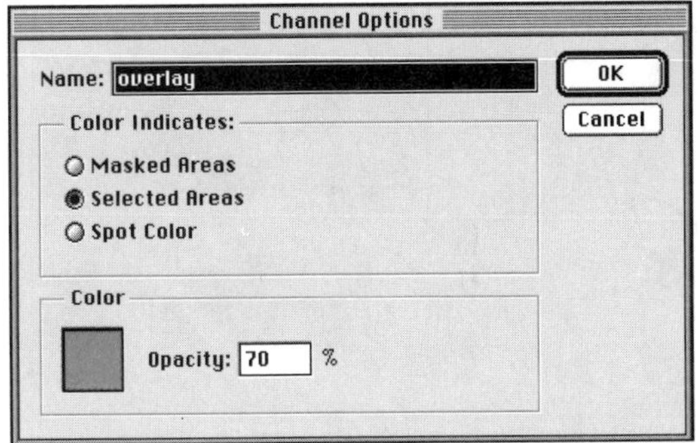

Paste the overlay art into this new channel, and move the overlay into its proper position.

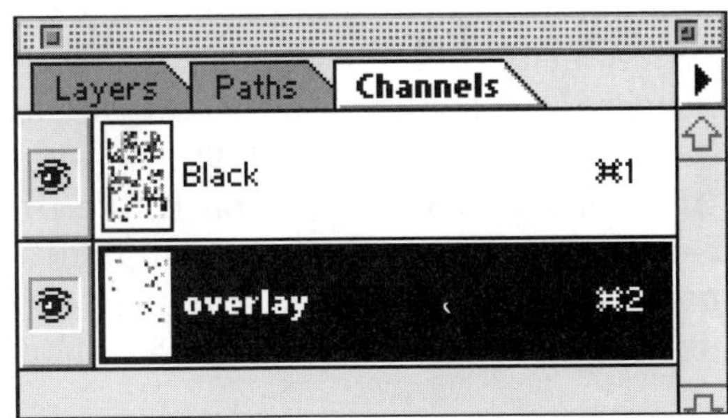

Save this document, and create the color document as usual. Remember this document is already in gray scale. If the color overlay is going to be added in Quark, as may be the case with separate color and black files, a bitmap TIFF will be needed of the overlay by itself. Simply click on the overlay channels name in the gray scale document and convert to bitmap, which will discard the art channel. Save this document as a TIFF with the letters OL added to the name. This new document has the identical proportion constant as the black line art, and should fall in its correct position in Quark.

figure 3-06: shows the opacity level and placement of a color overlay.

Another type of additional art that may arise is the use of hand lettering overlays. Many companies try to save time on a project by lettering pages on vellum using full size photocopies of the pencil art as a guide. This allows a book to be lettered and inked at the same time. In the past, an approach like this required each individual balloon to be pasted onto the finished art, using rubber cement and white opaquing medium.

Nowadays, this same approach can be done on the computer, with more precision and less chemical goop. The process is similar to color overlays, however, it utilizes the layers palette as opposed to channels.

Open the lettering overlay scans first, and change its constrained resolution to the proper printing resolution.

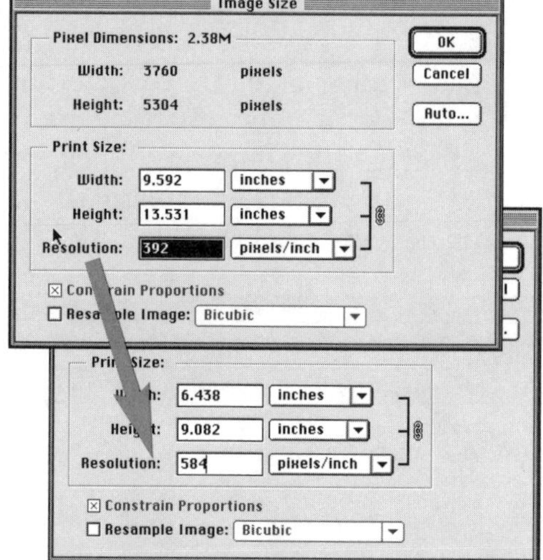

Clean up any dirt, dots, or smudges that should not be present by using the eraser tool or by deleting selections made by the marquee tool. Zooming in on the page may be required to see some of these artifacts. At this time determine if the lettering is closing up or becoming illegible.

Close any open balloons or caption boxes. The easiest way to do this is to use the line tool. It is important that the new lines intersect with the black lines of the balloons. The white on the inside of the balloon ***cannot*** touch the white of the background.

Convert the document to gray scale. In the layers palette double click on the word 'BACKGROUND.' A window will appear with the following information about LAYER 0: OPACITY 100, MODE: NORMAL.

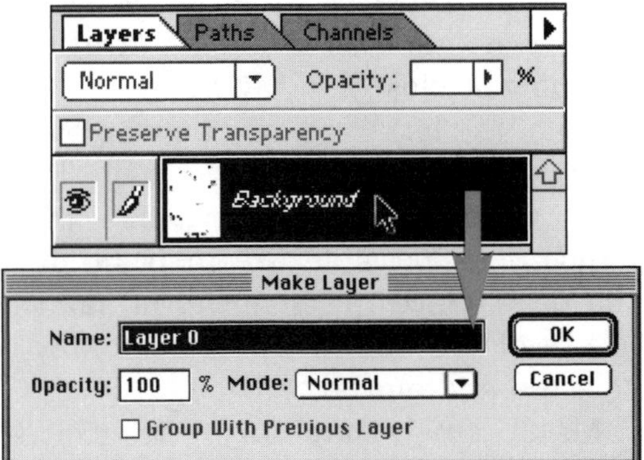

If there is any artwork cutting in front of balloons or sound effects which cannot be closed off using the line tool, use the lasso tool or eraser to delete small areas between the interior of the balloons and the background. Make sure that 'feathering' is set at 0 in the option palette of the lasso tool.

Select the magic wand tool, and set its tolerance to five in the options palette. Then click on the white background of the page. The selection indication, often referred to as marching ants, should appear along the outside of the document, and on the *outside* of all the balloons. They ***should not*** appear on the inside of the balloons or around any lettering inside balloons or captions. If they do appear inside the 'forbidden zone,' the balloons have not been closed off properly. If necessary, zoom in to find the offending gap, it may be as small as a single pixel.

Hit the delete key once the background alone has been selected. A checkerboard pattern should appear in the deleted area. Deselect and save the file, but do not close it.

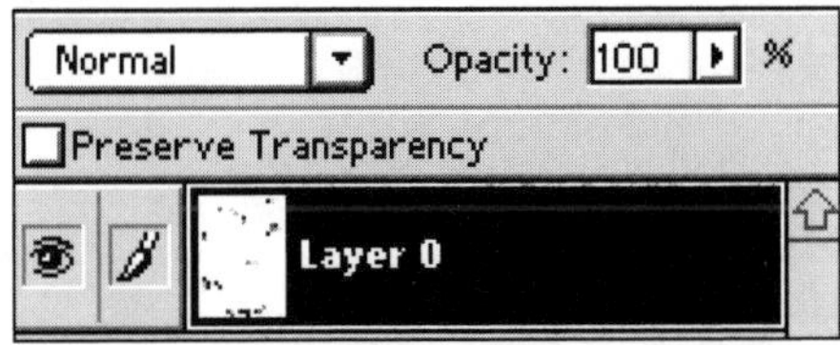

Open and set up the corresponding black line art, and convert the mode to gray scale. Return to the lettering document and choose the move tool from the tool box. (The move tool looks like four arrows originating from a central point, and it can be found directly under the lasso tool). Click and drag the selected lettering, moving the entire selection until the curser is inside the black line art document The document

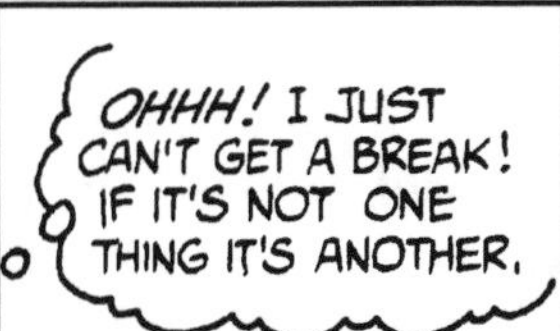

figure 3-07: shows the steps taken to close off an open thought balloon.

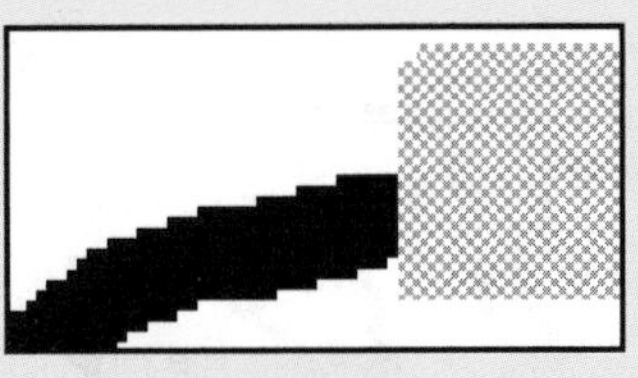

It is crucial to make sure that the deleted area touches the black outline.

The eraser tool was used to separate the inside of the balloon from the outside.

The end product will butt up to the panel border while still covering the art underneath.

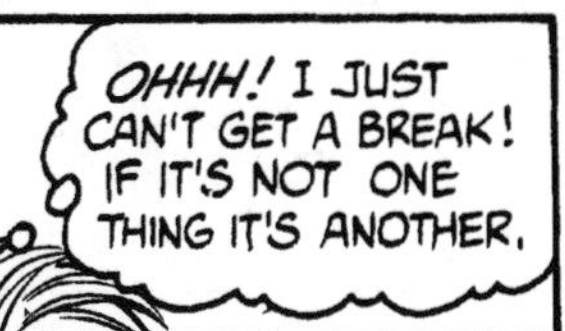

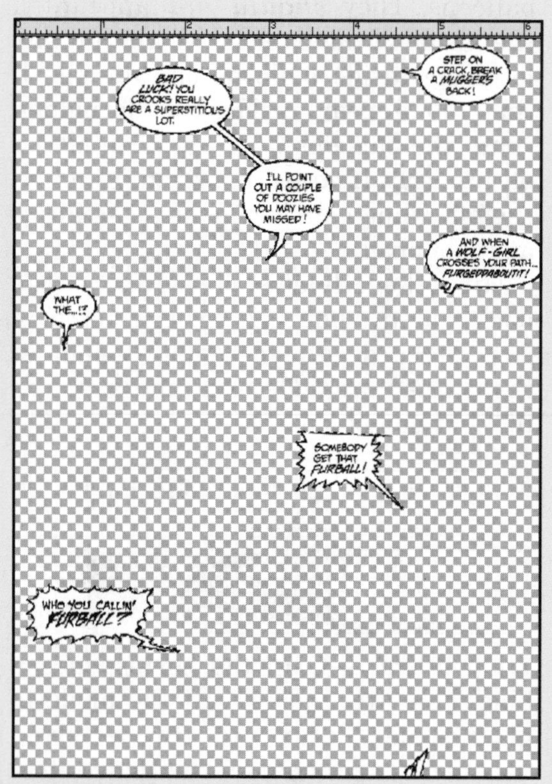

figure 3-08 shows layer 0 with the white background deleted. Note that the interior whites of the balloons remain intact. It may be necessary to zoom in on sound effects to delete the interiors of closed letters using the wand tool.

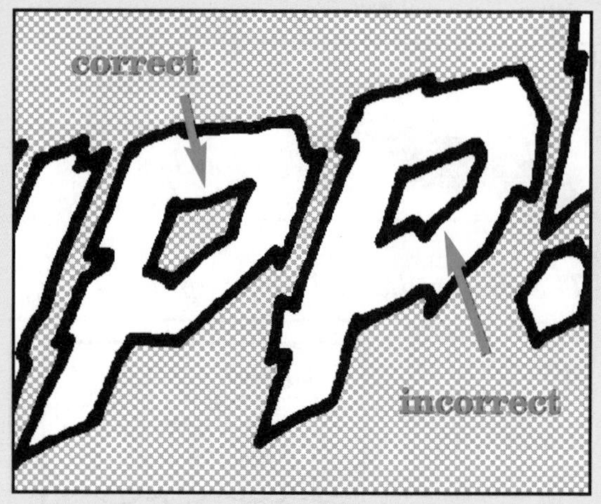

should have a bold line around its window, indicating the selection is now inside the document. When the mouse button is released, the lettering will appear in a new layer. The lettering scan can now be closed.

All of the lettering may now be moved *in unison* with the move tool. Place the lettering so that as many balloons as possible are in position on the page. Once the majority of balloons are in place, individual balloons may be selected and moved.

Make sure that any art that is supposed to cut in front of a balloon or sound effect is clearly visible. Delete the lines that were added to close off balloons if they interfere with the artwork underneath.

figure 3-09: Delete the lines that were added to close off balloons, so that they butt to panel borders.

At this point , after all balloons have been properly placed and cropped , ***it is important to save a copy of this document*** (always save periodically while working, but this is the point at which work ***must*** be saved). This is the document to return to if any future corrections need to be made. This document will now be referred to as the ***gray scale document.***

After the gray scale document has

Cutting Art in Front

figure 3-10: To strip art in front of word balloons, change the opacity of the lettering layer for better visibility.

Select and delete the appropriate areas from the balloon. Note that the selection need only be precise where black lines meet. Once this is complete, return the layer opacity to 100%.

been properly saved. Click on the triangle at the upper right corner of the layers palette and go to flatten image, and then convert the image mode back to bitmap with a 50% threshold. Save the file as a TIFF and the job of setting up is now complete.

Double-Page Spreads

If double-page spreads need to be scanned in sections, these separate scans need to be recombined during the set up process. This will be done much in the same way as compositing hand lettering, with only a few modifications.

Begin by doubling the width if the left-hand page. Go to IMAGE>CANVAS SIZE, type in the new width, and position the image marker in the left-hand square. This will create blank space only to the right of the image. Convert the document to gray scale. Copy and paste the right hand page art into the enlarged gray scale document, creating a new layer.

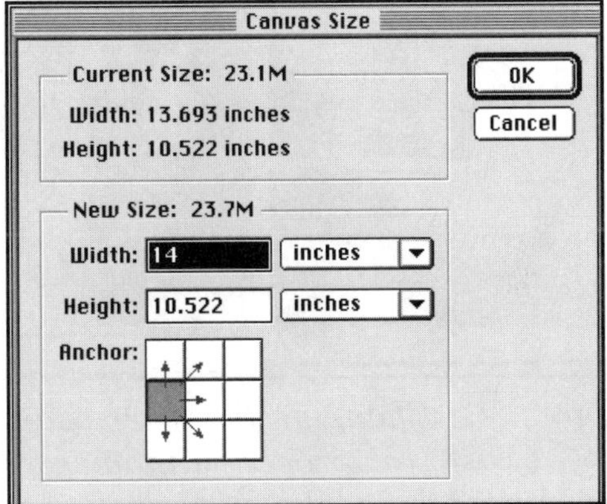

In the layers palette, change the mode of the new layer to darken to make the whites transparent. Consider changing the opacity as well, for this may facilitate more accurate placement.

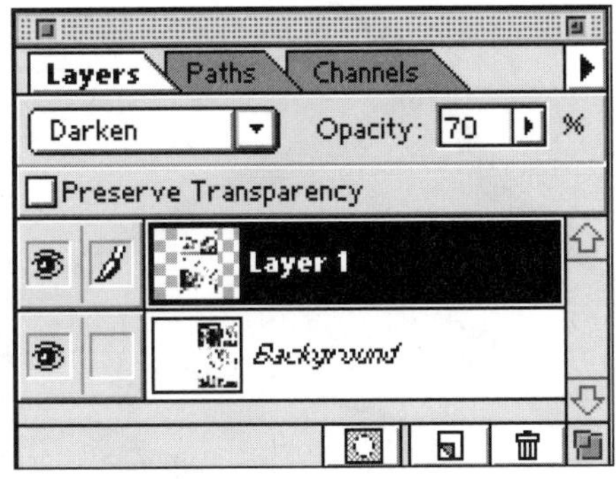

Align the scanned overlap as precisely as possible. Zooming in and rotating may be necessary. Also, areas in the overlapping sections may have to be smoothed out with the pencil and eraser tools to avoid a cut look where art can not be aligned properly.

Once this is complete, change the opacity back to 100%, and flatten image. Convert the image back to bitmap, and complete the set up process.

figure 3-11: Changing the layer opacity will assist in proper alignment of overlapping scan (above). Areas that are impossible to line up completely need to be touched up with the pencil and eraser tools (below).

Crop the file to just outside the art work, and canvas size. Remember that the width of a double-page spread ***is not*** twice the size of a single page, because there is no central bleed.

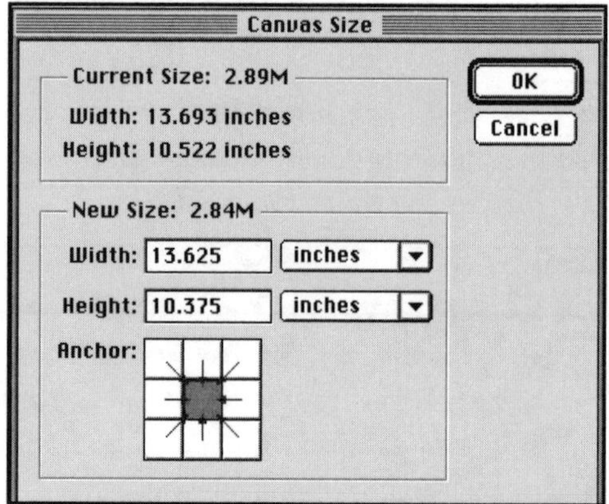

Naming Conventions and File Info

Organizing and naming files in a logical manner is far more crucial than most people realize. The more people working on a project the more important this organization will be. It is especially important once the job has left house, and has gone to the printer. All files and folders placed on a disk should be immediately recognizable for what they are by their name alone. Similar types of files should follow a consistent naming pattern so that they are easily found using FIND FILE.

The first folder encountered on a disk should contain the contents of the entire publication. The name of the folder should contain the full name of the magazine (if possible), the issue number, and the publication date or cover month. Inside this folder will be a folder for the covers, a folder for the interior pages, and folder containing all necessary fonts for the job at hand. The cover and interior page folders should also contain the name and issue number of the magazine in their name as well as identifying their contents, such as *Wolf-Girl#3.covers1-4* or *Wolf-Girl#3.pages 01 32*.

Inside the covers folder should be all the elements, documents, and other folders necessary to create a cover. There may be separate folders or Quark files for the inside and outside covers. The standard for identifying covers in the printing industry is as follows: outside front cover is cover 1, inside front cover is cover 2, inside back cover is cover 3, outside back cover is cover 4.

The Quark files should be floating free in the cover folder. Quark files should be named: title of book, issue number, period(.), 'C1/C4'(identifying the outside covers), and if necessary a dash(-), and market identification (newsstand, direct). Example: *Wolf-Girl#3.C1/C4-DIRECT* or *Wolf Girl#3.C2/C3* for the interior covers.

There should also be two document folders named PHOTOSHOP, and ILLUSTRATOR. These folders should be created as soon as a project is begun in order to facilitate updating Quark. Obviously all Photoshop files should be inside the Photoshop folder. Photoshop files should be named: title of book, issue number, period(.), cover identification, a dash(-), resolution. Example: *Wolf-Girl#3.C1-450*. Clipping path documents should have the resolution replaced with the word *'CLIP'*. Example: *Wolf-Girl#3.C1 CLIP*. The Illustrator files inside the Illustrator folder should be clearly labeled as to their contents, such as *LOGO, COVER COPY,* or *TRADEDRESS.*

The interior pages folder should follow a similar layout. The Quark file floating free and named: title of book, issue number, period(.), page numbers. Example:Wolf-Girl#3.pgs 01-32. There should also be two document folders named *PHOTOSHOP* or *ART*, and *ILLUSTRATOR* or *LETTERING*. The files contained in both should be named: title of book, issue number, page number, a dash(-), and resolution for art files or LET for lettering files. Example: *Wolf-Girl#3.01-450* or *Wolf-Girl#3.01 LET.*

If there are separate black and color plates for the project, they may be further divided into folders within the Photoshop folder. This may sound like a chinese box of folders inside of folders inside of folders, but it makes things far easier to keep track of, especially when placing or updating files in Quark.

It is also a good idea to place the name of each Photoshop file inside a caption in the file info window (go to FILE>FILE INFO). This allows the name of the document to appear on any printout made directly from the Photoshop application. Companies that employ several set up people or color separators have the individual who works on a page enter his name or initials into the caption writer section of this window in case corrections need to be made.

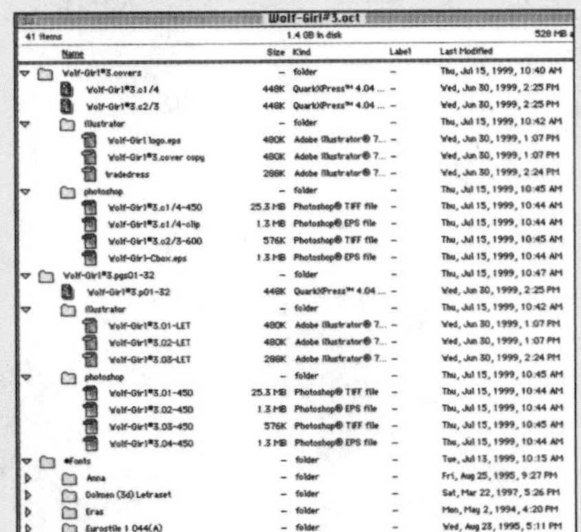

Wolf-Girl#3.oct

41 items — 1.4 GB in disk — 528 MB a

Name	Size	Kind	Label	Last Modified
Wolf-Girl#3.covers	–	folder	–	Thu, Jul 15, 1999, 10:40 AM
Wolf-Girl#3.c1/4	448K	QuarkXPress™ 4.04 ...	–	Wed, Jun 30, 1999, 2:25 PM
Wolf-Girl#3.c2/3	448K	QuarkXPress™ 4.04 ...	–	Wed, Jun 30, 1999, 2:25 PM
illustrator	–	folder	–	Thu, Jul 15, 1999, 10:42 AM
Wolf-Girl logo.eps	480K	Adobe Illustrator® 7...	–	Wed, Jun 30, 1999, 1:07 PM
Wolf-Girl#3.cover copy	480K	Adobe Illustrator® 7...	–	Wed, Jun 30, 1999, 1:07 PM
tradedress	288K	Adobe Illustrator® 7...	–	Wed, Jun 30, 1999, 2:24 PM
photoshop	–	folder	–	Thu, Jul 15, 1999, 10:45 AM
Wolf-Girl#3.c1/4-450	25.3 MB	Photoshop® TIFF file	–	Thu, Jul 15, 1999, 10:44 AM
Wolf-Girl#3.c1/4-clip	1.3 MB	Photoshop® EPS file	–	Thu, Jul 15, 1999, 10:44 AM
Wolf-Girl#3.c2/3-600	576K	Photoshop® TIFF file	–	Thu, Jul 15, 1999, 10:45 AM
Wolf-Girl-Cbox.eps	1.3 MB	Photoshop® EPS file	–	Thu, Jul 15, 1999, 10:44 AM
Wolf-Girl#3.pgs01-32	–	folder	–	Thu, Jul 15, 1999, 10:47 AM
Wolf-Girl#3.p01-32	448K	QuarkXPress™ 4.04 ...	–	Wed, Jun 30, 1999, 2:25 PM
illustrator	–	folder	–	Thu, Jul 15, 1999, 10:42 AM
Wolf-Girl#3.01-LET	480K	Adobe Illustrator® 7...	–	Wed, Jun 30, 1999, 1:07 PM
Wolf-Girl#3.02-LET	480K	Adobe Illustrator® 7...	–	Wed, Jun 30, 1999, 1:07 PM
Wolf-Girl#3.03-LET	288K	Adobe Illustrator® 7...	–	Wed, Jun 30, 1999, 2:24 PM
photoshop	–	folder	–	Thu, Jul 15, 1999, 10:45 AM
Wolf-Girl#3.01-450	25.3 MB	Photoshop® TIFF file	–	Thu, Jul 15, 1999, 10:44 AM
Wolf-Girl#3.02-450	1.3 MB	Photoshop® EPS file	–	Thu, Jul 15, 1999, 10:44 AM
Wolf-Girl#3.03-450	576K	Photoshop® TIFF file	–	Thu, Jul 15, 1999, 10:45 AM
Wolf-Girl#3.04-450	1.3 MB	Photoshop® EPS file	–	Thu, Jul 15, 1999, 10:44 AM
•Fonts	–	folder	–	Tue, Jul 13, 1999, 10:15 AM
Anna	–	folder	–	Fri, Aug 25, 1995, 9:27 PM
Dolmen (3d) Letraset	–	folder	–	Sat, Mar 22, 1997, 5:26 PM
Eras	–	folder	–	Mon, May 2, 1994, 4:20 PM
Eurostile 1 044(A)	–	folder	–	Wed, Aug 23, 1995, 5:11 PM
Eurostile 2 130(A)	–	folder	–	Wed, Aug 23, 1995, 5:11 PM

figure 3-12: An example of a disk window utilizing naming conventions

BOINK!
SHRACK
BOOM!
ZAP
ARRGH!
THWACK
TERMINATE
UUGH!
POP!
POP!
D.Z.Z.Z.T.
CRACKLE
END PROGRAM!

CHAPTER 4
DIGITAL LETTERING

Not of the letter, but of the spirit: for the letter killeth, but the spirit giveth life.
II Corinthians 3:6

The single driving force behind the computer revolution in comics, with the possible exception of the computer itself, is the advent of digital lettering. Even the earlier introduction of computerized color separations cannot compare to the sweeping changes to the industry that resulted from that first letterer converting his hand-lettered alphabet into a computer font. From that point on, it was a runaway train picking up speed. On the other hand, many hand letterers and production personnel have good reason to compare it more to a tornado in a trailer park.

A little history lesson may be in order here. Hand lettering, or calligraphy, is an art form that precious few can master. In many ways, this style of lettering is as much a cultural icon as the comic book itself. Despite the many and varied styles within the industry, a vast majority of 'ordinary citizens' will recognize, and identify, certain fonts as 'comic book lettering.' Including people who may never have read a comic in their life!

In the beginning, lettering was done directly on the art boards. The letterer would received the penciled art and a script. The job of the letterer included not only lettering the script, but also: laying out the balloon placements, drawing balloons and sound effects, inking panel borders (often with the infamous ruling pen), and designing and drawing logos. Only after the lettering was complete could the pages be sent to the inker.

Everything ran fairly smoothly with this method for over fifty years. Then, sometime in the late '70s and early '80s someone came up with a desperate plan to save his own skin. No one knows exactly who or when, but they all know why: *The Dreaded Deadline Doom,* the scourge of the entire industry. Faced with this impending peril, the idea was formed to have the lettering completed on a vellum overlay while the art pages were being inked. The production department could then paste the lettering onto the art boards as the job was completed.

At first this was intended to be a last-ditch effort to avoid disaster. But, as the years passed, more and more books began falling behind schedule. By the late '80s, many people thought this was the way it was supposed to be done, nay, how it had always been done. Even books that were on schedule–a rarity to be sure–were done in this fashion. Production departments expanded, filled with employees whose only job was to 'paste-up' word balloons and sound effects.

In the early '90s, a few letterers began experimenting with computers. Initially, this did not drastically change the production process. Some letterers would actually print out computer generated balloons and paste them on the vellum overlay. Others just sent in the printouts alone. The problem that quickly arose was that most of these printouts could not survive the production process. They would break up and smudge, requiring constant lettering corrections. These printouts needed to be photostated, increasing both costs and production time. This process lasted little more than a year before changes were demanded.

By this point, print shops and separation houses had already replaced their stat cameras with scanners and imagesetters many years earlier. It was decided to send the unlettered art boards, with a floppy disk containing the digital lettering files, directly to the printers and have the separators place the lettering on the computer. As editors became more enamored with snazzy three dimensional logos, and the apparent time savings (for them alone), this process became more prevalent.

In less than a year, the printers reached a breaking point. An ultimatum was delivered to the comic publishers involved. ALL work must arrive one of two ways: completely analog (pasted up by hand), or completely digital (art and lettering placed in computer files). If the work continued coming in as a mixture of both, the printers would cease printing comics. Period.

figure 4-01:
An example of a hand lettered overlay.

Resolution Free Vectors

Illustrator and Freehand are ***vector based*** programs. This means that the objects created in these programs are defined by mathematical lines and curves. By contrast, painting programs, like Photoshop, are pixel based. They create ***raster images*** based on a grid pattern (or ***bitmap***) made up of small squares (***pixels***).

The lines of vector graphics are defined and edited by ***anchor points***. Curves are edited using handles attached to the anchor point. This type of curve is called a ***Bézier curve***. The entire length of a line that creates a distinct shape is called a path. The section of line between two anchor points is called a ***vector***. Vectors and paths do not print, but can be given a ***stroke*** and a ***fill*** of any color that does print. The width of a stroke is centered on a path. The fill of an object stops at the vector.

Since vector graphics are mathematically based, they have two distinct advantages over raster images. The first is that they take up far less memory than bitmaps (which have to remember every single pixel). The second is that they are ***resolution independent*** or ***resolution free*** and ***scaleable***. This means that the resolution of a vector is determined during printing. When an illustration is being outputted, the imagesetter uses the mathematical definitions to calculate the line being set at the optimum quality of the imagesetter. The illustration will be the maximum resolution of the printing device used.

This is true even if the size of the illustration has been altered in a page layout program. No matter how large or small a graphic is made in the layout program, it will still print at the maximum resolution of the printing device used. This is what is meant by scaleable. However, the width of any stroke that is given to a path will also increase or decrease in size when scaled. This can affect trapping, therefore all vector graphics should be imported into page layout programs at 100% during the trapping phase of a project.

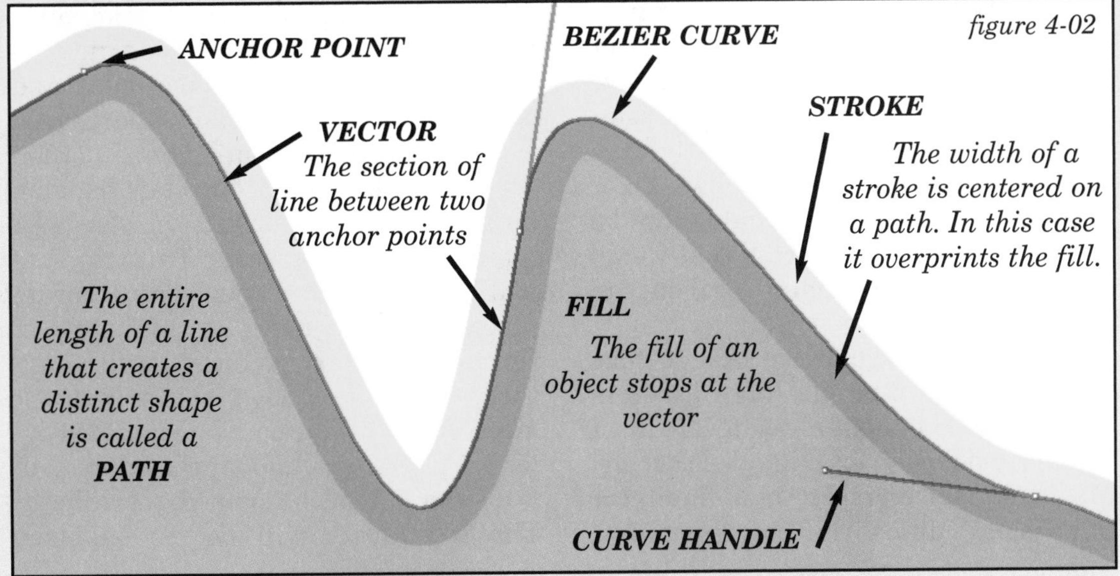

figure 4-02

The snowball was now turning into an avalanche. Entire production departments had to be computerized, and it had to be done yesterday. Even those who wanted to move slowly and cautiously found it was now impossible to make this transition in anything less than broad sweeping steps. It also became apparent to the comic companies that, despite the initial large capital expense, this method would prove to be faster and less expensive.

Digital letterers can now do more work, faster by hiring assistants to help with the workload. The lettering is no longer being done simultaneously with the inking, but at the same time as the coloring and separations. Comic companies no longer have to pay for, often hazardous), production supplies such as rubber cement thinner and razor blades. Nor do they have to pay printers and separators to scan and set up pages, for this is now done in-house.

There are other advantages as well. Since the lettering files are resolution free, the reproduction quality is vastly increased. Lettering files are no longer physically connected to the art or separations. This allows for inexpensive translations into different languages, which previously required costly film stripping, as well as new color separations. Late books could now be lettered overnight, a process that would have taken an individual several days to complete by hand.

The disadvantages were less obvious to the majority of people. A few letterers had positioned themselves to create a virtual monopoly on digital lettering. Most hand letterers are now finding it increasingly difficult, if not impossible, to find work. Production artists unable to make the transition to computers are now unemployed.

Within a few short months the entire industry had changed. As the price of computer hardware and scanners became more affordable, small independent companies, and even some individuals, now had the tools in hand to produce their own unique comics. However, throughout this mad rush to digitize, people began to lose sight of, if not outright ignore, basic production principles. Thereby, bringing about the need for this book.

The Page Template

Now that everyone knows how we got here, where do we go from here. First and foremost, is the need for a font. Customized fonts can be created, but require the skills of a hand letterer. Therefore it is far easier simply to purchase a comic font than to create one. Most font suppliers carry some kind of comic book font–most notably and often overused is called *Whiz Bang*. Comic-related lettering companies also sell a variety of comic fonts. This variety is especially useful when creating sound effects. Many of these can be purchased over the Internet, or through mail order.

However, before you can start banging away at the keyboard, a master-page template must be created. This template will help to insure a swift and accurate placement in Quark. A minimum of three layers are required, although there are usually five, six, or more if necessary. The bottom two layers will be for art placement, and for the ***bounding box***, and should be named accordingly. The top layers will be for balloons,

Font Creation

The font creation application of choice for most type designers is Macromedia Fontographer. This will be the best choice if creating a personalized hand-lettered comic book font. The users manual is excellent for learning how to use the program, so this section will only briefly cover some pitfalls and suggestions for creating a comic font.

Although fonts can be created from scratch on the computer with a great deal of patience, most comic fonts are lettered by hand first. Once an acceptable complete alphabet has been lettered, it is scanned–letters can be scanned in separately. These scans are imported into Fontographer, auto-traced and edited. After the editing is complete, the program converts the lettering into a font that can be used as such with application programs, and typed out on a keyboard. Make no mistake, this process takes some time to complete.

Create a complete font that includes numerals, punctuation marks, and any other symbol that is found on a keyboard. Bold face and italics should be created as well. This can be done by altering the original font in Fontographer, though it may be better to hand letter a bold and italic alphabet.

Comic fonts are usually upper case only. Many letterers create two complete alphabets that are similar, but whose individual letters are noticeably different. When the final font is generated, one alphabet is loaded as upper case, the other as lower case. This furthers the illusion of hand lettering by providing a slight variety to the letter forms, which is particularly useful when double letters are used in a word.

The biggest pitfall that arises for the beginner, is improper letter spacing, leading, and kerning. Letter spacing is the space that falls in between letters. Too much or too little spacing can make words difficult to read. Leading (pronounced *ledding*) is the space between rows of type stacked on top of each other. The measurements for leading is taken from baseline to baseline.

Kerning improves the legibility of certain pairs of letters that do not work well together with normal letter spacing. These characters are referred to as kerning pairs, and for all capital comic lettering include: AV, AT, AY, AW, CO. In a font that includes both upper and lower case, there are many more troublesome pairs.

If left unedited, these kerning pairs will appear to have too much space between them when typed out. The letter 'I' can be a problem, and may appear too close to some neighboring letters, such as the combination of 'LI' may combine to look like the letter 'U.'

Another difference with typography fonts and calligraphy fonts is that the curve of round letters does not sit on the baseline, but falls slightly below. This creates a more natural hand-lettered feel to the font.

All font editing should be done in Fontographer before the font is actually generated. This is especially true with kerning. Many beginners rush through, or even skip, this phase of the process because it can be tedious. However, constant kerning in Illustrator is far worse!

WAIT WAIT

figure 4-03:

BOUNDING BOX

The bounding box is the same dimensions as the bleed guidelines. This box has no stroke and no fill.

TRIM

The trim is the dimensions of the final printed book. Lettering that is to close to this guide risks being cropped.

BLEED

The bleed is the area of art that is trimmed off during printing.

SAFE COPY AREA

The safe copy area is the same dimensions as non-bleed pages. All copy that is supposed to print, should fall within this area.

lettering, and sound effects. The balloon layer should exist underneath the lettering layer so that balloons themselves do not cover the dialog.

Generally, the document set up for the Illustrator document is set up as tabloid (11" x 17") to prevent any typesetting problems later on. Guides should be created in the bounding box layer. These guides should be created by three boxes that correspond with the bleed, trim, and safe copy area of the book.

To create a box with specific dimensions, simply double click inside your document with the box too. Type the precise dimensions into the window that appears. Select all three boxes, and align them using the center option of the alignment palette. Group the boxes and center them inside the document layout. With the boxes still selected, go to VIEW>MAKE GUIDES.

Set the ruler axis coordinates to zero/zero at the upper right corner of the guide box that will correspond with proportion constant. It is important to be absolutely precise, and align the axis with the guide lines. Some people prefer to zero the center point, however, the upper-right corner may prove less confusing if precise changes need to be coordinated with Quark.

Now create the bounding box inside its proper layer by double clicking with the box tool. The bounding box is the single most important element in the lettering document, and yet it never sees print. This invisible box is what allows

Bounding Box

The bounding box created in Illustrator lettering files is absolutely critical for proper placement in Quark because it defines the area used by a document. To understand why this box is so critical, one must understand how placement is determined for Illustrator files.

Documents are placed in Quark by aligning the uppermost left corner of an imported document to the upper left corner of the layout programs art box. If a document is non-rectangular, such as a series of word balloons without a bounding box, Quark must calculate where the upper left corner should fall.

It does this by creating an intersection of two imaginary perpendicular lines whose locations are determined by the top of the uppermost graphic object, and the left-most object in the document. If a document is then centered in Quark, an imaginary rectangle is created touching the outermost objects, and the center of the rectangle is used for placement.

Keeping these calculations in mind, it is easy to see that without the bounding box, lettering files would be initially placed beyond the trim. Centering these documents will be of little use, especially on pages that only have one or two balloons. The bounding box forces Quark to use consistent dimensions for every page despite its content. Since the bounding box uses the exact dimensions of the Photoshop document, they should always align in Quark whether they be centered or placed at the default upper left corner. If the dimensions are not *identical*, misalignment will occur.

Any object placed outside the bounding box will invariably throw off the Quark calculations, causing misalignment. This is why it is so important to delete any stray point or object beyond the box before Quark placement.

figure 4-04 Quark creates an imaginary box (in red) around Illustrator objects in order to determine upper-left corner and center points for placement. Creating a bounding box equal to the proportion constant is the only way to insure proper placement.

for proper alignment with all other software. The size of this box will be determined by the proportion constant of the printed job. The box that appears should be given no fill and no stroke, making it transparent.

Type the number '0' into the x-y coordinates in the transform palette. Make sure the upper left corner is selected in this palette in order to align the box in its proper position with the guides. Once this is done, lock this layer in the layers palette. Save this template, and keep multiple back-up copies in case the original is damaged. If, at some point, the proportion constant for the comic should change, a new template should be created.

Info | Transform | Align

X: 0 in W: 0 in
Y: 0 in H: 0 in
∠: 0° ▱: 0°

figure 4-05:
An example of balloon placements and proofread script.

Lettering

Now it is time to begin lettering. However, it cannot be stressed enough that digital lettering is far more than just typing. As a matter of fact, the ability to type is not even required. Lettering is still an art form that requires an eye for good layout and design. Intrusive lettering will detract from the art and story.

Before you begin, take the script and a printout of the black line art, and create balloon placements with a color magic marker. Decide the least intrusive areas of the art to place balloons and captions. Try to visualize how to break up excessive dialogue into multiple, small balloons. Indicate to whom balloon pointers are directed, and number each balloon and caption to correspond with its intended dialog in the script. This balloon placement can be done as each page of art and script are completed, and will be the layout guide used when actually lettering the page.

Open the lettering template to begin a page. Place the low res Photoshop file into the art layer by going to FILE>PLACE. Zero the art once it appears, and lock the layer to prevent accidental movements. The dimensions of the art should correspond with the bounding box guide.

Many letterers will make the artwork gray so that they are better able to see there work. This is done by going to the *layer options* for the art layer, and clicking on *'dim images.'* The color of the art can also be altered in this window.

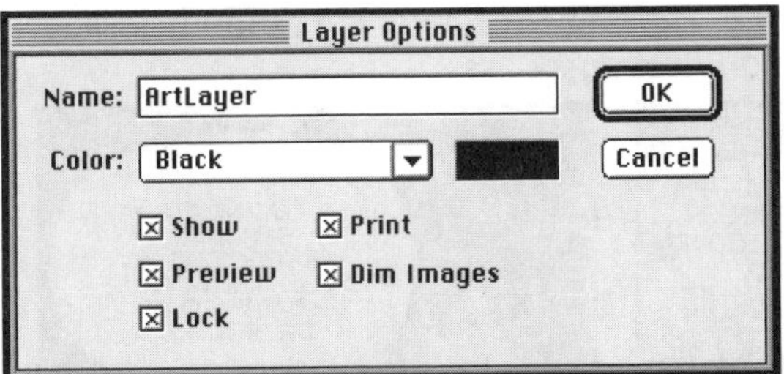

Some letterers prefer to type the balloon lettering as they go along. However, an easier way does exist for slow typers. Entire pages of script can be copied from the word processing file, and pasted into Illustrator. This paste up should be placed outside the live art area in the lettering layer, so that individual dialog can be cut and pasted for placement. Change the type to the correct font and point size. Point sizes vary greatly among different fonts, so individual judgement is required to determine what is too big or too small. Also, italic and boldface indications may not translate between the word processing file and the Illustrator file, or between fonts. These indications may have to be redone where indicated in the script.

Illustrator creates sections of type as individual units that can be edited or moved as a whole. Therefore, the contents of each balloon should be created as a separate unit unto itself, independent of all others. This allows for easier movement and placement. Add line breaks with an eye for creating pleasing balloon shapes, and avoid hyphenating words. Once all of the appropriate blocks of dialog, including boldface and italic conversions have been created, delete the script existing outside the live-art area. Lock the lettering layer to prevent accidental movements.

figure 4-06: Visualize a diamond shape over the lettering in order to create pleasing text layout and balloon shapes.

Creating Balloons

There are two distinct ways of creating balloons. Each has its own advantages and drawbacks. Personal preference will be the deciding factor in which process to choose. Although the industry has no names to distinguish these types of balloons, this book shall refer to them as ***whole balloons*** and ***layered balloons***.

Whole balloons are faster to create and easier to trap. Simply create the balloon shape behind the appropriate dialog. The average balloon has a white fill and a 1 point black stroke which overprints. Overprints and knockouts are chosen in the attributes palette, and stroke widths are chosen in the stroke palette. Alter the balloons shape so that there is an appropriate amount of white space around the lettering. Occasionally, creating the most pleasing shape may

A certain amount of design sense must be applied when writing, lettering and creating balloons and captions. The most effective lettering will not be noticed. The reader's eyes should flow smoothly across the page without interruption, and the lettering should not interfere with the artwork. Here are a few basic guidelines that can make the difference between good and bad lettering.

SPEAKING OF COVERING UP ART...
THAT'S THE STRANGEST THING I'VE EVER SEEN!
DO NOT COVER UP IMPORTANT SECTIONS OF ART WITH BALLOONS OR CAPTIONS.
PLACEMENT IS ESSENTIAL.
BE CAREFUL OF WHAT YOU DO AND DON'T HIDE.
SO DOUBLE-CHECK THOSE BALLOON PLACEMENTS.
THERE IS NOTHING WORSE THAN OUT OF PLACE BALLOONS.

POINTERS SHOULD AIM TOWARD THE SPEAKER.
GENERALLY, TOWARD THEIR MOUTH.

BUT DON'T MAKE THE POINTER TOO LONG.
YOU COULD POKE SOMEONE'S EYE OUT WITH THOSE THINGS.

AVOID LONG, MEANDERING CONNECTORS...
...BETWEEN MULTIPLE BALLOONS...
...NOT TOO MENTION USING AREAS AS ROADMAPS.

ALSO, THINK ABOUT THE ORDER...
...IN WHICH...
...YOU READ BALLOONS...
...OR CAPTIONS.
MOST PEOPLE...
...READ IN A SWEEPING...
...CURVED MOTION.

If people notice that the lettering as too big, too small, too intrusive, out of place, or too anything, then the letterer hasn't done his job properly.

require altering line breaks in the lettering layer.

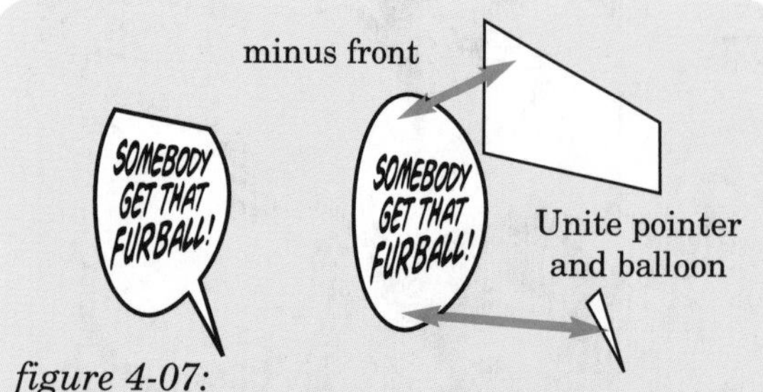

*figure 4-07: The **minus front** filter subtracts the top object from the bottom object. **Minus back** does the opposite. The two objects must overlap. Pointers are added using the **unite** filter, to create a single object.*

Create pointers using the pen tool. The pointers should overlap, and have the same attributes as, the balloon shapes to whom they will attach. Edit the pointers so that they are directed to the right speaker, and curve accordingly. Select both the pointer and balloon shape and apply the unite filter. In Illustrator 8 all path filters are found in the pathfinder palette, however in version 7 go to OBJECT>PATHFINDER>UNITE. The balloon and pointer are now one whole object. This same technique is used to alter the shapes of balloons and captions, such as creating a dripping effect.

To square off a balloon with a panel border, use the pen or box tool to create a shape outside of the panel. Try to be precise when aligning the edge of the box with the panel border. Again, this shape should have the same attributes as the balloon. Select both objects–more than two objects may not combine properly–and apply the minus front or the exclude pathfinder filter. Make sure the stroke appears to be a natural part of the panel border.

Layered balloons, although created in a similar fashion as whole balloons, are a group of multiple objects layered one on top of the other. These objects are, from top to bottom: the interior balloon shape; the pointer complete with stroke; and the outside balloon shape. All similar objects on a page will be given their own separate layer, for example ALL pointers on a page will be located in a single pointer layer. These separate layers are crucial for efficient trapping.

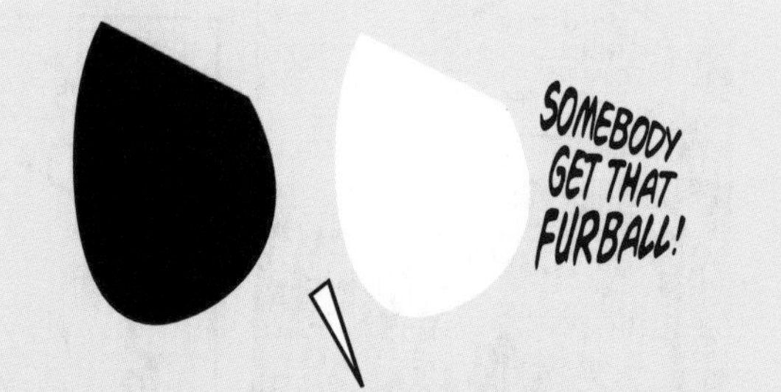

*figure 4-08: A **layered balloon** is broken into four pieces: the colored balloon shape, the pointer, the interior balloon face, and the lettering itself.*

When trapping layered balloons, the stroke on the pointer should overprint and the fill should knockout. If the interior balloon is white, or contains a gradation, it should have no stroke and should knockout. Applying a color fill, set to knockout, will require a stroke of the same color set to overprint –assuming the foreground color is lighter than the background color. The background balloon will also have a fill that knocks out and a stroke that overprints. If this background balloon is black the fill should be 60C 40M40Y100K, and the stroke should be 0C0M0Y100K. All colors should be

Balloon Shapes

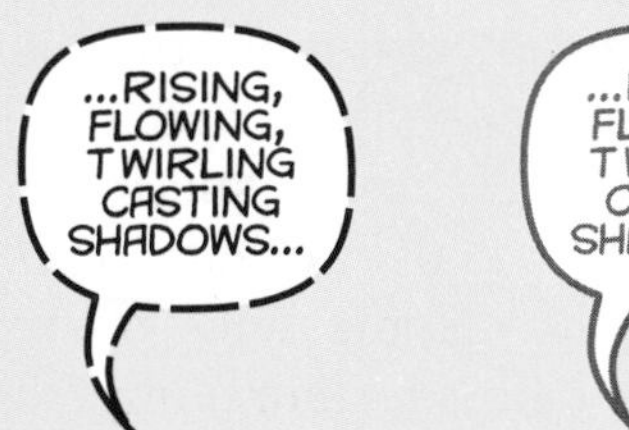

Whisper balloons are done one of two ways. The traditional dashed line which is created using a whole balloon, or by using a shade of gray for lettering and balloon outlines.

Thought balloons are created by uniting varying-sized circles to a pre-existing balloon shape. The circles should fall more on the inside of the balloon than outside.

A double balloon is nothing more than two overlapping layered balloons.

When creating burst balloons, use an oval shape as a guide. Draw the burst using the pen tool, where the inside points touch the oval. Eliminate the oval after the burst is complete.

A second way to create burst balloons is to add extra points to an oval balloon, and run the punk filter at a –15 setting.

To create a balloon that mimics the shape of a sound effect; duplicate the sound effect and give it a large stroke, outline the path, and unite it with the balloon shape.

CMYK, Do not use RGB.

Obviously, the drawbacks of creating layered balloons is that they are more time consuming to create and trap. The advantages are twofold. It is easier to alter the position of a pointer at any time, and the weight of the outline may vary slightly and appear less mechanical. One way to ease the time dilemma is to create and maintain a library of balloon shapes and sizes. This is also a good idea for whole balloons, however the 'adaptable' pointer advantage of layered balloons will become more apparent.

figure 4-10: The advantages of creating layered balloons is the ability to vary line weights (as seen in comparison to the single balloon above); and the ease of moving and editing pointers. The pointer must be sandwiched between the two balloons in order to appear attached.

Sound Effects

Creating sound effects is much like creating layered balloons in that a number of large shapes are used in combination to create a specific look. Even though small sounds can be created as letter forms with a stroke, larger noises look far more impressive when designed with numerous layers. Having access to a variety of different types of fonts will be a great asset, and do not be limited to only comic fonts. Mainstream fonts can be very useful, especially when creating logos.

figure 4-11: These sound effects are small enough that they do not require layers. They only require strokes in order to trap to the Photoshop document. Note the different font usages.

Type out the sound effect and increase its point size so that it is roughly the right size. As long as the computer has many fonts open, it is possible to change from one font to another while searching for the appropriate look. As the fonts change, the size of the letters may also

figure 4-12: Create separate objects out of large strokes, and reserve strokes for trapping purposes. Both objects have a dark overprinting strokes in order to trap properly.

change, sometimes quite drastically. Once an appropriate font and size has been reached, convert the letters into individual objects by going to TYPE>CREATE OUTLINES.

Layout the letter forms, keeping in mind they may end up surrounded by an extra large stroke. As soon as the positioning has been finalized, group the letters together so that they will be easier to handle. Make duplicates of the effects on different layers. The best way to do this is while the grouped objects are selected, go to the layers palette and option drag the colored selection dot from one layer to another. This will create a copy in exactly the same position as the first, but in a different layer.

figure 4-13: In this example, the center object creates the illusion of a gradating stroke. It requires no trapping stroke because it shares the color black with the other layers. The bottom-most object must have an overprinting stroke in order to trap to the Photoshop document.

Now go to each layer and add strokes of different sizes and colors. A good rule of thumb for designing sound effects is that they should remain legible if the entire effect, strokes and all, were printed as one solid color. It is all right to break this rule occasionally, but it is important to follow this rule in order to maintain variety and interest.

figure 4-14: In the above example, notice that 'zap' remains relatively unchanged when converted to a single color; where as 'shrack' becomes completely illegible.

At the final stage, large strokes must be transformed into objects and given a trap. Do this by going to OBJECT>PATH>OUTLINE PATH, followed immediately by OBJECT> PATHFINDER>UNITE (or using the pathfinder palette in version 8). OUTLINE PATH converts a stroke into an object surrounding the original un-stroked object. This can be useful when creating a smaller stroke on top of a larger stroke, or for creating a see through window frame. UNITE turns numerous selected objects into one singular object.

figure 4-15: Outline path turns the stroke of an object into a separate object unto itself, and leaves the original object without a stroke.

Now give the unified object an appropriate trapping stroke. Once the trapping for the entire effect has been complete, the multiple layers may be combined into a single sound effect layer. However, this is not absolutely necessary. The number of layers in Illustrator does not in any way affect the imagesetters ability to process the file.

Three types of imagesetting problems can occur involving sound effects, strokes, and grouping. Different objects with differing stroke weights, colors, and overprints which are grouped together can cause the imagesetter to revert to a default 'knock-out all' setting for the ***entire*** document. This will effectively render the file untrapped, so make sure to ungroup all unrelated objects.

The second error can occur if large overprinting strokes are not converted into objects. Although this occurs very rarely, the imagesetter may overprint these strokes on top of objects in the foreground layers.

figure 4-16: If large strokes are not converted to objects, there is a small risk that the imagesetter may overprint the stroke over objects on top of the stroke. The end result may appear as the bottom example, as opposed to the top.

Also, do not create objects which contain too many anchor points–too many is too many to count. An object with (literally) thousands of points can cause postscript errors, and can even crash an imagesetter. Remember: more is not necessarily better and simplicity can be a really good idea.

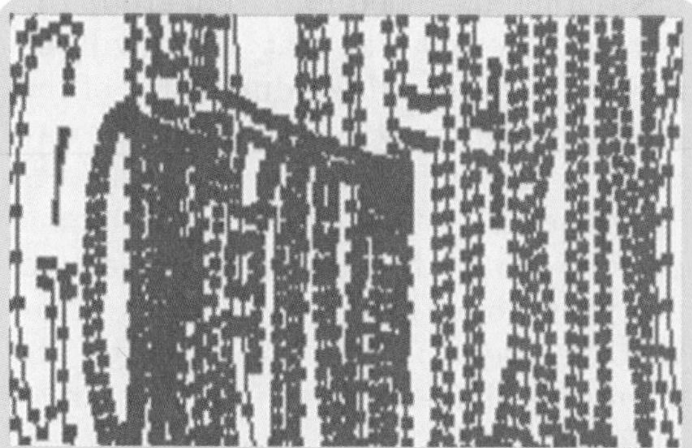

figure 4-17: Avoid creating sound effects, cover copy, and logos with too many anchor points. The example above was so complex, it created several errors with the film outputter.

Creating varied and different types of sound effects can be a very difficult task. The use of multiple fonts and filters is a must when creating these effects on the computer. Some letterers still do sound effects by hand, and then scan them into the computer. For many of them, this way is actually faster, despite the extra trapping that is required.

Cutting Art in Front of Lettering

Occasionally, art needs to appear to go in front of balloons or sound effects. This could be done in Photoshop, and in some cases this is the best way to proceed. However, in most cases this method is either to inconvenient or is unacceptable, such as with multiple language editions. Fortunately, there are at least two ways to proceed.

The first way is the minus filter approach discussed earlier. Simply create an object in the same shape as the art that is intended to cut in front of the elements involved. If cutting in front of layered objects, copying the object by option dragging across layers will be the best approach. This allows for minusing each layer separately. It would also be a good idea to import the high-resolution black line art into the file for creating a more precise cut.

The advantage to this approach is that proper trapping can be maintained. The disadvantage is that slivers of lower layers may peak out from below. This approach will not work on whole balloons, because the stroke of the balloon will run around the art.

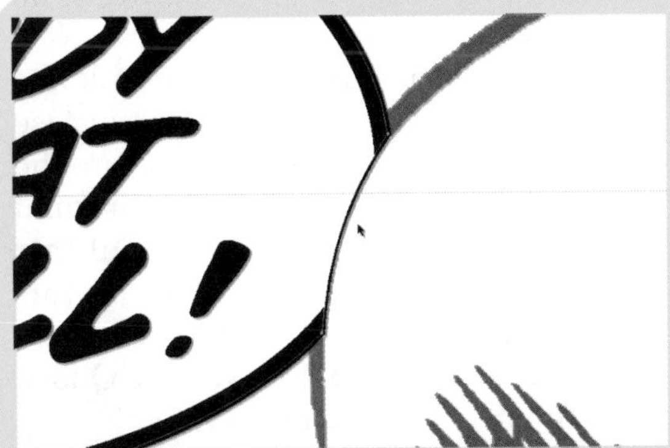

figure 4-18: Using the minus filter on layered balloons may result in slivers of the back balloon showing between the artwork and the interior balloon.

On the other hand, the stroke of a whole balloon will follow the shape of the balloon after using a minus filter (below). This may look unusual on more complicated cuts.

The second approach is to create a mask which will allow the art to show through without physically affecting the Illustrator objects. To create a mask, make an object or path around the area of the balloon that is to remain intact and visible. Select both object and mask and go to OBJECT>MASKS>MAKE. The art will now be visible. But remember, both the object and the mask are still intact and can be moved independently of each other.

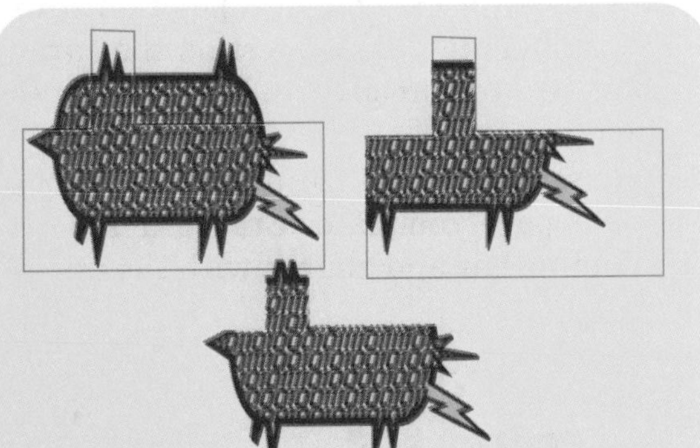

figure 4-19: A mask is created around art that remain visible. Since the art remains intact, different areas of the art will be seen if the mask should shift. The art will not be trapped along the edge of the mask.

The advantage here is its simplicity and precision. The major disadvantage, however, is that the areas where the masks cut an object will not be trapped because strokes disappear behind the mask. This may or may not be a major problem depending on what colors are involved. Obviously in the case of black and white, trapping is not even an issue.

Again, it would be wise to point out that the high res art or color files should be used for creating or editing precision masks. It is also a good idea for fine-tuning balloon placements, especially those which square off with panel borders.

Double-Page Spreads

Working with double-page spreads can be tricky. A spread template can be created using the proper proportion constant. Make sure that nothing falls outside the document set up.

However, many comic companies today require an individual Illustrator document for each printed page. This facilitates proper page imposition during film making. The question that arises, is how to spread sound effects across the fold.

First place and zero the art in a single page template. Create a second bounding box and align it with the upper right corner of the art. The left side of this new box will be just outside of the right-hand safe-copy guide, creating an overlap with the original bounding box. Letter the page as normal.

Once the lettering is complete and trapped, select the new bounding box and its entire contents. Copy and paste into an empty page template. Delete any art or sections of art that fall outside the new bounding box. The use of the minus front filter may be required to square sound effects to the inside of this bounding box. After completing this task, select all and zero the art. Now that the lettering is in position, delete the new bounding box. Its only purpose was to allow for proper zeroing in the new document. Return to the original document and delete, or minus, all art that falls outside the guides of this document. These two separate documents should align well in Quark with the necessary overlap intact.

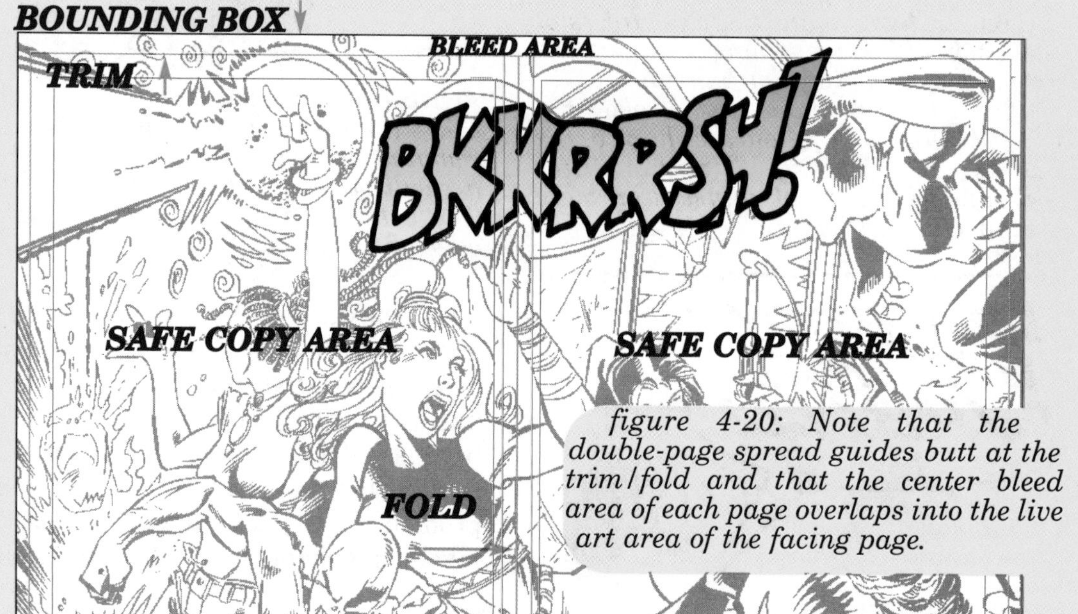

figure 4-20: Note that the double-page spread guides butt at the trim/fold and that the center bleed area of each page overlaps into the live art area of the facing page.

figure 4-21:
If separate lettering files are required for each page of a double-page spread, sound effects that cross over the fold will have to be broken apart. This is done by creating a duplicate in the exact same position, and deleting the section that falls outside the bounding box for each page.
It is important to create an overlap within the bleed areas so that the cut will remain unseen when printed. It is equally important that nothing falls outside the bounding box to insure proper placement in Quark.

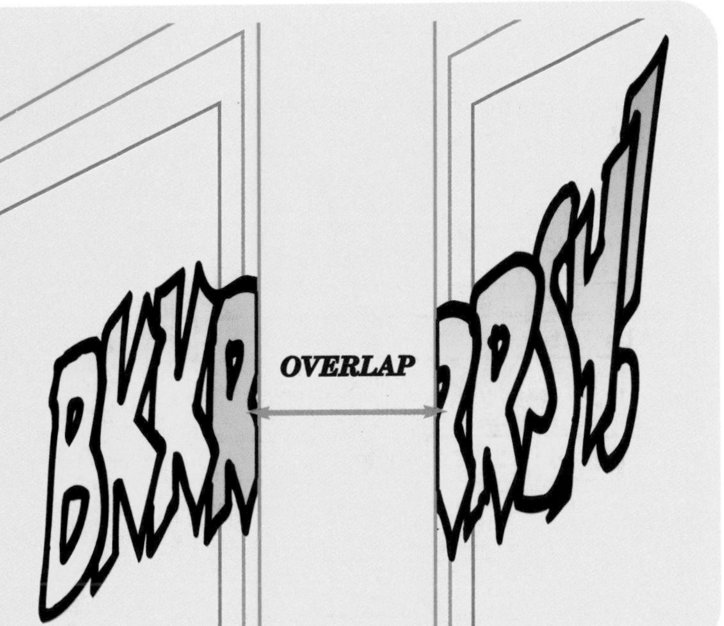

Pre-Flighting Documents

Before the lettering documents can be imported into Quark, certain steps must be taken to insure that they will align and print correctly. These steps are referred to as ***pre-flighting*** the document.

First, select all lettering still existing as fonts and convert them to outlines. This will prevent any possible font errors, both human and computer. Next, delete anything that falls outside the bounding box. The quickest way to accomplish this is to select all, then drag a de-selection marquee across the interior of the guides, and hit delete. Any object that falls outside the bounding box will throw off the alignment. Anything that falls outside the document set up can cause imagesetter errors.

double-check all trapping and make sure all colors are in CMYK only. Ungroup any objects with different trapping attributes, this too can cause imagesetter errors. Delete all Photoshop line art, there is no use for them inside a completed Illustrator document, and they will print better from Quark.

If using multiple fonts in a single Illustrator file, it is often suggested to copy and paste the entire contents from one document into a brand new document after outlines have been created. This copy and paste process can eliminate frequent font errors that can occur between Fontographer and Illustrator. One of the most common errors in this category, is when Illustrator or Quark request fonts that are no longer present within the lettering file.

Once these steps are complete, save the documents in EPS format. This is the only Illustrator format Quark will recognize and print correctly. EPS documents can not be trapped in page layout programs, which makes it all the more important to trap properly in Illustrator.

Trapping in Illustrator:
General Guidelines:
1) Generally the stroke is set to overprint and the fill is set to knockout. An x in the box indicates overprint. No x means the color will knockout.

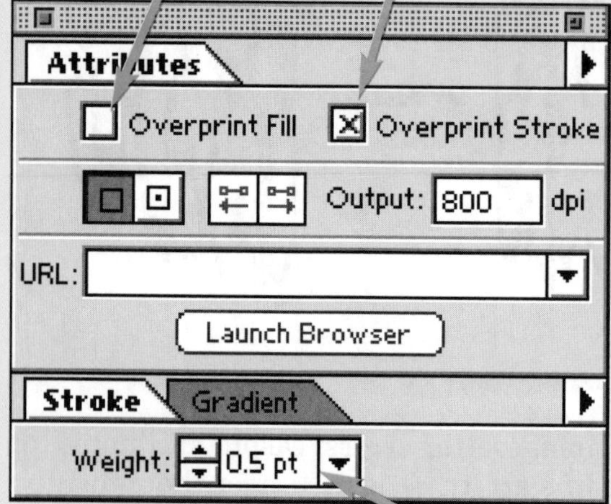

2) To create a .25 pt trap in Illustrator you must set the stroke at .5 pt, because the stroke is centered along the path.

3) Trap Illustrator documents to the Photoshop and Quark documents that they will be placed on. Be aware that Illustrator knocks out all colors by default; you must tell the computer when to overprint.

4) Don't forget to create blacks with underprintings in Illustrator.

Simple sound effects should have a fill that knocks out and a half-point stroke (.5 pt) that overprints. The stroke and print are the same color.

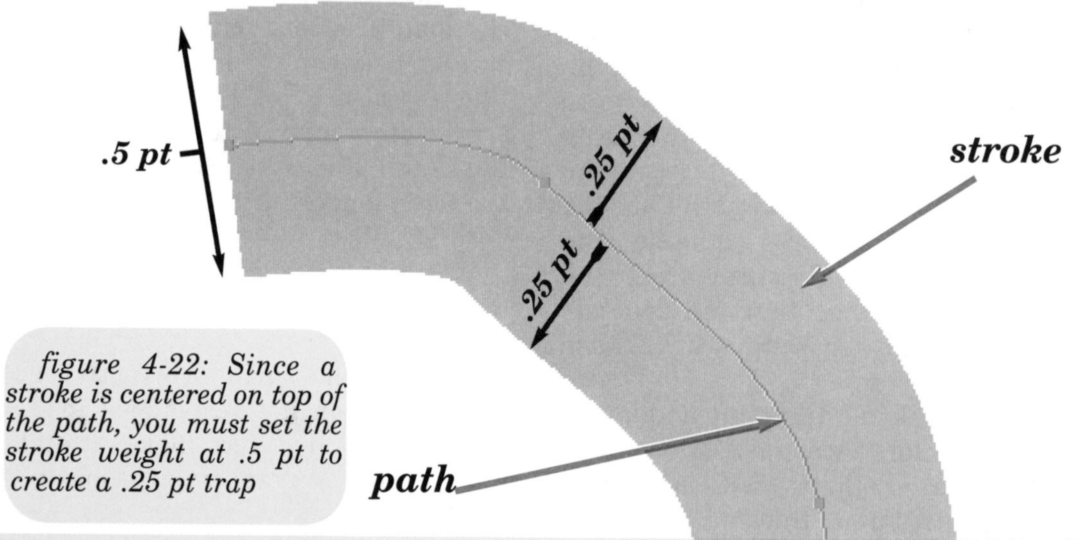

figure 4-22: Since a stroke is centered on top of the path, you must set the stroke weight at .5 pt to create a .25 pt trap

Word balloons and caption boxes should have a fill (any color) that knocks out plus a stroke (100K) that overprints. Colored strokes 1 pt or less should knockout.

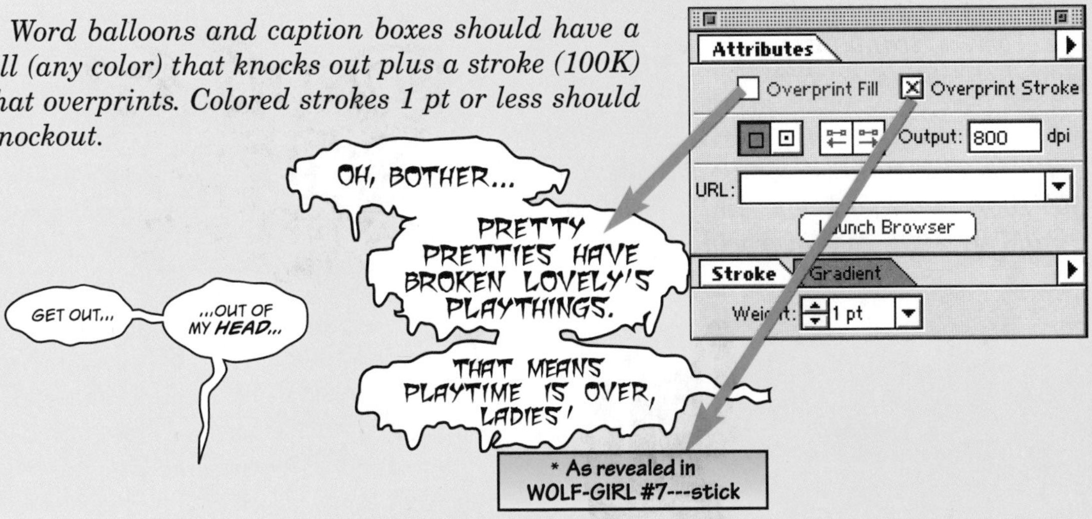

Attributes
Overprint Fill ☐ Overprint Stroke ☒
Output: 800 dpi
URL:
Launch Browser
Stroke Gradient
Weight: 1 pt

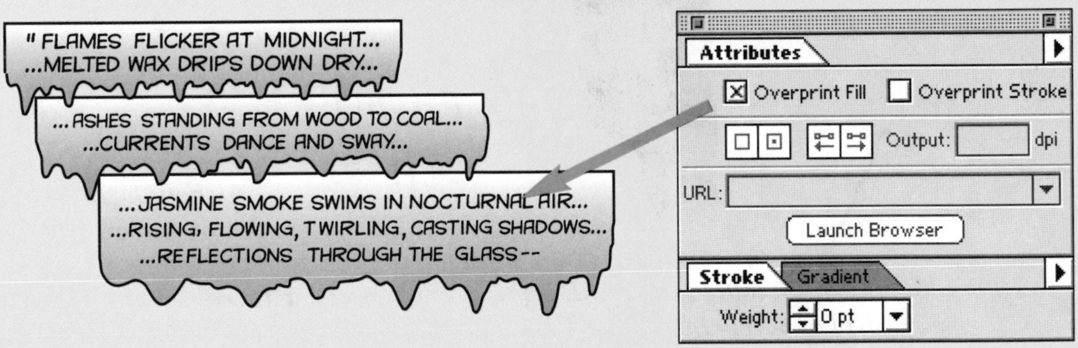

OH, BOTHER...
PRETTY PRETTIES HAVE BROKEN LOVELY'S PLAYTHINGS.
THAT MEANS PLAYTIME IS OVER, LADIES!
GET OUT...
...OUT OF MY *HEAD*...
* As revealed in WOLF-GIRL #7---stick

"FLAMES FLICKER AT MIDNIGHT... ...MELTED WAX DRIPS DOWN DRY...
...ASHES STANDING FROM WOOD TO COAL... ...CURRENTS DANCE AND SWAY...
...JASMINE SMOKE SWIMS IN NOCTURNAL AIR... ...RISING, FLOWING, TWIRLING, CASTING SHADOWS... ...REFLECTIONS THROUGH THE GLASS--

Attributes
Overprint Fill ☒ Overprint Stroke ☐
Output: dpi
URL:
Launch Browser
Stroke Gradient
Weight: 0 pt

Do not trap small fonts with strokes. Lettering inside balloons and captions have fills that overprint, or knockout in cases of light lettering on dark backgrounds.

Some letterers are concerned about how trapping strokes look when added to sound effects. The example at left is how the stroke will appear on the screen. At right is how it will print.

The examples at right and below show the correct trapping and layering for sound effects / cover copy.

Black objects have a fill of 60C40M 40Y100K that knocks-out and a stroke of 0C 0M 0Y 100K that overprints.

Gradation fill knockouts, 0B0R0Y100K .5 pt stroke (overprint)

100Y100R fill (knockout) 100Y100R .5 pt stroke (overprint)

Although this gradation knocks-out, it does not require a stroke because it traps naturally to the red color underneath.

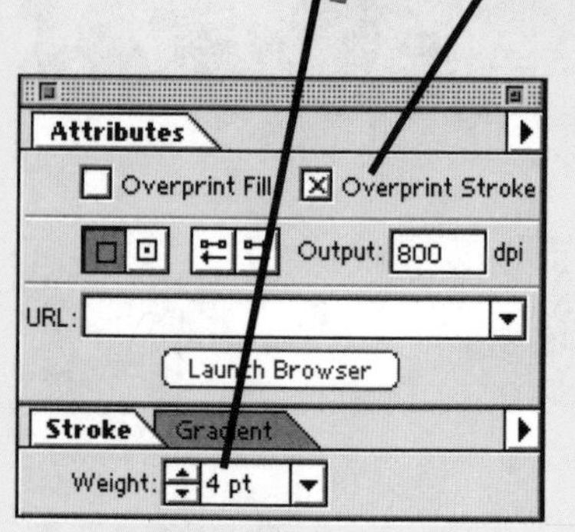

The sound effect on the left was created incorrectly. Both dropshadows have a 4 pt stroke that overprint. Not only will the imagesetter have problems with this approach, but the Photoshop document will be visible inside the red color.

The two dropshadows should have been combined into one object (OBJECT>PATH>OUTLINE PATH followed by OBJECT>PATHFINDER>UNITE); and then given a .5 pt stroke (overprint).

Avoid cover copy, sound effects, or logos that have overly complex layers.
Below is an example of a logo that can cause an imagesetter to mis-print due to complexity.The unnecessary layers were created in an attempt to trap.

The original logo had over ten layers, where as the final logo only needs four.

The example at left was created by using strokes as large as 10 pt on multiple layered objects. There is an incredibly large number of points used to create the letterforms.

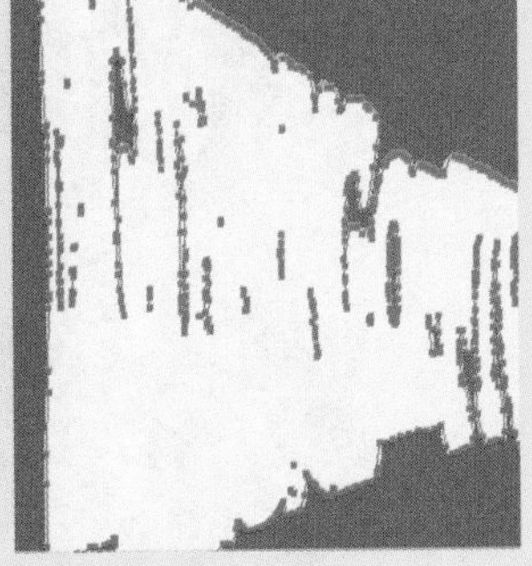

The two green layers should have been combined into one layer (at right), and converted into a single object by: (1) going to OBJECT>PATH>OUTLINE PATH followed by (2) going to OBJECT>PATHFINDER>UNITE; the object is then given a .5 pt stroke that overprints.

...MELTED WAX DRIPS DOWN DRY...
...FROZEN RED AND BLUE...

...JASMINE SMOKE SWIMS IN NOCTURNAL AIR...
...CURRENTS DANCE AND SWAY...

...RISING, FLOWING, TWIRLING CASTING SHADOWS...
...ASHES STANDING FROM WOOD TO COAL...

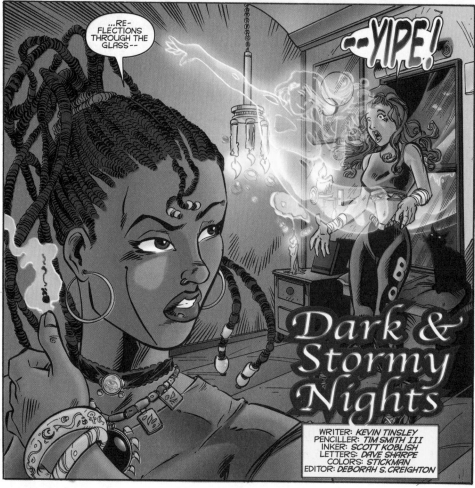

...RE-FLECTIONS THROUGH THE GLASS--

--YIPE!

Dark & Stormy Nights

WRITER: KEVIN TINSLEY
PENCILLER: TIM SMITH III
INKER: SCOTT KOBLISH
LETTERS: DAVE SHARPE
COLORS: STICKMAN
EDITOR: DEBORAH S.CREIGHTON

CHAPTER 5
COLOR SEPARATIONS

But yield who will to their separation,
My object in living is to unite
My avocation and my vocation
as my two eyes make one in sight.
-Robert Frost, 1936

Most people did not notice when computers first entered the field of comics. Their first appearance was in the separation houses. Even though they completely revolutionized this area of the publishing industry, it was a completely utilitarian endeavor. Computers were simply a tool used by low paid wage slaves. Certainly not anything an *artist* would want to use.

These days, anyone who even remembers how color separations were done before computers is showing their age. Most people can not remember, nor even conceive of how it use to be done. There are even those few, so spoiled by technology, who refuse to believe when they are told of the 'good old days.' What a horrid fate to be forced to do color separations ... *gasp* ... by ***hand***.

From the very beginning of printing itself, different colors required different plates. As mass production printing developed, so too did the separation houses. When comics were introduced into the mass market, certain limitations were imposed to save time and money. Originally, only three percentages of the three printing colors (cyan, magenta, and yellow) were allowed: 25%, 50%, and 100%. By mixing different percentages of these colors, 64 colors could be produced. That number was later increased to 125 with the (re)introduction of 75%.

Colorists would work on photostats (there were no photocopiers either) using special watercolor dyes that were absorbed into the photo emulsion. Nothing fancy, just flat colors. These colorists would then use a color chart showing the 64–or 125–colors to label each color with a percentage code. Somewhere along the line cyan and magenta got labeled B (blue) and R (red).

These color guides were then sent to the separation house. Each separator would take a page to separate. Acetate or amber lithe was placed over the original black line film, the film positive that would be used to create the black printing plate. A different overlay was needed for each percentage of each color (that is 9 to 12 separate overlays).

Amber lithe is a piece of acetate with a red film attached. This red film could be cut and removed with an X-acto knife. The red color reproduced as a flat black when photostated. The alternative to amber lithe, was to apply a thick black ink to a clear sheet of acetate. These were stated using a screen to break up the solid black into small rows of black dots. A different sized dot for each percentage.

An example of a hand-colored guide, with printing codes..

The separation process was made easier with the introduction of Litho-Paque. This product was a series of grey and black 'ink' about the consistency of gouache. A different shade of grey for a different percentage of color. Now each percentage could be applied to a single overlay, one overlay per color. These

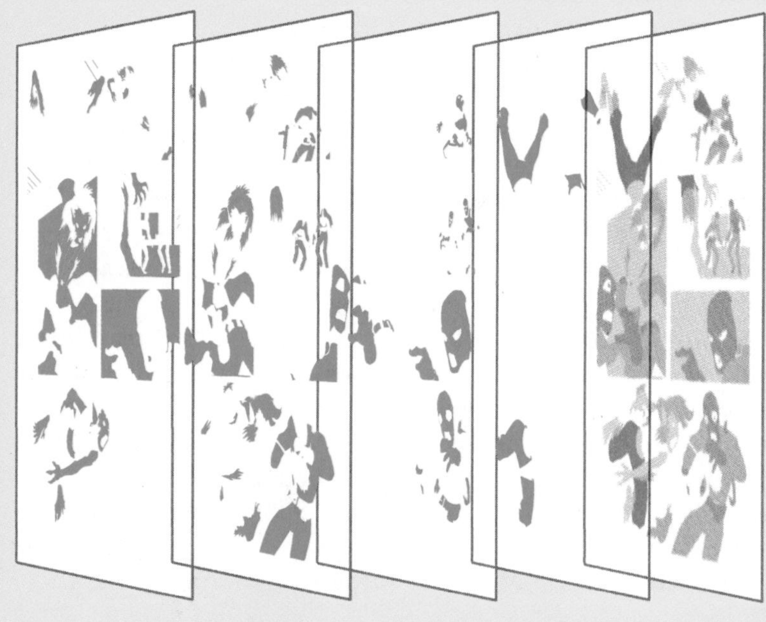

figure 5-02:When using Amber Lithe or Ruby Lithe, color separators needed to cut a separate overlay for ***each percentage*** *of each color. Since each overlay was a solid mask, percentages were created photographically using screens (etched glass filters placed in front of the photostat lens). The film percentages were then used in unison to create a single printing plate.*

overlays were now halftoned by the photostat, using a single screen.

Any type of gradation would require the use of an airbrush. Any color hold had to be cut out of the black plate and stripped into the color plate, unless drawn as a separate overlay. These were both costly and time consuming, and were almost never done in comic books. The introduction of computers did little to change this fact. Not at first anyway.

As computer hardware and software improved, so did the capabilities of separators. Many new colorist entering the field had backgrounds in separations. They began to exploit these new capabilities. Beginning in the late'80s, a few select colorists began buying computers and started there own coloring and separation studios. Two jobs for one low price. As time moved on, computers became faster and less expensive. More and more studios popped up, and coloring and separations improved exponentially. Although there are some who will, with good reason, argue this last point.

What good reasons? For many of the same reasons that prompted the writing of this book. Basic printing, design, and production techniques no longer seem to be taught in college. They have been replaced by computer classes that teach the use of hardware and software, but not their real world application. This results in graduates who are highly skilled, but ultimately ignorant and unprepared for the tasks that lie ahead. These people are capable of producing intricately rendered computer art that displays beautifully on screen, but which is rejected as completely unprintable and uncorrectable.

The intended nature of this book is to deal strictly with production issues, and to avoid questions of aesthetics and artistic techniques. Entire books can be written on these subjects, and many volumes already have. However, when dealing with the concept of computer

figure 5-03: The advent of Litho-Paque meant only one overlay per plate. The percentages were still created photographically, but now using a single halftone screen. Note that there were still no K-tones, and the line art was never screened, so that it remained crisp. A similar technique is used in computer production by combining high resolution black bitmap art with low res color files in Quark.

coloring, production is integrally incorporated into the art technique. Please understand that this chapter will stress production, and will only introduce techniques as a starting point for beginning separators.

CMYK vs. RGB

Let's begin by jumping head first into the middle of controversy. Computer colorists are divided into two camps on a key production issue. This issue revolves around using the RGB color space to separate pages. The RGB camp argues that their color space requires less memory, is faster to work with, has more variety of vivid colors, and is of equal quality to CMYK. Many also argue (incorrectly) that most art filters in Photoshop only work in RGB. The CMYK camp will argue that RGB does not translate well, printing dark and muddy colors, and create a host of production headaches. Be forewarned, as a production artist myself, I fall squarely into the CMYK camp.

RGB is a color space based on light. Light can be broken down into three dominate wavelengths, red, green, and blue. The combination of these colors produce all other colors, and 100% of all three colors produce white. All scanners, monitors, and televisions operate in RGB. Even the rods and cones of the human eye are attuned to RGB.

CMYK are the cyan, magenta, yellow, and black printing inks used in the four color process. These colored inks absorb RGB light waves. Herein lies the first problem. A fully saturated color in RGB may contain 100% of any wavelength –say blue–to create an intense color. Translate this into 100% ink and the colors are not as intense. The more ink that is present, the more light waves that are absorbed; the more light waves that are absorbed, the darker the color appears. Remember, the absence of color/light in RGB is black.

Adding to the dark-translation problem is Photoshop itself. The method used to translate RGB to CMYK is a very familiar mathematical principle.

figure 5-04: White light is made up of 100% RGB. Yellow ink absorbs all of the blue light, reflecting the red and green wavelengths, creating yellow light.

The RGB color space is indeed much larger than, and completely encompasses, CMYK. If an RGB color is out of ***gamut*** (outside the CMYK printing parameters), Photoshop converts it to the closest color ***geometrically***. More precisely, the shortest distance between two points is a straight line. The mathematically closest number is very rarely the closest visual approximation. This process usually results in a little bit of each printing ink added to any color, none of which may reach full saturation.

At this point the colors would need to be corrected, which in some cases is

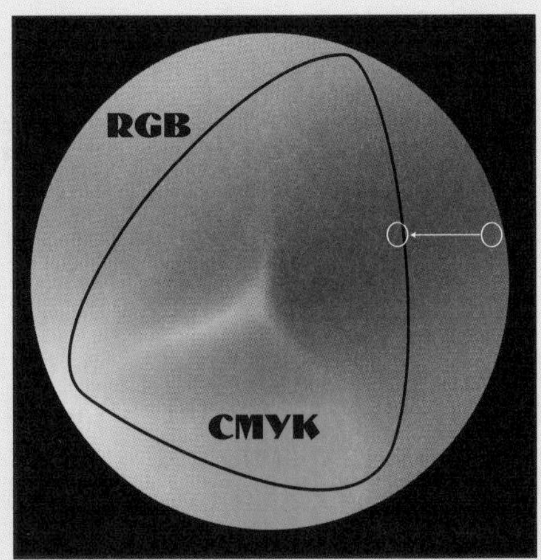

figure 5-05: The RGB color space is larger than, and completely encompasses, the CMYK color space, and Photoshop's conversions are mathematical, not aesthetic.

equivalent to recoloring the art. There are a small number of computer colorists who do an excellent job of correcting their colors, and I tip my hat to them. However, most RGB zealots do not convert their work at all, or convert it at the wrong stage of the process without corrections.

The wrong stage of the process? Let us now discuss the biggest production problem that accompanies RGB coloring: trapping and ink saturation. Where is the black plate? In RGB, black is the absence of all color, which translates as equal amounts of all inks in CMYK. This conversion of black results in untrapped line art, with an ink saturation between 320% to 400%. This is well above the limit of the majority of paper made these days. A magazine would look like it was run through the rinse cycle of a washing machine at these limits.

The trapping filter in Photoshop will not help, because its functions only allow for spreading colors, making them larger. The type of trapping required here is to choke, make smaller, the colors underneath the black. Furthermore, some of the undercolor may actually spread outside of the black because cyan and magenta spread equally into each other when butting. This filter was never intended to be used on line art or continuous tone images.

If coloring in RGB is done, the color space ***must*** be converted and color corrected before the black plate is added. This is the only way to insure proper trapping and prevent oversaturation.

It is true that RGB files are smaller by as much as 20% than CMYK files. It is also true that this may increase processing time. However, all the time saved may be lost again during the conversion and correction stage. If all

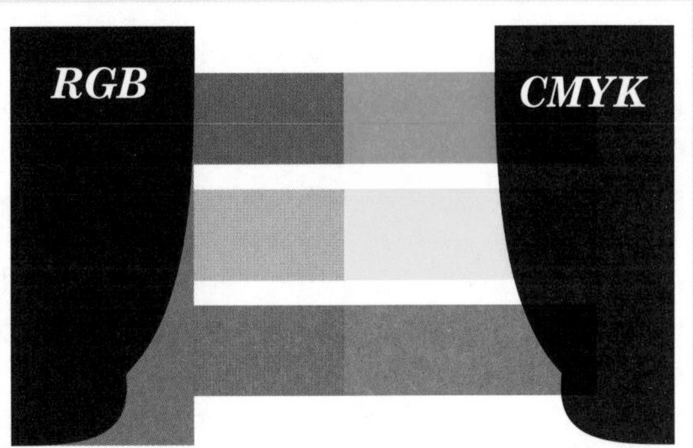

*figure 5-06: To test how RGB colors change during conversion create strips of pure ink colors in CMYK, and add an overprint of 100%K (EDIT>FILL> DARKEN) over a section of the colors as shown above. Convert the file to RGB, then back to CMYK. Check to see how the colors have changed. Also note if the black section is oversaturated and how it has eliminated the colored blocks underneath. To complicate matters further, the CMYK setup under **Color Settings** will alter the conversion process. Change the setting, and repeat these steps to see the difference.*

pages are eventually printed in CMYK anyway, why not color it that way to begin with? Working on inappropriate computer equipment is a poor and extremely unprofessional excuse. What editor would accept thumbnail drawings as finished art because the penciler did not have enough pencil lead? The cost of upgrading a computer is negligible compared to getting the job done right on the first try.

Monitor Colors and Printing Codes

Onto another RGB related topic. There are many computer colorists who choose colors based on what they see on the computer screen. Even if they are working in the CMYK color space they are forgetting that monitors only display RGB. Not to mention each individual monitor is calibrated, and displays color, differently. In other words: what you see is most definitely ***not*** what you will get.

The computer revolution has not changed the fact that printing codes are still the industry standard. People can argue all day over color hues and values. One person's crimson may be another's sienna, but everyone can agree that 100%Y100%M is RED, and 100%Y70%M is **not** (it's vermillion, actually). Printing codes, or CMYK values, are the only way

Channels and Layers

The differences between channels and layers often creates a great deal of confusion, even among seasoned professionals. Channels can be thought of as masks, the digital equivalent of air-brush frisket. Channels serve several purposes. They are used to create the printing plates during color separation, and this may include spot colors for additional ink plates. They are also used to save selections for key areas of art that may need repeated editing. This saves time over selecting the area multiple times by hand.

Channels play a key role during the production process of covers. They are essential for stripping in and trapping logos. Logos are usually placed in one channel, while a mask is created in a separate channel for art that cuts in front of the logo. These two channels are then used in conjunction to create the full color logo.

Layers, on the other hand, are actually a part of the printing art and contain information for all four printing plates, therefore, requiring more memory than individual channels. However, they are separate from the background, similar to an overlay. Individual layers can be edited without effecting the whole of the art. They can also be used to create editable special effects over specified areas of art.

One of the most valuable additions to Photoshop is the ***adjustment layers***. These provide the ability to make tonal and color changes without permanently effecting the pixels of the art. They are fully editable at any time, and their position in the layer palette can be moved, effecting only the layers that fall below.

Both layers and channels are powerful editing tools. One should become familiar with both their uses and their differences in order to utilize Photoshop to its full potential.

K-Tones

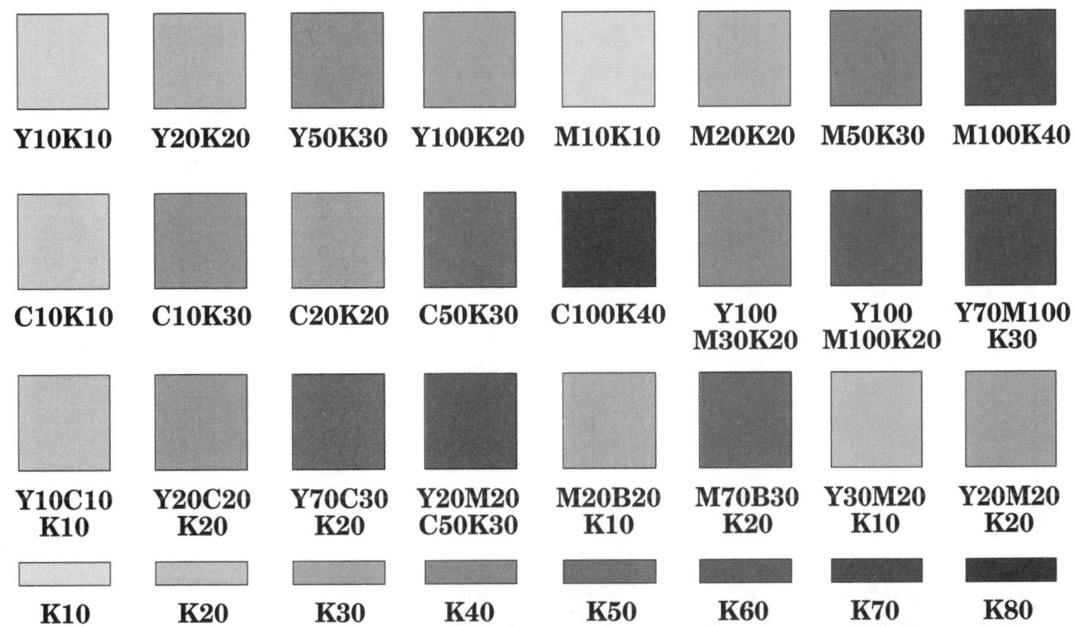

The proper use of K-tones in color separation is perhaps the most misunderstood subject facing computer colorist. Adding black to a color does **not** make a darker version of that color, it creates an ***entirely new*** color. Adding too much black can create mud. Relying too heavily on K-tones to define value changes and modeling can result in disastrous effects. These problems are so prevalent in the industry today, that many companies have issued a restriction against the use of any K-tones at all.

This restriction may seem extreme, but it is often the only way to insure an acceptable product. There is a proper approach to the use of K-tones. Using more than 20% of a K-tone in combination with other colors is usually unnecessary, and 30% is generally the recommended maximum. An 80% K-tone by itself appears almost black when printed, adding additional colors to this mix lowers the percentage value that appears black.

It is very important to remember that adding K-tones changes the actual hue of the colors present. Adding a K-tone to yellow creates a muddy green color. Adding K-tones to a red does not make a dark red, but instead makes a dark sienna. To create a dark crimson or burgundy color with K-tones, decrease the percentage value of yellow in relation to the K-tone added.

Keep the use of K-tones in skin colors to an absolute minimum. They can make flesh appear dead and muddy.

And one final word of warning: never create an underprinting using a line channel that contains K-tones. The K-tones themselves will be underprinted, further contaminating the colors present.

Flesh Tones

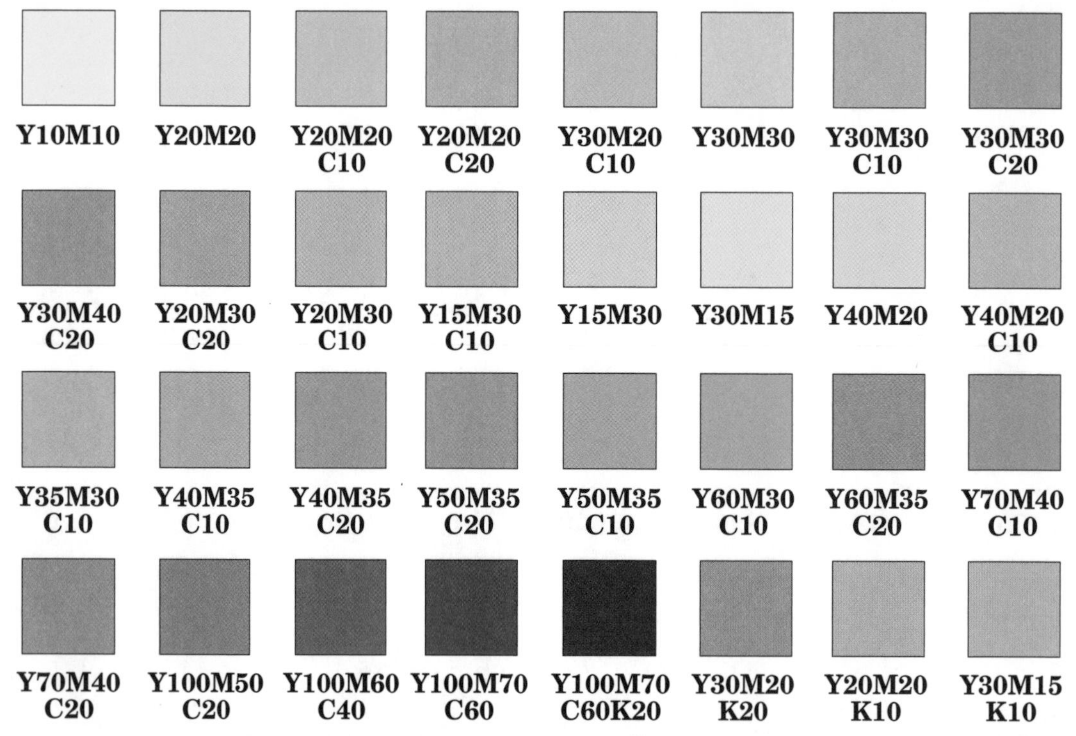

In the days of 25% ink values, the range of appropriate skin tones were severely limited. When line screens became tighter, the range reduced even further because colors became darker or brighter. However, the 10% range of colors have opened up a wide variety of subtle variations that can be used effectively.

Originally the base color for caucasians was M20Y20, and for C20M50Y100 for African flesh. These are still good starting points. But keep in mind that M20Y20 falls towards the light end of the spectrum and should rarely be made lighter, unless the individual is extremely pale. On the other hand, C20M50Y100 falls towards the darker end of the spectrum. Making this color darker moves it closer to the red or green areas of the spectrum.

When studying photographs, one may find caucasian flesh tones in the range of 8C35M40Y to 10C40M50Y. But remember that there are no holding lines in the real world. These colors may appear unnatural or dark when used as a base color in line art. They can, however, make excellent shadows. Also, K-tones can be found in photos to create value ranges. The use of K-tones in skin colors should be restricted. They can make flesh appear dead and muddy. Even professional color correctors strive to avoid them when working on photographs, and color separators have far more control over their ability to eliminate them.

to communicate efficiently.

It would be a good idea to obtain a color chart. Many printers have them, or there are books which can be purchased that contain nothing but pages of CMYK color grids. These codes do not have to be followed religiously, but should be used when choosing colors in the CMYK sliders palette. Otherwise, that vibrant red on the computer monitor may turn out brown.

Resampling

Before the separation process can begin, certain decisions concerning the production process must be made. To save time and increase the imagesetters processing speed requires the creation of smaller file sizes. This is done by placing a high-resolution black plate and separate color overlays over a lower resolution color file containing no line art. The reproduction quality does not suffer, but there are extreme limitations involving the use of special effects. Cover production may also become unnecessarily complicated (*see Chapter Eight*).

Having the full array of 'bells and whistles' will require (eventually) combining the black line art with the color channels. This demands a higher resolution to print with the appropriate line quality. It does not necessarily mean beginning the project at this higher resolution. Many separators color most of the job at a lower resolution, and increase the resolution when it is time to add the black plate and special effects.

The only rule written in stone concerning changing resolution or ***resampling*** is: never increase the resolution of *line art*. It is acceptable to res-down line art (only in gray scale mode), but this should be avoided as well because lines can become soft or fuzzy.

Resing-up line art can cause a stair stepping effect, particularly evident in curves and diagonal lines. Any such effect in the color plates will be hidden by the overprinting black plate, or de-emphasized by the line screen angles of the imagesetter. But remember, color holds are considered line art.

All processes begin with ***flats***. This requires making each selection a flat color with no gradations or modeling, until the entire page is filled. Flats allow for swifter magic-wand selections when adding modeling and gradations at a later stage.

Initially, all selections will have to be made using one of the lasso tools. This job is made easier if using a light pen and tablet which allows for more natural 'drawing.' Make selections well inside,

figure 5-08: An example of flats. Note how the colors butt together leaving no white spaces where the black line art will eventually fall. This is part of the trapping process.

or under, the black line art. This is part of the trapping so don't be timid, put as much color as you can under the black; and since this area is hidden, precision is not a major concern. Since the line art is located in a separate channel it will remain unaffected by the color (as long as the channel remains inactive).

A good way to work is to color from the background and move forward. This allows for large imprecise selections to begin with, by simply ignoring the foreground images entirely. Objects closer to the foreground require more and more precise selections. Intricate or overly complicated selections may be saved in additional channels if there is a possibility of a later color changes or special effects.

Usually, the magic wand can not be effectively used at this point, due to hatching techniques and broken or open line work. If the line work does accommodate the magic wand, the selection must be expanded considerably. Good judgement is necessary when expanding or contracting wand selections for trapping purposes. Again, you want as much color underneath the black as possible, without going 'outside' the lines. If the underprinting will be contracted by four pixels (this will be covered later) then expend the initial color selection by six or eight pixels if possible.

figure 5-09: Working from background elements to foreground objects is a time efficient way to separate. It allows for fast selections at first, and creates better traps.

Modeling and Gradations

Computer colorist are distinguished from each other by their color palettes, and their modeling techniques. Color is highly subjective. Good and bad coloring is based on successful application of intent. Dark and muddy colors are fine ***if*** they are intentional. The intent of most coloring is to set mood, emphasize characters, and establish depth. Even though there are many highly recommended classes and books on the subject of color theory, ultimately it boils down to what the individual thinks looks good (and pray the editors and readers agree).

However, modeling techniques can be taught and copied, and are occasionally closely guarded secrets. Individual style and skill still play a key role in distinguishing a 'look,' but there are entire studios who color in a single style.

Modeling is the addition of highlight and shadow colors to define form and lighting conditions. Without modeling art and coloring may appear flat and uninteresting. But be careful! Over-rendered modeling can be far worse to look at, and some art looks much better with flat colors.

Modeling can be achieved using a

wide variety of tools. Flats can be selected with the wand tool, and rendering can be drawn into the selection using the pencil, brush, airbrush tools, or even the eraser tools. The pencil tool creates a hard-edged flat color. The brush tool creates a soft-edged flat color, or may have varying translucency if the 'wet' option is selected. The airbrush tool mimics its namesake, and is arguably the most overused. If *all* modeling is done with the airbrush, it can appear 'mushy' and have no form.

Another way to create modeling, is to render it with selections and gradations. This is achieved by 'drawing' areas with the selection tools and filling them with colors or grads. The freehand lasso gives a more organic look, whereas the polygonal lasso gives a straight line 'cut' look. This technique can be expanded upon by filling the selection with a gradation, contracting the selection a few pixels (possibly repositioning it), and refill the grad. This can be repeated a number of times, while changing only the position of the gradation, and not its color.

When modeling dark skin tones it is usually a good idea to keep the highlight areas very small. If the highlights are to large, they may appear to be the actual skin tone. It can also be difficult to create a good shadow color without shifting towards a dark green or sienna caste.

Secondary Light Source

It is wise to border secondary colored light effects with 'shadowed' colored skin tones (bottom center). Many colors used for light effects are actually darker in value than skin tones and may look like shadows (bottom left). Placing them next to skin tone with a darker value will give the illusion of colored light. This is similar in effect to the addition of inked shadows added by the artist (bottom right). Also note how the white and dark backgrounds affect the appearance of the colors

Modeling Techniques

In addition to color choice and color theory, the style and approach used to add shadows and highlights to art is what distinguishes most computer colorist and separators from each other. Although their are many different aesthetic styles, there are only a few basic techniques used when separating artwork. Most colorist use a combination of all of these techniques. The style of artwork may determine which approach will predominate any given job.

The most important things to remember while modeling artwork is to avoid oversaturating the colors, for not only may this lead to printing problems, but it can create colors that are too dark or muddy. Also avoid over-rendering figures. This can lead to a super-slick plastic 'texture.' This may be fine for shiny wet objects, but can make human skin appear unrealistic.

Airbrush modeling is the fastest modeling technique available to the computer colorist, particularly when using a drawing tablet. Once flats are selected using the wand tool, the separator uses a variety of brush sizes, opacities, and modes to create highlights and shadows. The drawback to using this technique **exclusively**, is that the figures may start to appear overly soft and 'mushy,' as if they were made out of clay.

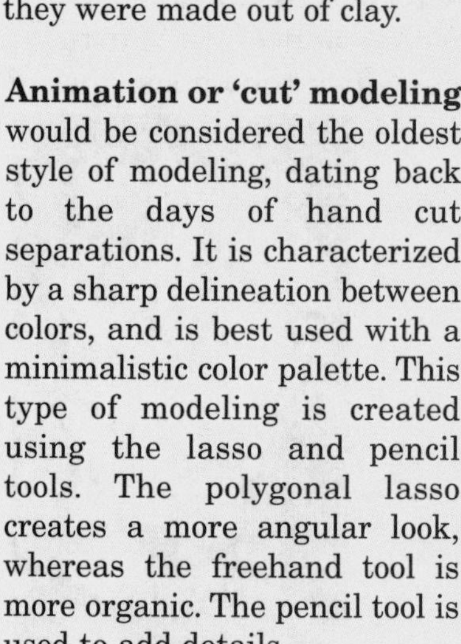

Animation or 'cut' modeling would be considered the oldest style of modeling, dating back to the days of hand cut separations. It is characterized by a sharp delineation between colors, and is best used with a minimalistic color palette. This type of modeling is created using the lasso and pencil tools. The polygonal lasso creates a more angular look, whereas the freehand tool is more organic. The pencil tool is used to add details.

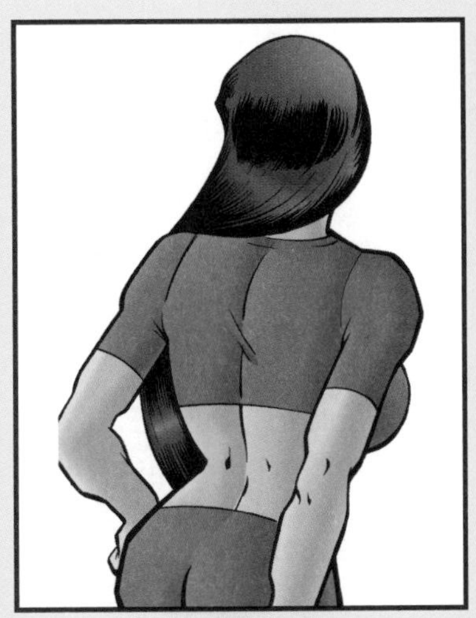

Gradation modeling is a simplified form of modeling generally used on relatively small objects, or for expediency. The lasso tool is used to select relatively large areas, and the gradation tool is used to add highlights and shadows. The airbrush or brush tool can be used to add some detail. This type of modeling is used to give the *illusion* of detail to secondary objects. Gradation modeling is also the basis of more complex modeling styles.

'Soft Cut' modeling uses a combination of all other forms of modeling. Highlights are added with the airbrush tool. Shading is applied using the the lasso tool. Selections are feathered to to soften the cut lines, and the gradation tool is used to add dimension to the shadows. Generally, the shading will be darkest near the interior part of the selection, and lightest near the horizon of the form (the black outline of the drawing).

Complex modeling is a far more intricate version of the gradation modeling technique. Muscle forms are selected with the lasso tool, and shading is added using any number of tools. Smaller selections are used to add highlights. These selections are then contracted to add further highlights, usually using the gradation tool set to screen mode. This selection may be contracted several times to create the characteristic 'penlight' effect.

Learn and apply a variety of modeling techniques, and by all means, experiment. This will keep the work visual interesting to both the audience and the colorist.

Conversions and Underprinting

Once all of the modeling has been done, it is time to make all of the necessary conversions relating to the production techniques that will follow. Increase the resolution if necessary, and replace the line channel with art that has not been resampled. If working in RGB, it is time to convert to CMYK and correct the colors. It would also be wise to double-check the saturation levels of the colors at this point (the info palette can be set up to read both CMYK values as well as ink saturations). And finally, –barring any color holds or texture effects–add the underprinting and check the trapping.

figure 5-14: The underprinting should be contracted from the black plate to create a proper trap. The trap is the area of color beneath the black plate which butts to the underprint color.

It is important to create the proper trap when adding the underprinting. The correctly trapped underprinting is created by making the black line art a selection. Go to SELECT>MODIFY> CONTRACT. Contract by one pixel for every 100 ppi of resolution, therefore a 500 ppi file would be contracted five pixels. Failure to contract properly may result in the destruction of the trap.

Fill with the appropriate underprint color. This color will be 110 to 120 points less than ink saturation limits, and will contain equal portions of magenta and yellow, and slightly more cyan ink. A good undercolor for a 250% saturation book would be 60C40M40Y. Make the black line art a selection for a second time (***do not contract***), and fill with 100%K only by going to EDIT> FILL>DARKEN. This will add the black plate to the art without deleting any colors underneath.

Now double-check the trapping; you must zoom in close to an edge or thick outline of black line art. Click the eye icon on and off several times. The underprinting ***should not***

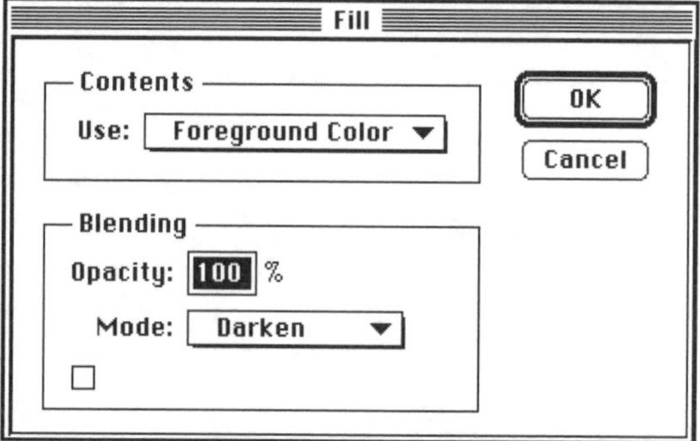

identically match the black line art, but be noticeably smaller. The background colors should go underneath the black line art and butt to the underprinting. There should be no noticeably large areas of white beneath the black line art.

Technically, underprinting is not utilized for any trapping purpose. It serves two important functions in the printing process. The first function is to create a rich, even black. If 100%K is printed on white paper with no underprinting, it will appear less dense (or washed out) than many of the colors surrounding it. On the other hand, if that same black ink is printed on top of several colors of varying values, the value of the black itself will vary with the colors it overprints. This will give the noticeable appearance of an uneven black tone.

However, the primary function of underprinting is to prevent oversaturation of the paper with ink. If black ink were to overprint a large area of YR, the saturation would be 300% (small trap areas have no real impact). This would be unacceptable if the saturation level is 250%. Therefore, we avoid this problem by creating an underprinting for black that is equal to 240% (60C40M40Y100K).

figure 5-15: Note that you can see the color bars behind the overprinting black on the left. The underprinting on the center bar is 30C70M40Y. On the right bar it is 60C40M40Y. Is there a difference?

It should now be clear how proper trapping is incorporated into the actual process of coloring. As special effects are added, careful attention must be paid so as not to destroy the trapping already established.

Adding Special Effects

Obviously the use of special effects add to the appeal of computer coloring. Unfortunately, certain effects and filters can hinder production, or destroy trapping if handled improperly. Also, filters are given as a reason for coloring in RGB. There are many filters that do not work in CMYK. These filters may be important for creating textures, and will only work in RGB or gray scale formats.

However, there is a solution that most people overlook. CMYK is made up of four separate gray scale channels. So even if a filter can not be run on all four channels at one time, they can be run on each separate channel. As soon as a filter is used, its name will appear at the top of the filters list. By selecting this name the filter will run automatically with the same preferences. Interesting effects can also be created if the preferences are altered slightly on each channel.

In the case of creating textures, it is usually a better idea NOT to run filters directly on color art. Instead create them in a channel. Have a separate channel for the selection area. Fill this area with

figure 5-16: The examples above show a before and after of an ocean ripple filter to give the impression of wet pane of glass. At right a frosted glass filter was run. In both cases the filter was run on each individual CMYK channel because they only run in RGB and gray scale.

a base color or gradation. Make a selection out of the texture channel, and de-select the area outside the masked area by option clicking with the wand tool. Then go to IMAGE>ADJUST> CURVES either darken or lighten the colors. Inverse the selection and de-select the outside masked area again. Finally, apply the opposite curve adjustment. This method gives more precise control over color content. It also allows for using multiple filters to create a single texture without damaging color or art. However, textures should be applied before the underprinting and black plate are added, but AFTER the file has been resed up.

Color holds can be tricky when dealing with a transition between color art and black line art. This effect is applied after the underprinting and black line art have been applied.

Applying Textures

The best way to create textures is through the use of channels and curves. In this example, the texture was created with the use of a cloud filter.

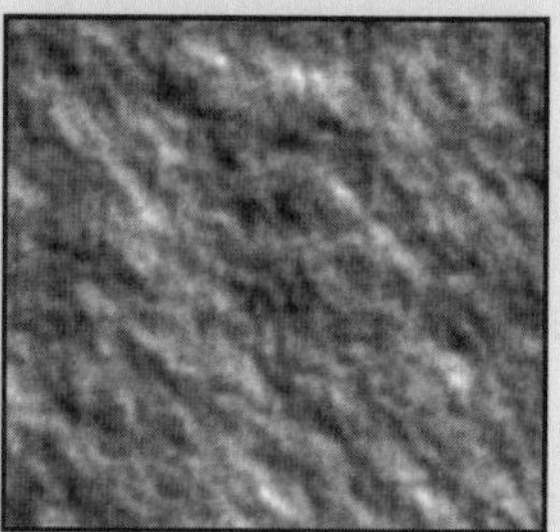

The pattern was then embossed to near maximum levels (height: 9/ amount:500). This gives us a rough-hewn rock texture.

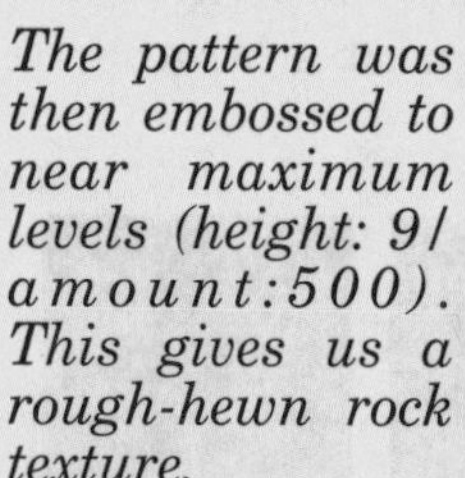

This channel was then made into a selection and applied to darken a flat color using curves. The use of curves allows for more precise control over each individual color channel.

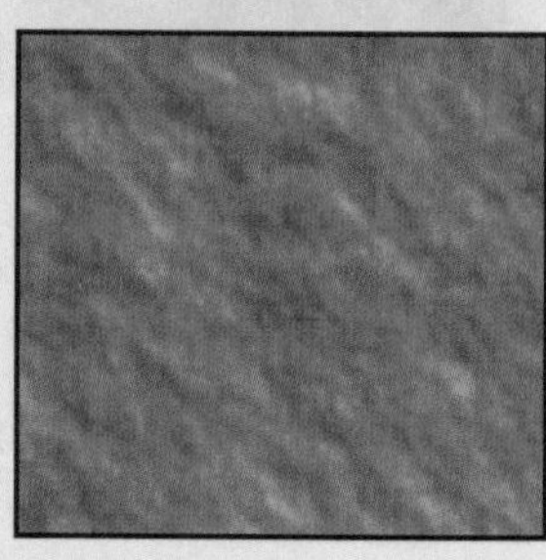

The selection was then inversed, and the color lightened, in order to apply highlights.

More on Textures

An inside joke through out the industry is that to some separators, asking for a texture means 'add noise.' Try not to fall into a 'texture rut' by using the same filters over and over again.

Experiment with multiple filters to create a single interesting texture. The combinations are boundless. The following textures began as 'clouds' to use as a base.

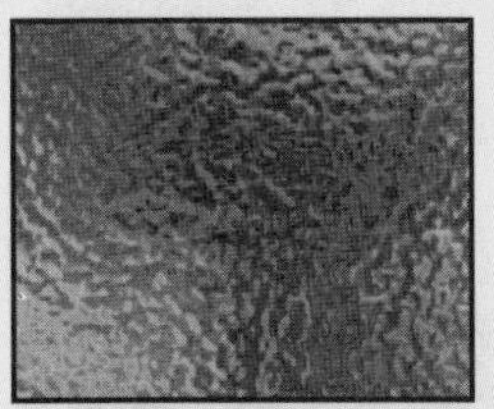

ocean ripple

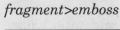

fragment>emboss

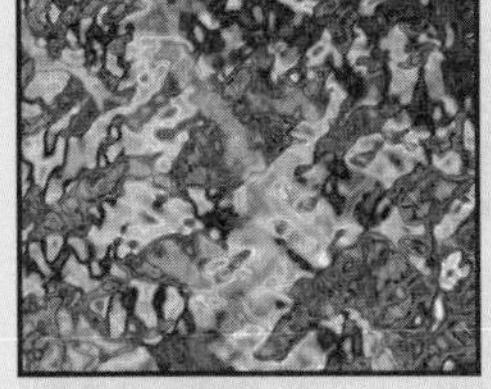

chrome

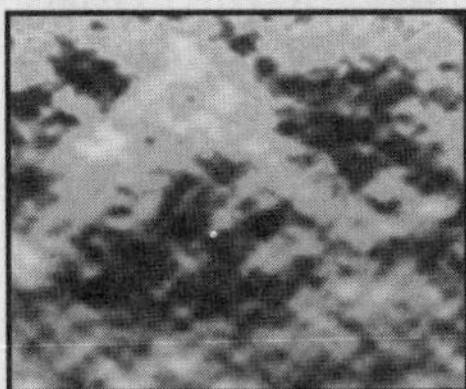

bas relief

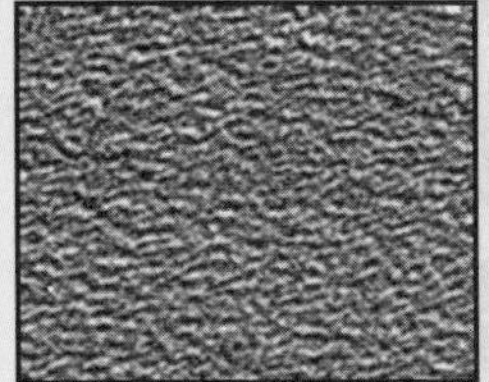

grain (clumped)> embossed

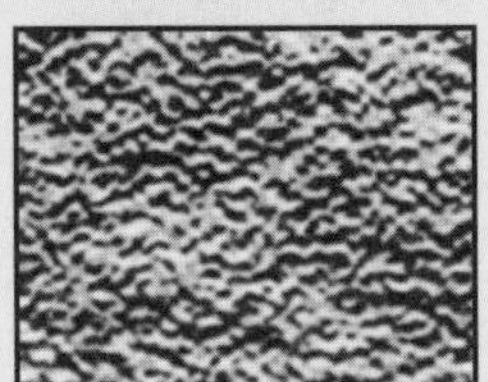

grain (clumped)> bas relief

Create a mask around the area to be affected. Make the appropriate selection using the line art channel and mask. Then use the gradation tool with the options set to go from a color to transparent. This will create a gradation from the chosen color to the trapped underprinted black. If this option is not selected, the trapping will be destroyed.

figure 5-19: In the example above, the glass jar, label, and liquid were all held in different colors.

Be aware that the colorize function in the HUE/ SATURATION window can also destroy trapping, even if the line art remains black.

Lens flares are the only consistent problem filter. They will not work in gray scale, only in RGB. Yet everyone wants to use them. My suggestion is to create them in a layer by hand in

figure 5-20: The candle flame color was added using an airbrush. The glow was added using a layer with 50% opacity.

figure 5-21: Note how a color hold gradation to black added after the underprinting is applied. The underprint color may be visible behind the gradation on the computer monitor, but will not be seen in the final print.

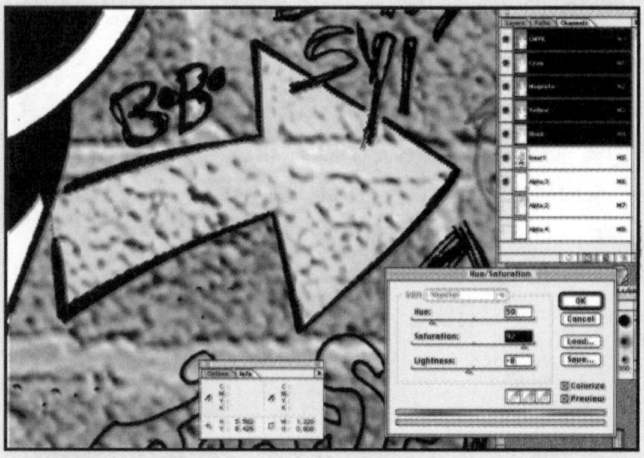

figure 5-22: The art in this example contained a photographic background with a distinctive texture. Graffiti was added by colorizing the photograph. A different color was applied for the inside (above), as well as the outline (below). It is a good idea to have the info palette visible, to keep track of color and ink saturation.

CMYK. They can be created using a combination of airbrush, smudge, and selection tools, using a variety of colors. Working in a layer allows for movements and rotations, as well as opacity changes. Also, they can then be copied into a 'library' for later use.

Lens Flare

The best way to create a lens flare is in a separate layer. Start by airbrushing a base color with a large brush.

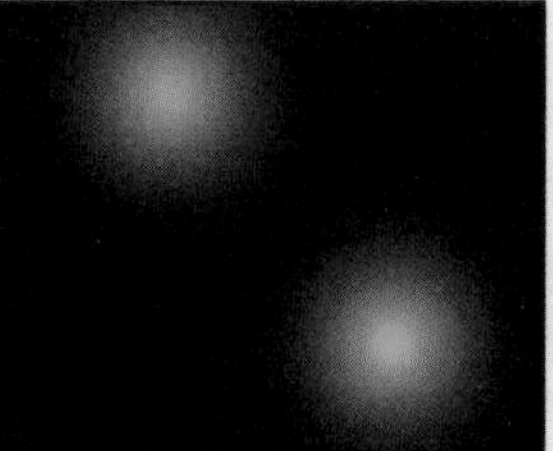

With a series of smaller brushes, add lighter colors, reaching white in the center.

The smudge tool is used at a low pressure to add spokes to the flare. Changing the size of the brush, changes the size of the spoke.

In yet another layer, add details using the circular marquee and the airbrush. Alter the opacities of the layers to create the desired effect.

Color Holds vs. Overlays

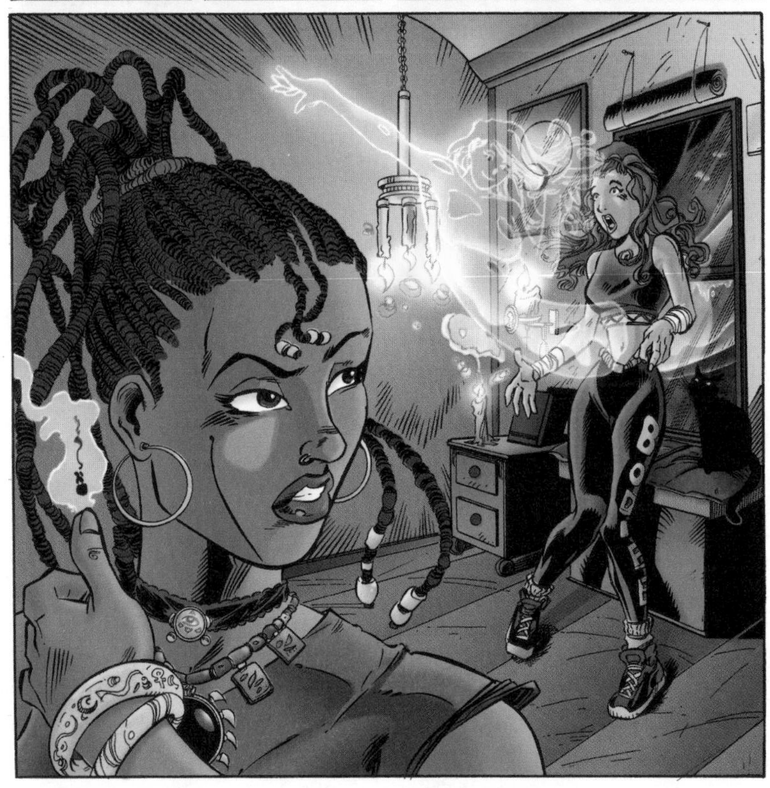

An area of confusion that often arises with pencilers and inkers is the proper time to use color overlays, and when to draw future color holds directly on the art board.

The answer lies in the intended effect, and in how difficult it will be to remove the color hold from the line art. Another factor is if the color hold will be added in Quark (which will be covered in Chapter 6), or in Photoshop (which is covered here).

If the art is relatively simple to select (such as the flames, smoke, and glass jar) it can be drawn on the art board with the black line art. On the other hand, if it is extremely complex, or consists of many, many tiny parts (such as rain, falling snow, or a million shards of broken glass), it should be drawn on a separate overlay.

Effects that are intended to interact with the black plate should also be drawn on an overlay. In this example, the ghostly apparition is intended to be translucent, so that the CMYK plates underneath can be seen at a different opacity.

This can be particularly effective for portraying holograms, or invisible people. This type of effect is usually colored in separate layers of varying opacities. Be advised that the background art will probably need to be ghosted behind the overlay to complete the visual effect, as well as prevent ink oversaturation.

Saving Formats

Once a job is complete, all layers should be flattened and extraneous channels discarded to create the smallest possible file. Quark will not recognize the native Photoshop format language, therefore the file format must be changed.

There a number of formats that these files can be saved in, and the printer may have a distinct preference. Some imagesetters process some formats faster than others. The formats to use are:

TIFF (*Tagged-Image File Format*): All black line bitmap art to be imported into Quark must be saved as TIFF's so that they can be trapped properly. Also, any bitmap line art that will be used as a color hold in Quark must be saved in this format. Color files may be smaller when saved as TIFFs.

EPS (*Encapsulated PostScript*): Although this format may create a larger file, it was created specifically to describe curves and angles associated with fonts and artwork. Most imagesetters use the postscript language to translate art into film, therefore this is usually the better format for saving color files. EPS files can not be trapped in Quark, and will automatically knockout. However, a printing option in Quark 4, allows for overprinting EPS blacks, which can assist in better traps, particularly for clipping paths.

EPS DCS (*Desktop Color Separations*): Color documents saved in this format create five different documents. The four-color channels are separated into gray scale documents, and a 72 ppi image preview that can be imported into Quark. This format can spool extremely quickly through the imagesetter, but can be somewhat fragile and prone to corruption. Once a file is saved in this format it no longer exists as a single document. The files would have to be reassembled if any editing were required. Also, proofing printers may only print out the 72 ppi preview.

There may or may not be problems with saving files as a **TIFF** with **LZW** (*Lemple-Zif-Welch*) compression. Some imagesetters and application programs can not open or decompress this format. It is best to check with the printer before saving any files in this format. If the printer has no problem with LZW compression it can save a great deal of disk space.

The format that must be avoided for publishing is **JPEG** (*Joint Photographic Experts Group*). Files in this format can be imported into Quark and will display properly on the screen, however they will turn into gray scale when imageset. The EPS formats can be saved with a JPEG preview, but this too should be avoided.

Most other formats do not support CMYK images, or can not be imported into Quark. Also avoid any compression standard that is considered 'lossy' because they throw away information during the compression process. Discarding data can damage image quality and cause stair stepping or change colors.

Photoshop & Memory

Of all the applications used in desktop publishing, Photoshop is the biggest memory hog. The minimum memory requirements of 32MB are just enough to open and run the program itself. They are certainly not enough to work on large files. It is important to understand how Photoshop uses RAM in order to overcome potential problems.

Open Photoshop files utilize both RAM and free hard drive space (referred to as the scratch disk). Earlier versions of Photoshop allowed one undo and a revert to last version saved. These two full copies of the file are saved to the scratch disk, and a full version is loaded into RAM as a working copy. This means that a file that is 10MB closed, utilizes 30MB when open, because there are three different copies of the file open.

Photoshop 5 allows for multiple undo's, and utilizes memory much better. The newer version still maintains the revert on the scratch disk, and the working copy in RAM. However, only edited pixels are saved as undo (now found in a history palette), not an entire copy of the document. Small changes take up a small amount of memory, larger changes take up more room. But be careful, changing all pixels in an entire document creates a copy of the document in memory. Do this four or five times, and the scratch disk memory decreases rapidly.

Adding layers and channels to a document will also increase its memory needs. Layers will increase the document by an amount equal to the base document. For example, each layer added to a 10MB document–with no additional layers or channels–will be 10MB. Add two layers and the document will now be 30MB. Channels enlarge the file by one-quarter for CMYK files, and one-third for RGB (not including layers). Therefore, a 20MB CMYK file will increase by 5MB for each additional channel. Adding layers will not effect the size of channels, nor vice-versa.

Now take into account the effect adding multiple layers and channels has on the 'undo' saved on the scratch disk, and you will realize how quickly one can run out of memory on large files. This is especially true in earlier versions of Photoshop.

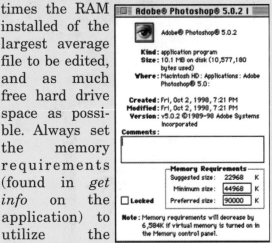

It is recommended to have three times the RAM installed of the largest average file to be edited, and as much free hard drive space as possible. Always set the memory requirements (found in *get info* on the application) to utilize the maximum amount of RAM without interfering with the system.

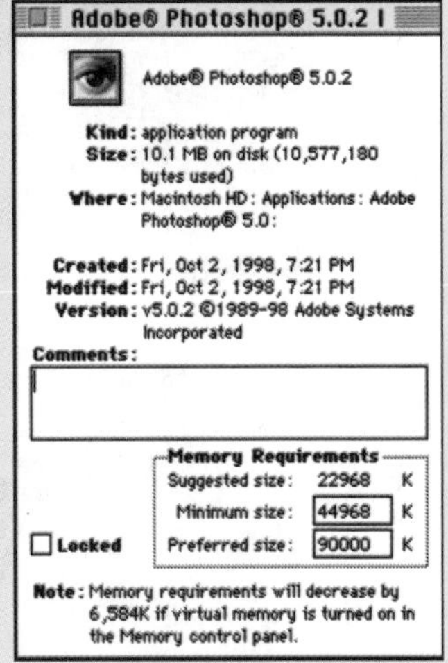

This particular recommendation is for Photoshop alone. A good rule of thumb for other applications is double the manufacturers recommendation. Also keep in mind, these other applications may have to be run at the same time as Photoshop during the production process. The total memory configuration of all open applications should not exceed the total amount of RAM available.

ISN'T THIS KIND OF ANIMATION UNUSUAL FOR ZOMBIES?!
THAT'S GOTTA HURT!
YES, BUT NOT FOR GHOULS.
NOW YOU TELL US!
hrmph!
OH, BOTHER...
PRETTY PRETTIES HAVE BROKEN LOVELY'S PLAYTHINGS.
THAT MEANS PLAYTIME IS OVER, LADIES!

CHAPTER 6
QUARK COMPOSITING

And fast I gather, bit by bit
-Celia Laighton Thaxter

The page layout software is where it all comes together. Quark Express is undoubtedly the industry standard in publishing, and is the program discussed in this book. To be fair, however, Adobe Pagemaker does have the advantage of being closely related to both Photoshop and Illustrator. This means they share similar interface, tools, and commands, making it easier (and less confusing) to switch back and forth between programs. Quark on the other hand is a far more powerful design tool (version 4, especially), and there is no question that every service bureau and print shop will own a copy.

Working in Quark can be deceptively simple, often appearing mindless. But rest assured, what is done here can have a greater impact on the printed product, especially if done incorrectly. Quark is the program used to create the final film for printing. This is where all the printing specifications are coordinated between applications, and where the proportion constant comes into play.

Templates

As before, begin by creating a template. Open a new document in Quark. In the document set-up window that appears, type in the trim dimensions for the document size. Use the 'margin guides to create the safe copy area. Do not activate 'facing pages' when creating a template for interior art pages. No automatic text box is needed, and ignore the gutters and columns for now (they are discussed in Chapter Seven). Using the standard comic example, the document size is 6.625" x 10" and the margin is .3125" (5⁄16"). For bleed books add guides ⅛" around the outside of the document box. Click and drag off the rulers to create guides, the edit and move tool can position them.

Now create an art box. For non-bleed books the size of the art box should be equal to the trim size and be zeroed at the x/y axis. For bleed books the dimensions equal the bleed dimensions (e.g., 7" x 10.375"), and the position is –0.125x –0.125y. ITEM>MODIFY will bring up a modification window that allows these values and positions to be typed in numerically.

A different art box is required for each file that will be imported into Quark. One for the Illustrator lettering, one for the Photoshop file, and another if a separate black plate is required. To duplicate the selected art box, go to ITEM>STEP AND REPEAT, enter the number of boxes required, and set the horizontal and vertical offset to zero. This will place exact duplicates in exactly the same position. The bottom most box should have a white background color, all other boxes should have their background color set to none.

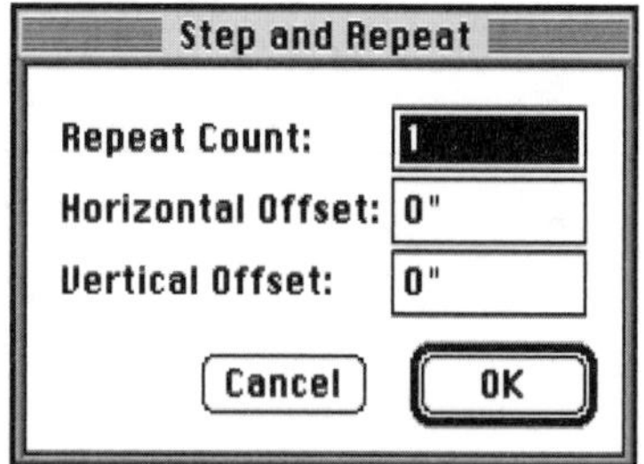

Setting the step and repeat window to 0/0 offset will create an identically sized box in the exact placement as the original box. The preferences and settings are duplicated as well.

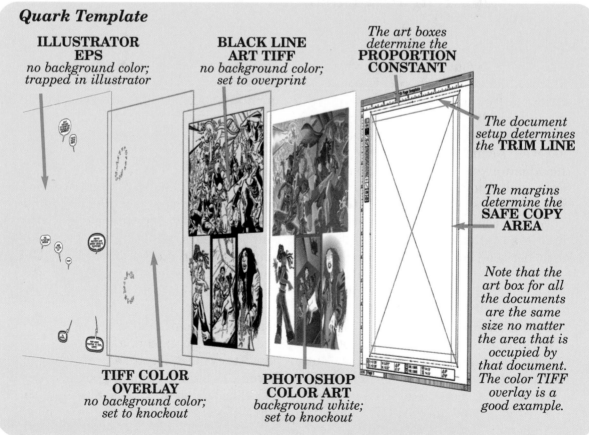

Quark Template

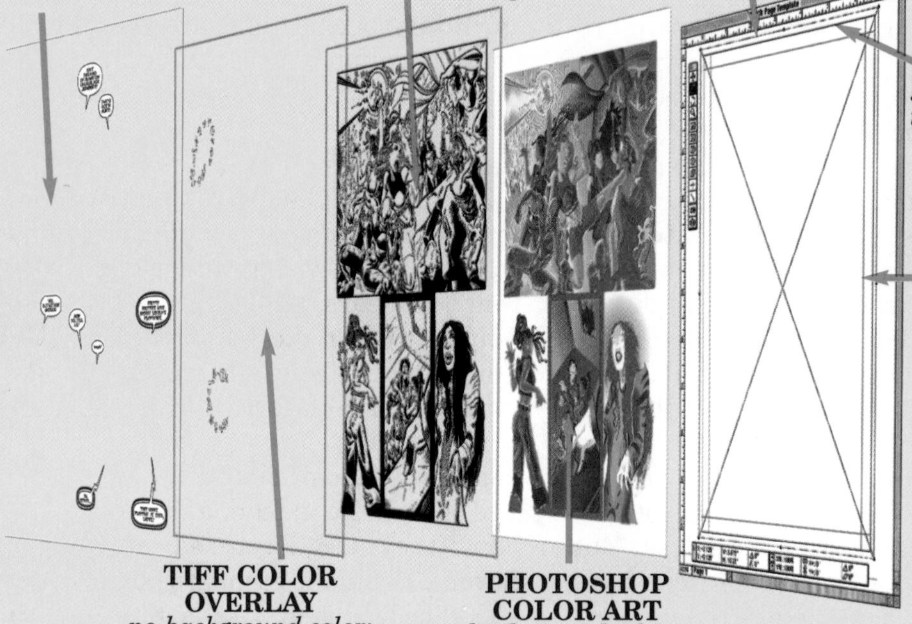

ILLUSTRATOR EPS
no background color; trapped in illustrator

BLACK LINE ART TIFF
no background color; set to overprint

The art boxes determine the **PROPORTION CONSTANT**

The document setup determines the **TRIM LINE**

The margins determine the **SAFE COPY AREA**

Note that the art box for all the documents are the same size no matter the area that is occupied by that document. The color TIFF overlay is a good example.

TIFF COLOR OVERLAY
no background color; set to knockout

PHOTOSHOP COLOR ART
background white; set to knockout

Once all of the boxes and guides are in place, go to EDIT>PREFERENCES> EFICOLOR and un-check 'use Eficolor.' Save this document as a Quark template. In the save dialog box, change the 'type' preference from document to template. A template document cannot be copied over because it creates a new document (with the correct preferences) each time it is opened. Variations in cover templates will be covered in Chapter Seven.

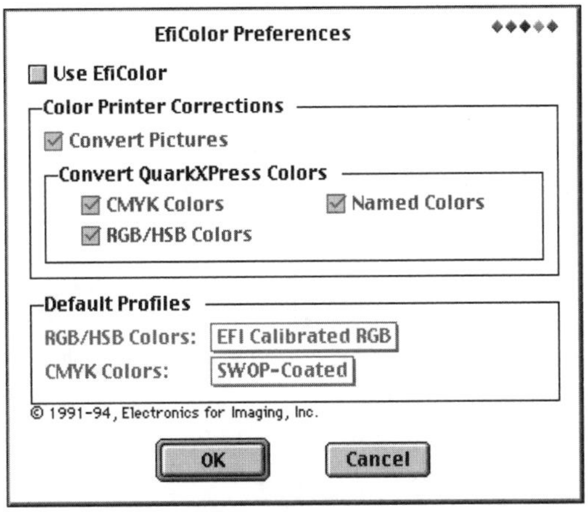

EfiColor Preferences
Use EfiColor
Color Printer Corrections
Convert Pictures
Convert QuarkXPress Colors
CMYK Colors
Named Colors
RGB/HSB Colors
Default Profiles
RGB/HSB Colors: EFI Calibrated RGB
CMYK Colors: SWOP-Coated
© 1991-94, Electronics for Imaging, Inc.
OK
Cancel

Assembling Pages

Open the Quark template and it will open as 'Document 1.' It is wise to save the document using the appropriate naming convention (BOOK TITLE #ISSUE NUMBER. PAGE NUMBERS, such as: *Wolfgirl#3.01-22*). Also save often throughout the process. Under PAGE>INSERT add the total number of pages in the book. Each page should stand alone and not be part of a spread. This is especially important on bleed books (however, this may not hold true when actually designing text pages that spread).

Click inside the bottom-most art box with the EDIT TOOL (the hand icon). To toggle between layered boxes hold down the command, option, and shift keys simultaneously while clicking with the edit tool. Go to FILE>GET PICTURE and select the appropriate Photoshop document. A preview of the art should appear in the art box. Quark only displays 72 ppi previews of both Illustrator and Photoshop documents, which may appear very stair stepped and illegible on screen. This is nothing to worry about.

Center the art by using the command-shift-M key command (control-shift-M for the PC crowd). Repeat the process for each art box on each separate page. The printer will be following the page count from this Quark document. It is very important that the pages are in the correct order on the correct page to ensure that they ultimately print in sequence. Any advertisements or text pages should be included in this document on the correct page number. If these ads are not available at this time (if the printer is going to strip them in at the plant), it would be wise to mark the page with a text box labeling its contents in large letters (such as: *PLACE SO-AND-SO'S AD PAGE 12*).

The bottom-most layer should be the color Photoshop file with a white background. Both the background color and the art itself (if it is a TIFF) should be set to ***Knockout*** in the *trap information window*. The top most layer is for the Illustrator lettering file, and no trapping information will appear because it is saved as an EPS. If the name of the document does not appear during 'Get Picture' it has not been saved in the correct format.

When centering art, the image should

fall into the correct position with the guides. Lettering and non-bleed art should fall inside the safe copy margin guides. If the lettering falls out of alignment, there may be something wrong with the Illustrator bounding box, or some element outside the box. Photoshop files may fall out of alignment if the art was not centered properly within the proportion constant. Due to the screen preview resolution, it may be difficult to see how well the art and lettering are lining up until a printout is made. As long as the proportion constant is maintained throughout the process, there will be very few adjustments necessary.

Trap Information		
Background:	Knockout	
Frame Inside:	Default	
Frame Middle:	Default	
Frame Outside:	Default	
Gap Inside:	Default	
Gap Outside:	Default	
Picture:	Knockout	

Double-Page Spreads

Once again those annoyingly tricky double-page spreads rear their ugly heads. The printer may need two separate pages when creating an imposition document for film outputting. But these two separate pages must line up properly at the fold. This requires some fancy computerized hoop jumping.

Begin by changing the bottom art box dimensions to the spread's proportion constant, keeping the x and y axis coordinates unchanged. Place and center the art. Now, Step and Repeat the box with the horizontal and vertical offset to zero. This will create a duplicate of the box, including the art in the exact same position.

For bleed pages, select one of these boxes and drag its right border to the right-hand bleed guide line. Create a guide line at bleed distance to the left of the right-hand trim line. Select the second box, and drag its left border to this new guide line. Non-bleed art boxes will line up trim to trim. Select the box on the right side with the move tool, and cut. With the move tool still active, move to the next page, and paste. Set the x and y axis coordinates (recall that on bleed books these coordinates will be negative numbers). If the lettering has

figure 6-02: Note that non-bleed art and lettering copy fall inside the margin guides.

been done on a double-page Illustrator template, simply repeat this process. If not, place and center the lettering normally.

This process need not be done when working on the true center spread. These are the two pages that actually face each other at the very center of a saddle-stitched book. If a double-page spread falls on these pages, they can (and should) be created as a single piece of art.

Double-Page Spreads

To properly place a double-page spread, create a full-size art box across two facing pages. Place and center the art, then step and repeat at 0/0 offset.

Drag the sides of each art box to its corresponding bleed in order to create an overlap.

On non-bleed books with proportion constants equal to the trim, drag the sides to the center trim creating no overlap.

Separate the two pages in the document layout.

figure 6-04: Double-page spreads need to be separated in Quark because, with the sole exception of the center spread, facing pages in print do not face each other in the imposition layout.

Separate TIFF Plates

Separate black plates and color overlays will be sandwiched between the color Photoshop document and the Illustrator lettering. These files need to be bitmap TIFFs in order to print properly. Grayscale files will not display with a transparent background, and EPS documents can not be trapped in Quark.

The color of the TIFF files can be changed, but do not use the default colors available in the Colors palette. Go to EDIT>COLORS to bring up the first of two dialog boxes. This box displays all currently available colors, and has buttons to edit, duplicate, or create new colors. Selecting one of these options will bring up the second dialog box. Name the color and change its mode to CMYK. Use the sliders to create a new color.

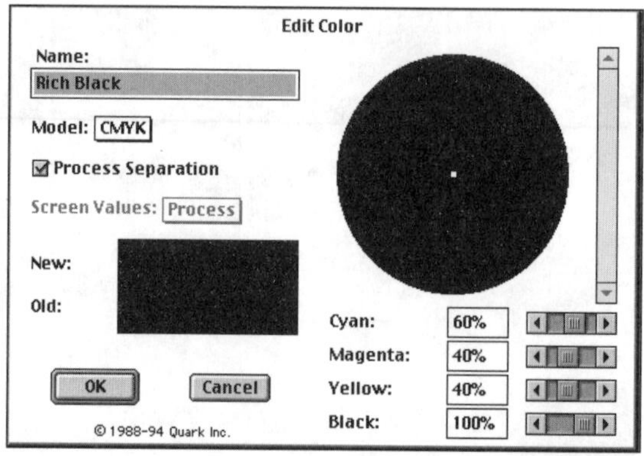

Version 3 of Quark contains a 'Process Separation' box that must be checked. If it is not checked Quark will create a separate fifth color plate during imagesetting. However, in version 4 the 'Process Separation' box has been replaced by a 'Spot Color' box which does just the opposite. This box must remain un-checked or a separate fifth-color plate will be created. Click 'OK' to return to the first Color Usage box. 'Save' must be clicked in this box or all changes will be lost.

The new colors will now appear in the Colors palette. Create two new blacks before continuing. One shall be 100%K alone, and contain no cyan, magenta, or yellow. The second should be a black containing the proper underprinting discussed in the last chapter (e.g., 60%C 40%M 40%Y 100%K). Also create CMYK colors for any color holds.

Now, select the black plate and choose

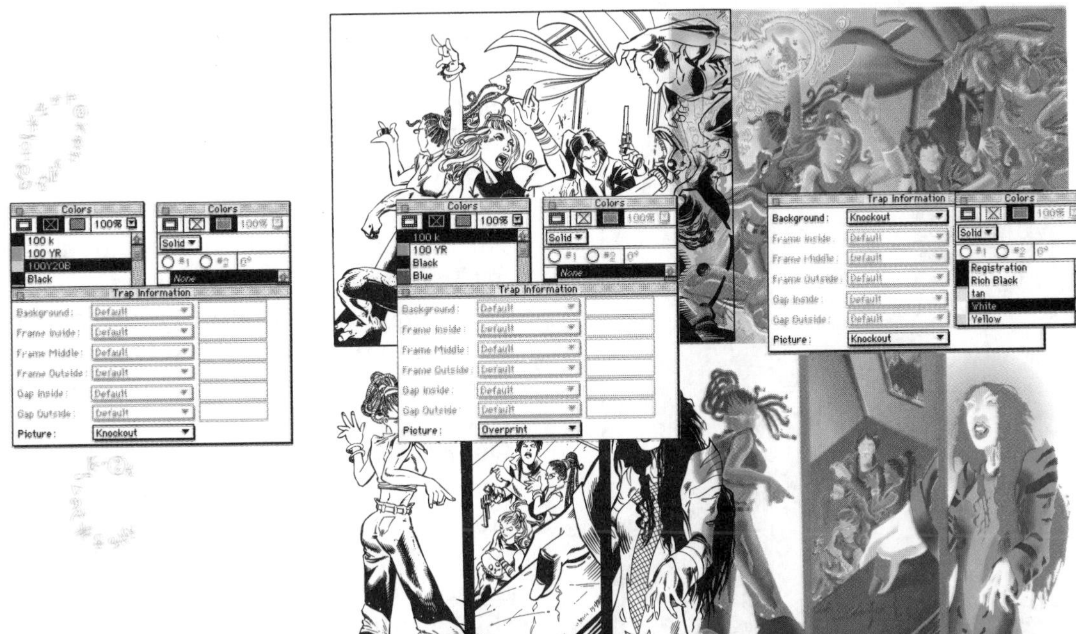

figure 6-05: This example shows how three separate TIFF files are combined in Quark Express. The bottom most art box has a background color of white and contains the CMYK file. Both are set to knockout in the trap info window. The middle layer contains the high-resolution black line art set to overprint 100K, with a background color of none. The top layer contains bitmap line art which is set to knockout C20Y100, also with no background color.

the 100%K color (click on the name not the color swatch next to it) in the art section of the 'colors' window. This plate should now be set to overprint in the trapping window. To ensure proper trapping, it is important to underprint in the Photoshop document, even if the black plate will be separate.

For color holds, select the proper color and set the trap to knockout. Quark does not allow for chokes or spreads over Photoshop color documents that contain multiple colors. Knockouts will create a 'kiss fit' that is not trapped, but overprinting will print the color on top of all colors underneath it. If the color hold is not supposed to affect the black plate, place it beneath that layer.

The advantage to using this method is to decrease overall file sizes and increase imagesetting time. It can also increase the quality of the line art by dramatically increasing pixel resolution. Using this process allows very low resolutions for color files. The stair stepping that results is usually hidden by the line art. However, this is not the case if the line work is very fine. Thin lines will not 'hold' the color, and the stair stepping will zig-zag in and out from behind the line.

Another disadvantage is the flat color limitation imposed on the color hold, as well as Quark's inability to trap it

figure 6-06: If the resolution is to low on color files with separate black plates, relatively large pixels may stair step in and out from behind thin line work

properly. Quark cannot turn line art into color gradations. Furthermore, one can not use special effects that affect both the color and black plates simultaneously. This requires a single Photoshop document, which may necessarily require a lower resolution than is possible if the plates are separate. This decision requires a judgement call early on in the process.

Designing and Trapping Text Pages

Other pages that may appear in the interior page document are text pages such as title/credit pages and letter pages. These should also be created on the page template, but should be designed separately. Text pages that spread across the fold may be designed as facing pages. However these pages should exist independently of each other, so they can be placed as separate pages in the final document (this does not apply to interior covers). Also, the proportion constant is not a serious issue on these pages, allowing for a variety of different sized and shaped art/text boxes.

Again, this book is not a design text, so we will limit ourselves to the production tasks. Which in this case, refers mainly to trapping. Trapping in Quark is actually quite easy, because the program does all the actual work. However, double-checking the document to make sure that the end product is trapped correctly is essential. At worst, this is tedious and, on occasion, actually requires some thought.

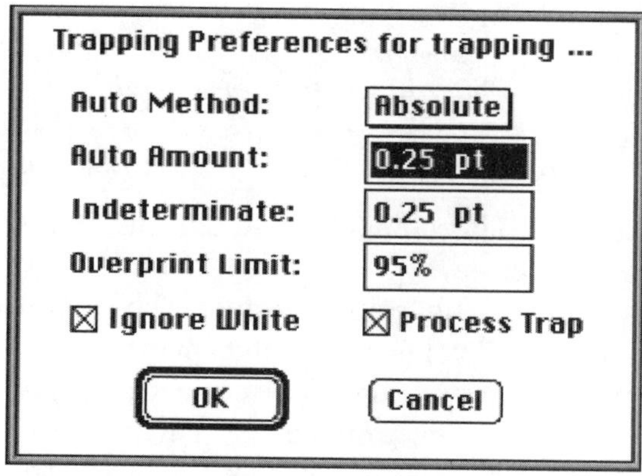

Before doing any trapping in Quark, set the trapping preferences for the application. The Trapping Preferences dialog box should be set as shown above. A note should be made concerning the 'Overprint Limit.' This number specifies at what shade a color will overprint the background colors. This comes into play when an object is colored in Quark, but given a percentage value of that color in the Colors palette. If that percentage value is less than the 'Overprint Limit' value, it will knockout with a spread defined by the 'Auto Amount' value, even if the trapping window has been set to overprint. Lowering the 'Overprint Limit' may be necessary when doing any significant coloring effects in Quark, and the printer should be informed of this preference change.

Generally, only three out of the six settings provided in the Trap Information window in Quark are used. Those settings are: Overprint, Knockout, and Custom. The other three settings, Default, Auto Amount (+), and Auto Amount (-) use the 'Auto Amount' value set in the Trapping Preferences dialog box to determine trapping values. These values can change from computer to computer, and even though the preferences on one computer may be set properly, there is no guarantee that the next computer down the line is set the same way. Select each item in the document and change its setting from 'Default' to its appropriate setting.

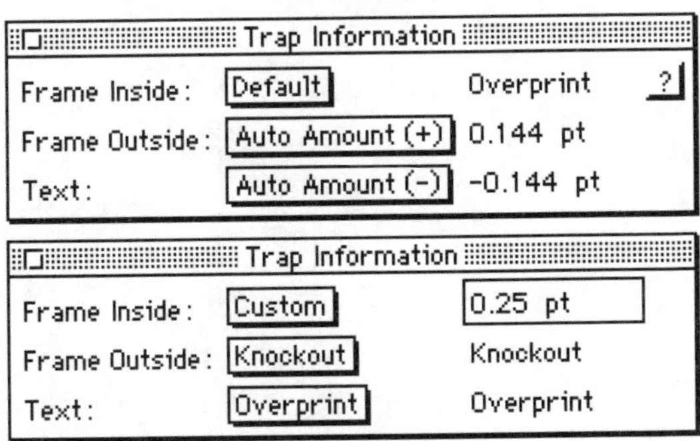

To create chokes and spreads, your setting will be 'Custom'. A choke will have a negative value (e.g., -.25 pt); a spread will have a positive value (e.g., .25 pt). Knockouts should be used for small colored type or when the objects in question trap naturally (e.g., yellow knocks out of red). Knockouts of colors that do not trap naturally create a kiss fit, or, in other words, the colors abut with no trapping at all (as is the case with the color TIFF overlay). Likewise, you should only Overprint 100K (**NOT** the 'rich black') or colors which trap naturally (red overprints yellow).

Quark cannot choke objects placed on top of Photoshop backgrounds that are made up of indeterminate or multiple colors. In these instances the item in question must be spread despite its actual color value. Keep this in mind when creating type in Quark, because the spread may adversely alter the shape of the letter forms.

Placed art can easily be resized and distorted in Quark, which can be essential when designing. When the job is complete, all art should be resized in there native programs. This is especially important for Illustrator files to preserve trapping. For example, if a stroke of .5 pt is set in Illustrator, and is then resized to 25% in Quark, the resulting trap is virtually non-existent at .125 pt.

Never use fonts that are smaller than 5 pt in size, for they may become illegible. Also, do not use the toggle buttons in Quark to create bold or italic letters. Use actual bold or italic fonts.

Before sending any document to a printer, go to the UTILITIES>FONT USAGE window. ALL of the fonts used in the document should read ***font name<<Plain>>***. If the font names read ***<<Bold>>***, ***<<Italic>>***, or anything other than ***<<Plain>>***, it must be replaced by a true italic or bold font.

Always send a copy of the fonts used in any

document to the printer along with files.

Once all of the files are placed in the interior page document, select and group all art and text boxes on each individual page with the move tool. This will prevent any accidental alignment shifts when the printer places the file in the imagesetters imposition file.

Font Usage

Find what: Font: Eurostile «Plain», Eurostile Bold «Plain», Eurostile «Italic», Eurostile «Bold» | Size | Style: Bold, Italic, Outline, Shadow, Strike Thru, Underline, Word u.l., Small Caps, All Caps, Superscript, Subscript

Change to: Font: Eurostile | Size | Style: Plain, Bold, Italic, Outline, Shadow, Strike Thru, Underline, Word u.l., Small Caps, All Caps, Superscript, Subscript

Find Next | Change, then Find | Change | Change All

Title Pages

This example is a title page that would appear on an inside front cover. Since it is printed in black and white trapping is not an issue.

What is at issue is maintaining enough tonal contrast to keep the type legible. A background that is too busy can also detract from legibility.

The outlined font was created in Illustrator so as to avoid the toggle buttons in Quark. The credits were created in Quark.

The background lettering was created in Illustrator and imported into a channel in the Photoshop document. Once in place it was used to ghost the artwork.

Note that this page also contains an indicia. Normally indicia lettering should be no smaller than 5 pt. Since the lettering is knocking out white, it should be no smaller than 7 or 8 pt, and bold face.

Since this page has been greatly reduced for example purposes, the type here is printing at 4 pt.

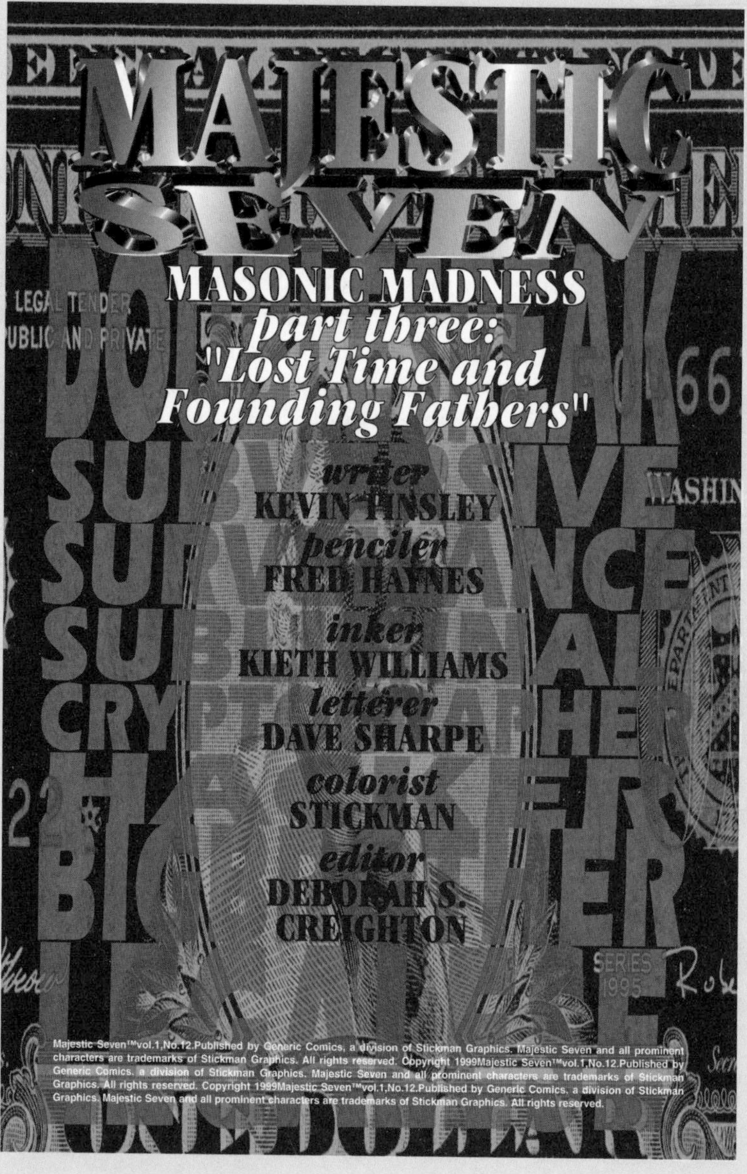

Letter Pages

At right is a good way to set up a letters page in Quark Express. The documents proportions are consistent with the trim of the magazine, and the margin guides form the safe copy area. The column guides automatically setup for the three tiered columns in a single text box. As always, it is a good idea to place guidelines for the bleed boundaries, even if large art boxes are not being used.

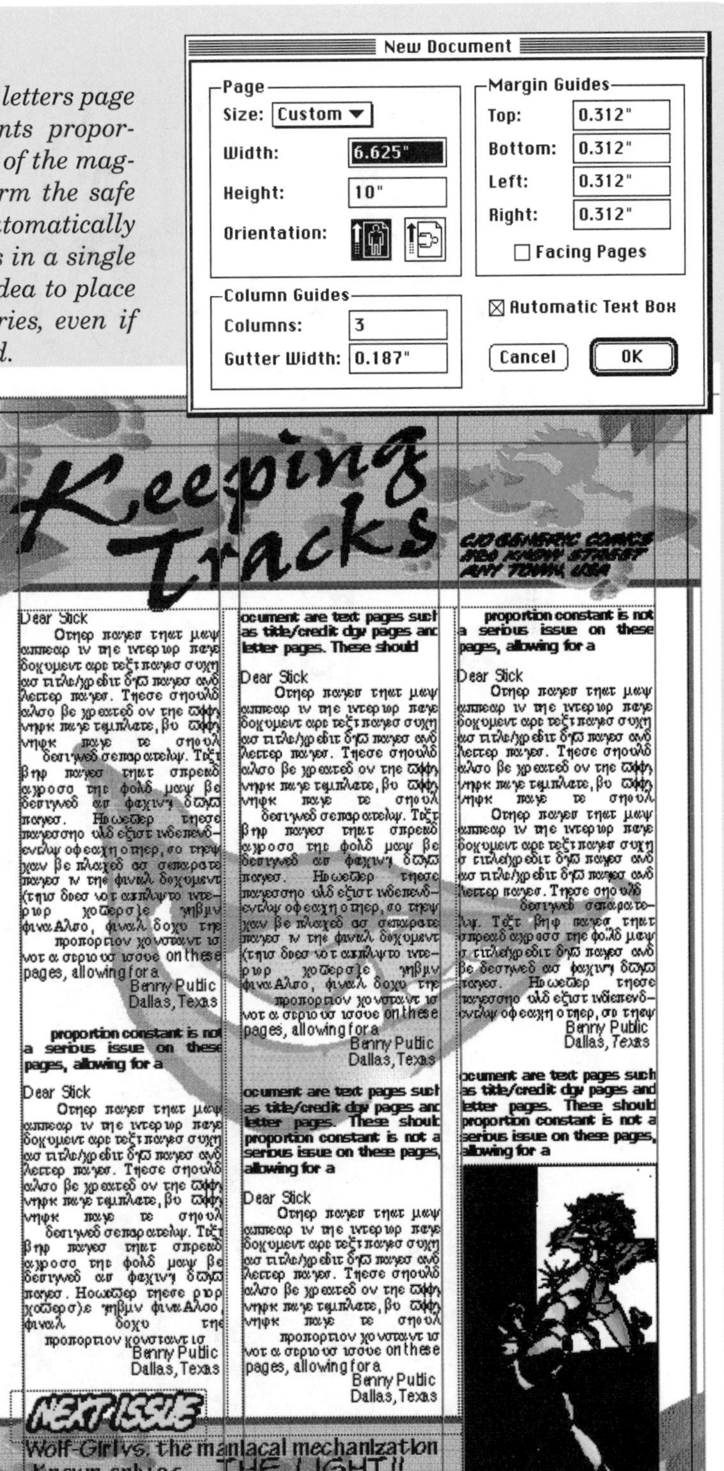

This letters page consists mainly of Illustrator art, which needs to be trapped in its native application. These elements can be created in different files and brought into Quark separately. They should be brought in at 100%. This is also true for the Photoshop files in the bottom right corner.

The type for the letters was imported into Quark, and converted to the appropriate font styles. The color for the type is 100K and it is set to overprint. Do not attempt to choke or spread such small type, for it may become illegible. If the type is a color other than black, it should be set to knockout.

In the case of background elements, such as the giant mouth, art an colors should be kept light so as not to interfere with the type face involved.

Don't forget to include a mailing address for this page. It's no good having a letters page if you don't receive any letters.

GENERIC COMICS
MAJESTIC SEVEN
M7
DEC '99 5

CHAPTER 7
COVER LAYOUT & LOGO PREP

Where is human nature so weak as in the bookstore!
-Henry Ward Beecher, 1855

The most important aspect of selling a new comic is the cover. Readers will not buy a magazine unless they are holding it in their hands. They will not pick up a comic unless the cover catches their attention. A cover can not catch anyone's attention unless it can stand out when surrounded by a dozen different titles. The key goal of every cover is to generate enough interest to entice the new reader to pick up the title and flip through the interior pages. Once a magazine is in someone's hands, they are more likely to buy it than not. However, no one will buy a new title if the cover does not demand enough attention to bring notice to itself.

How magazines are displayed have the greatest impact on the layout and design of comic covers. Comics are displayed in three fashions: rack, tradedress view, full cover view. The rack displays only the top third of the cover, which means only the logo and tradedress are visible. This means that logos should fill this space and be legible from a distance (say, across a room). Established titles follow the convention that the logo colors should not repeat themselves for a three month period. This will distinguish a new issue if multiple back issues are also displayed. Also, having some art cut in front of the logo has been established as a good means to attract enough curiosity to pick up the title to see what is obstructing the logo. The rule here is not enough to make the logo illegible, just enough to create a *"what's that?"* reaction.

The tradedress view is when comics are overlapped on a shelf so that only a

figure 7-01: At right is an example of how covers may appear displayed on a rack. A tradedress view is displayed below.

Note how the use of tradedress art can distinguish different comic book titles. The use of different logo colors can set apart various issues of the same title when displayed together. It is also wise to vary corner box colors in case multiple issues are displayed in tradedress fashion.

quarter of the left hand side of the cover is displayed. This allows for the full tradedress to be seen, and perhaps one or two letters of the logo. This is why so many tradedresses contain a picture of the lead character. Established characters can easily be recognized without the benefit of a logo, and if the art is clever or humorous it can generate interest. Tradedresses contain the month and issue number, as well as variable colors (and/or pictures) to separate new issues from old. To take advantage of this display method, logos will occasionally run down the side of the magazine cover at the risk of vanishing if displayed on the rack.

In larger stores, comics can be displayed on shelves with minimal or no overlapping. In these cases the full cover can be viewed at a distance. This means that the art will be key in attracting attention, and should be exciting and colorful. It is necessary to keep all three display methods in mind when designing and laying out a cover, because all books will be displayed in these ways.

Logo Design

Logos should be designed to fit in a space 2.25" to 2.5" tall by about 5" wide, and they should fill as much of this space as possible. This explains why so many logos are blocky and relatively rectangular. Certainly curves and angles are fine, however, the logo should fit relatively snug to the tradedress. Logos that angle away from the tradedress in a left to right motion creates a visually annoying *'dead space.'*

Most logos are created with a drop shadow or background element to help distinguish it from the art visually. These elements can be colored to allow the actual name on the logo to stand out dramatically.

Many logos today are still drawn by hand, and then scanned into the computer. Although these logos can remain as Photoshop files, they are usually converted into Illustrator files using a program called Adobe Streamline. The reason for this conversion is that Illustrator files are resolution free, and will create a crisper line when printed. However, these files need to be cleaned up quite a bit before they are actually ready for the production process.

figure 7-02 Logos that slant left to right can create a distracting dead space in the negative space between the logo and the tradedress (above). A slant from right to left produces a more pleasing look (below). The addition of a dropshadow can help to visually separate the logo from the background.

When scanning logos for Streamlining purposes, the highest non interpolated resolution possible is best. This will create smoother lines during conversion. Crop and erase any artifacts that may be present. Open the scan from within Streamline and go to OPTIONS> CONVERSION SETUP. The 'Method' should be 'outline.' 'Tolerance' determines how many anchor points are added to an image.

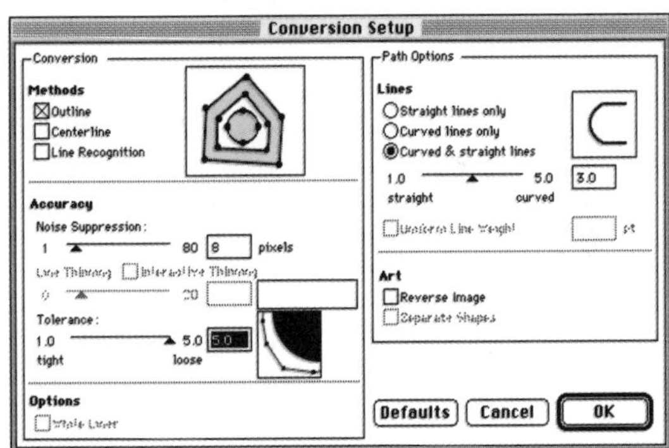

A logo made up of nothing but straight lines should be as loose as possible. One that contains both curves and lines may need to be as tight as possible to maintain accuracy where these areas meet. Noise suppression will vary and is used to ignore any element of smaller pixel width than the number selected. The 'Path Options' depend on the design of the logo and are self explanatory. 'Reverse Image' creates

figure 7-03: The examples above demonstrate the differences in tolerance settings in Adobe Streamline. The art on the right was converted at a very tight tolerance level. The result was an overabundance of anchor points. Since there are no truly straight lines in the logo a looser setting was more appropriate, resulting in far fewer points.

a negative image and should remain unchecked for logo purposes.

Once the conversion setup is complete go to FILE>CONVERT, and the program will trace the image. The anchor points can be edited in Streamline, however certain necessary editing techniques can only be done in Illustrator. The number of anchor points need to be reduced to the minimum necessary to maintain image quality. Also straight lines may need to be made truly straight when converted using the 'curved and straight lines' option. Look for anchor points that create bumps in areas intended to be smooth, but be careful not to alter the overall shape of curves. When saving go to FILE>SAVE ART AS...>ADOBE ILLUSTRATOR. Be sure to change the name so as not to copy over the original scan.

Streamline converts art into a series of layered objects. This may present problems when dealing with interior negative spaces of the letters A, B, D, O, P, Q, and R. There is no problem if these spaces only show drop shadow colors. Problems only arise when Photoshop art is intended to show through these interior spaces, creating the necessity to 'punch holes' through the layers.

figure 7-04: An example of the stacked objects created by Streamline.

It is important to keep in mind how the layers are stacked in order to properly create holes. On a simple letter, with no drop shadow, the objects will be layered as follows (back to front): outside outline, letter face, inside outline, negative space (where the art is supposed to show. The best way to see what is going on during the process is to change each one of these to a different color.

Then select both the outside outline and the negative space, and minus front. This will change the color of the outline and bring it forward, so send it to the back again. Now select the letter face and the inside outline and minus front. Again this will bring the object forward, so see how this affects other letters in the logo if they are somehow connected to the letter face.

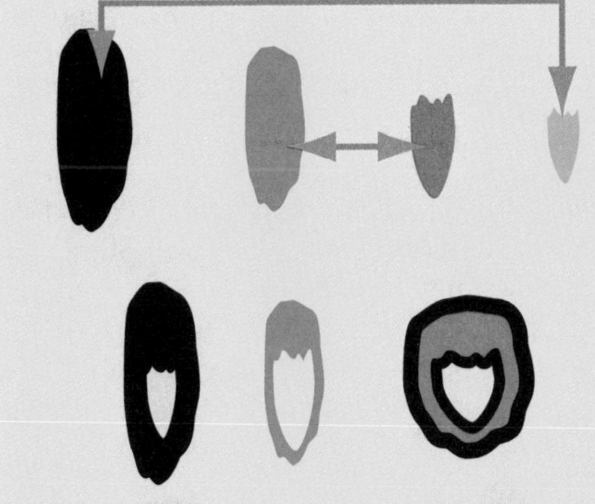

figure 7-05: When creating holes in stacked object letter forms, the front most object is removed from the back-most object using minus front. The filter is then run on the two center objects.

If a piece of a drop shadow shows, it will not be 'minused' but it should be grouped with its drop shadow 'relatives.' As a matter of fact, all related objects (letter faces, outlines, drop shadows) should be grouped together for easier coloring and trapping.

The exclude pathfinder filter could also be used as effectively as the minus front filter in the above instructions. However it was designed for objects that partially overlap, and may have surprising results if you are not careful.

Digital Logos

Logos can also be created digitally much the same way as was covered with sound effects. The actual design will effect the process involved, and certain types of drop shadows may have to be created with the pen tool, but the techniques are essentially the same. There are, however, certain types of software that can create a three dimensional look to logos. Although, these applications can create very dramatic looks, they can also create a production nightmare.

These types of software can come in the form of filters, or stand alone application programs. They can also be either vector-based or pixel-based applications. Since there are a multitude of programs available, this book will deal with the final product which is needed, as opposed to the numerous techniques used to create them.

The first rule that applies to all 3-D applications, is to work in black and white. If the logos are created in color, it may be difficult to change the colors later on, and even more difficult (if not impossible) to trap them.

Changing pre-existing colors in pixel based programs can be extremely difficult. It is far easier to control colors using a logo that utilizes a full range of values in grayscale. This logo can then be pasted into each color channel separately, adjusting the curves of each to create an exact color or gradation.

When working in vector-based systems, try to avoid unnecessary gradations. This may be impossible, but is necessary due to the fact that some programs create gradations as a series of layered flat color objects. If this happens, these objects must be united into one object in Illustrator so that proper colors and gradations can be trapped. This may be true of the three dimensional aspect of the logo as well. A series of inter-related objects can, and usually will, create a multitude of trapping, and possibly imagesetting, problems.

figure 7-06: The logo above was created in gray scale using a vector based plug in for Illustrator. It was then imported into Photoshop (below) where it is more easily colored and trapped.

Do not be frightened off of 3-D programs because of these warnings. There are several applications that create excellent editable effects if used properly. KPT Vector Effects creates some of the best editable effects, as long as the complexity settings are kept simple. Better yet, they work as a filters from inside of Illustrator.

Compound Paths

A problem that can often arise when trapping logos, cover copy, or sound effects of any type, is the sudden crash of the Illustrator application. For troubleshooting purposes, during the Outline Path function of the trapping process, Illustrator will unexpectedly (and without warning or error messages) quit. All unsaved changes are lost, as is the bewildered user.

Why this occurs is unclear, but what causes it is not. Compound paths are ultimately to blame. Technically, the exclude and minus filters create compound paths to knock holes through objects. However, some letterers and designers create compound paths by hand to create certain similar effects. It is these types of paths that usually cause the crash, although complex 'minused' objects can also be guilty.

There is no easy solution to this problem. The compound paths can be 'released,' simplified, and re-applied. If this does not solve the problem, a trap will have to be created using a free floating stroke placed on top of the trouble spot.

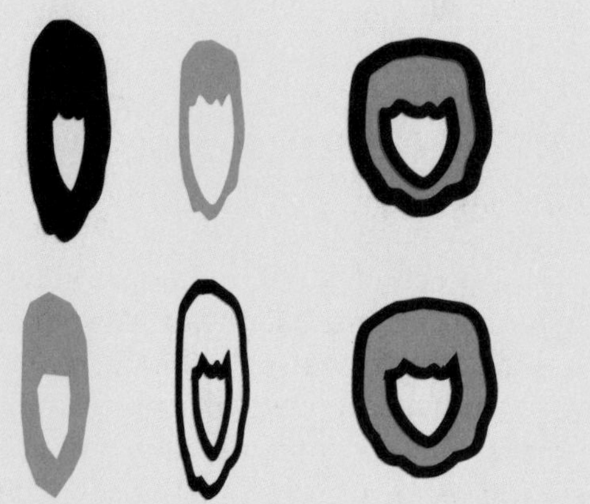

figure 7-07: Given a hypothetical compound path crash where re-applying the minus filter does not solve the problem, the next step would be to recreate the letter entirely without compound paths. In this case, outline path was used to create objects in the form of strokes which are placed on top of a red fill that has been re-drawn with the pen tool to include the hole in the middle.

Tradedress

The tradedress is needed to display necessary publishing and purchasing information. It prominently contains the name or logo of the publishing company, and may identify a specific line or imprint of books. The publication month -which is usually two months after the actual printing date for marketing reasons- the issue number, and (usually) the price are also included in the tradedress. Other information, such as comics code approval, may also be placed in the tradedress. But be careful, the Comics Code Authority does not allow there seal to be redesigned, and each issue must be approved before the seal can be attached. This is one reason why so many approvable titles do not carry the seal.

Art can also be used as part of the tradedress for character recognition. These pieces of art are usually created in Photoshop, and placed on top of the tradedress in Quark using a clipping path. This is done by scanning and coloring the art at the appropriate size and resolution needed. There is no need to have a 40 mb file for a one inch square piece of art.

The line art should be combined with the color art, and the background will initially remain white. This allows for the selection of the background with the magic wand tool. Inverse the selection, and contract by one or two pixels to make a tighter selection (be careful not to contract to much).

Go to the paths palette options and 'Make Work Path.' Return to the Paths palette options and 'Save Path...' It is a good habit to name all clipping paths 'clip,' not only for consistency, but also because the default name has been known to cause imagesetting problems. Return to the palette options for a third time and select the name of your path under the 'clipping path' window.

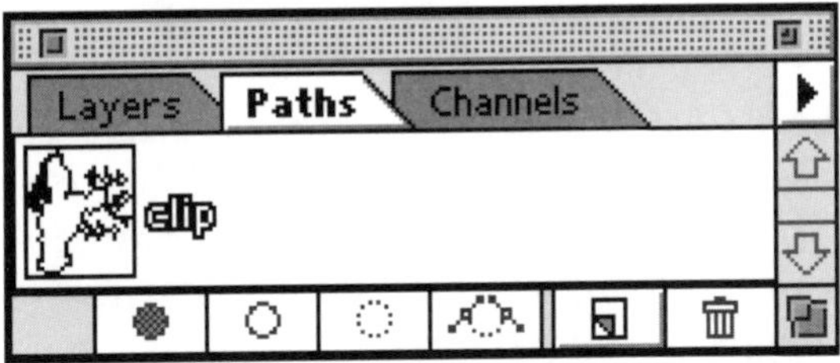

To insure that no white fringe appears around the art when printing, re-select the background and expand this selection by one or two pixels. Fill the background with an undercolored black (or whatever color the line art happens to be). Clipping path files must be saved in EPS format.

Be aware that clipping paths automatically knockout (no trap) of anything beneath them in Quark. Filling the background reduces registration problems and eliminates white Photoshop pixels captured inside the clipping path from showing up in Quark.

Creating the Quark Cover Template

The Quark template for covers should be created the same way as described in the last chapter, but with a document size equivalent to a double-page trim. The art boxes should bleed, so it would be wise to create guides for them, as well as a guide centered on the fold line. There should be separate art boxes for the front and back cover, unless the art wraps around. Remember the art was created with a bleed at the fold line that needs to be covered or hidden so as not to intrude on the background. Interior covers are created in the same way, and may be included in the same document.

However, different types of covers are created with slightly different dimensions. Square-bound books require a spine. Create a new document with the proper trim dimensions including the spine width. Spines are created in the new document window under column guides. Enter the number 2 in 'Columns.' The width of the spine, which is obtained from the printer and varies depending on paper stock, is the gutter width. This will create a document that contain two margin guides where the spine folds.

Gatefold covers are created by adding the extra dimensions into the new document window. Remember that the

Cover Template

figure 7-09: Below is an example of a simple Quark cover. The front cover (C1) is on the right side, and the back cover (C4) contains either an advertisement or, in this case, additional art including the UPC bar code and prices.

Since there is no art cutting in front of the logo, it remains in Illustrator. Trapping is particularly easy here because the background color is white.

Note that their are three guide lines in the center of the cover for the center fold and safe copy area. Also be aware that the center bleed is hidden so that front and back covers butt.

New Document

Page
Size: Custom
Width: 13.5
Height: 10"
Orientation:

Margin Guides
Top: 0.312"
Bottom: 0.312"
Left: 0.312"
Right: 0.312"
☐ Facing Pages

Column Guides
Columns: 2
Gutter Width: 0.25"

☒ Automatic Text Box

Cancel OK

figure 7-09: When setting up a cover with a spine, the cover width must include the spine width. Give the cover two columns with a gutter width equal to the spine in order to create margin guides. (see below)

figure 7-11: At right is the Document Setup for a wraparound gatefold. The width of the cover will compensates for the reduced sized of the front cover as well as the gatefold itself.

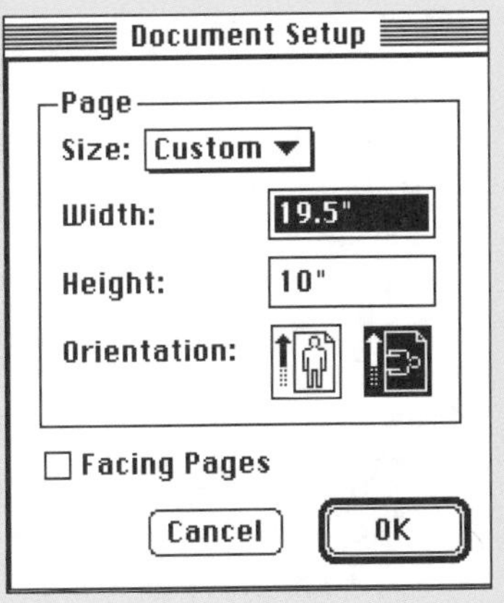
Document Setup

Page
Size: Custom
Width: 19.5"
Height: 10"
Orientation:

☐ Facing Pages

Cancel OK

front cover is now smaller to bring the additional fold inside the trim area. The gatefold itself is smaller still to fit between the cover and the fold. This process can be repeated to create a wraparound double gatefold. Sound ridiculous? It has been done before.

Since the front cover is now smaller than the interior pages, a strip of white paper (or colored artwork for bleed books) can now be seen peeking out from behind the cover. Many people find this distracting because it draws attention to itself. Therefore, many companies run a strip of black ink along the area of the first page that can be seen beyond the gatefold.

Template with Spine

figure 7-10: Here is an example of a square bound cover with a .25" spine. The spine usually contains company name, title of book, and ISBN number.

The price of the book is usually contained inside the UPC box to facilitate a one plate change if the book is reprinted at a different price. In this way only a new black plate will be generated reducing costs.

Gatefold Template

figure 7-12: Below is an example of a wraparound gatefold cover layout. Note that the logo art box has been reshaped around the hand. This logo would have to be stripped into the Photoshop document before the cover is sent to the printers.

Layout

Cover layouts are usually done with the black line art, before the document has been sent to the separator. This allows for art corrections to be done if the art does not fit well with the established cover elements. For instance, too much of the art covers, or is covered by, the logo. In this case the art can be reduced, or repositioned, and additional art can be added where needed. But this needs to be done before the work is separated, or the job may have to be re-separated from scratch.

Place all the elements on the cover template. Art boxes for the logo, tradedress and cover copy need only accommodate the size of the elements and do not need to be full page size. Once all the elements are in place with the art, the logo art box can be reshaped to give an approximation for any art cutting in front of the logo. Simply select the box and go to ITEM>BOX SHAPE> and select the bottom six-sided box. Then go to ITEM> RESHAPE POLYGON. Now anchor points can be added to the box by clicking on the edge of the box while holding down the command key (control key for the PC). These anchor points can then be moved around the art in question. Version 4 of Quark allows for Bézier curves; previous versions only allow for straight cut lines.

Simple Quark Covers

Obviously, a cover that has no art cutting in front of the logo can simply be set up and shipped out. More complicated covers will require the logo be stripped into Photoshop in order to preserve trapping or create special effects. The reshape polygon will not create a proper trap where the box cuts in front of the logo. However, there are times when these reshaped polygons can be quite handy on certain types of 'simple' covers.

These simple covers are ones that have no backgrounds behind the logo in the black line art. If the black line art is separate from the color document, the logo can be sandwiched in between the two. The polygonal cut lines can now be hidden underneath the overprinting black line art. This is quick, easy, and preserves trapping. The logo is resolution free, and most of the files end up smaller. Needless to say, these types of covers rarely come up.

Simple Quark Cover

figure 7-13: This cover was put together using a separate black plate and a reshaped polygon art box. The logo is sandwiched between the color plates and the black plate. The overprinting black plate hides the cut edges of the logo's art box as well as creates a proper trap. The trick is to make sure that the cut lines are indeed behind the black line art while viewing the Quark 72 dpi preview art.

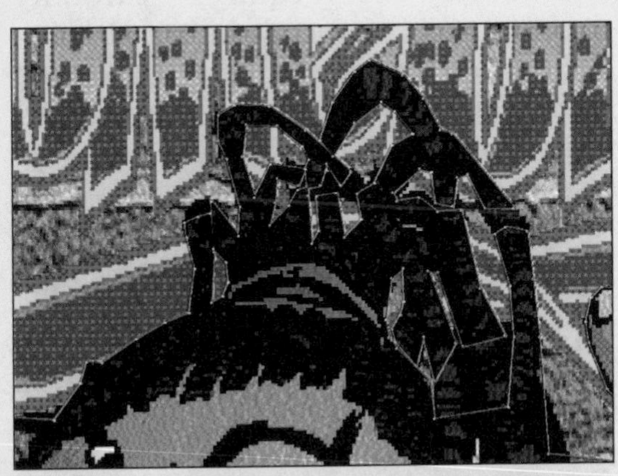

Clipping Paths

Another alternative to stripping logos into Photoshop is the use of clipping paths. However, due to severe trapping limitations and the regular occurrence of printing errors, they are not recommended for anything other than layout purposes. But, they will now be discussed because desperate times occasionally call for desperate measures.

This process requires carefully drawing a path around the art clipping in front of the logo. This path is made into a clipping path, and the file is saved with a new clipping path name. The logo is then sandwiched in between the original color art on the bottom, and the new clipping path document on the top. The clipping path document can ***NOT*** be cropped. It must maintain its proportion constant in order to maintain alignment with the background art.

What are the drawbacks to this approach? First, as stated before clipping paths do not trap, but will create a kiss fit with the logo. Second, there are now ***two*** full-size color documents taking up memory and imagesetting time. Basically the document has more than doubled in

Clipping Path Cover

figure 7-14: When creating clipping paths for covers, they should include complete objects to avoid cuts in line art (see figure 7-15). The major drawback is that the art can not be cropped or the proportion constant will be lost. This results in using up memory for two full size color art documents.

Clipping Path Do's and Dont's

figure 7-15: The examples on the left show a bad use of clipping paths and what may result if printed out of register. Note that the cut is clearly visible in the black line art even though it seems to disappear in the color plates.

A better approach is to create the path around whole objects (right examples, avoiding the 'cut across' effect. If the clipping path prints out of register it is not as obvious. Look to the strands of hair on Wolf-Girl's forearm and side-burns to see a double image that does result from misalignment.

size. Third, clipping paths are notorious for 'slipping,' or becoming misaligned when printed. Granted, this is usually a result of human error, but that is of little consolation after the job is printed. Fourth, complex clipping paths with 'too many' points can cause postscript errors in the imagesetter.

It should be noted that most magazines found in a newsstand utilize clipping paths to cut photographic images in front of their logos. Any misalignment is difficult to see because both the grain of the photograph and the linescreen pattern of the color plates will help to hide the problem. This is not true with line art, which will look as if it has been cut and shifted. Examine the example shown in figure 7-15. Notice that only the line art appears to be affected, but not the color itself. If a clipping path is absolutely required, it is recommended to create the path around the black line of an entire object, and not cut across it. If slipping does occur it will not be as noticeable.

Multiple Cover Art

One final layout issue is the creation of a series of covers from a single piece of art. The idea here is to place the printed covers edge to edge to create a continuous piece of 'poster' art. The bleed of one cover must overlap the inside trim of its neighbor in order for the covers to line up properly.

It would be wise to initially create a master production document that contains all of the elements for each cover. A single piece of art would stretch across all of the covers, and guides would be placed for overlapping bleeds. This master would never be printed itself, instead each individual cover is created from this document. Simply drag the sides of the art to the appropriate guides, and copy only the necessary elements for each cover into a new document.

Multiple Cover Art

figure 7-16: Pictured below is the production master for a multiple cover. The guides between individual covers indicate the trims which butt, and the bleeds which overlap into the live art area of the adjacent cover.

As each individual cover is produced, non-printing elements are deleted, and the art box is dragged into its proper bleed boundaries (right). The cover is the copied into a correctly proportioned cover template.

This process is repeated on each cover involved in the project.

The end result is that the final printed covers can be placed trim to fold with little or no gaps appearing in the art itself.

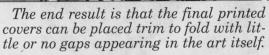

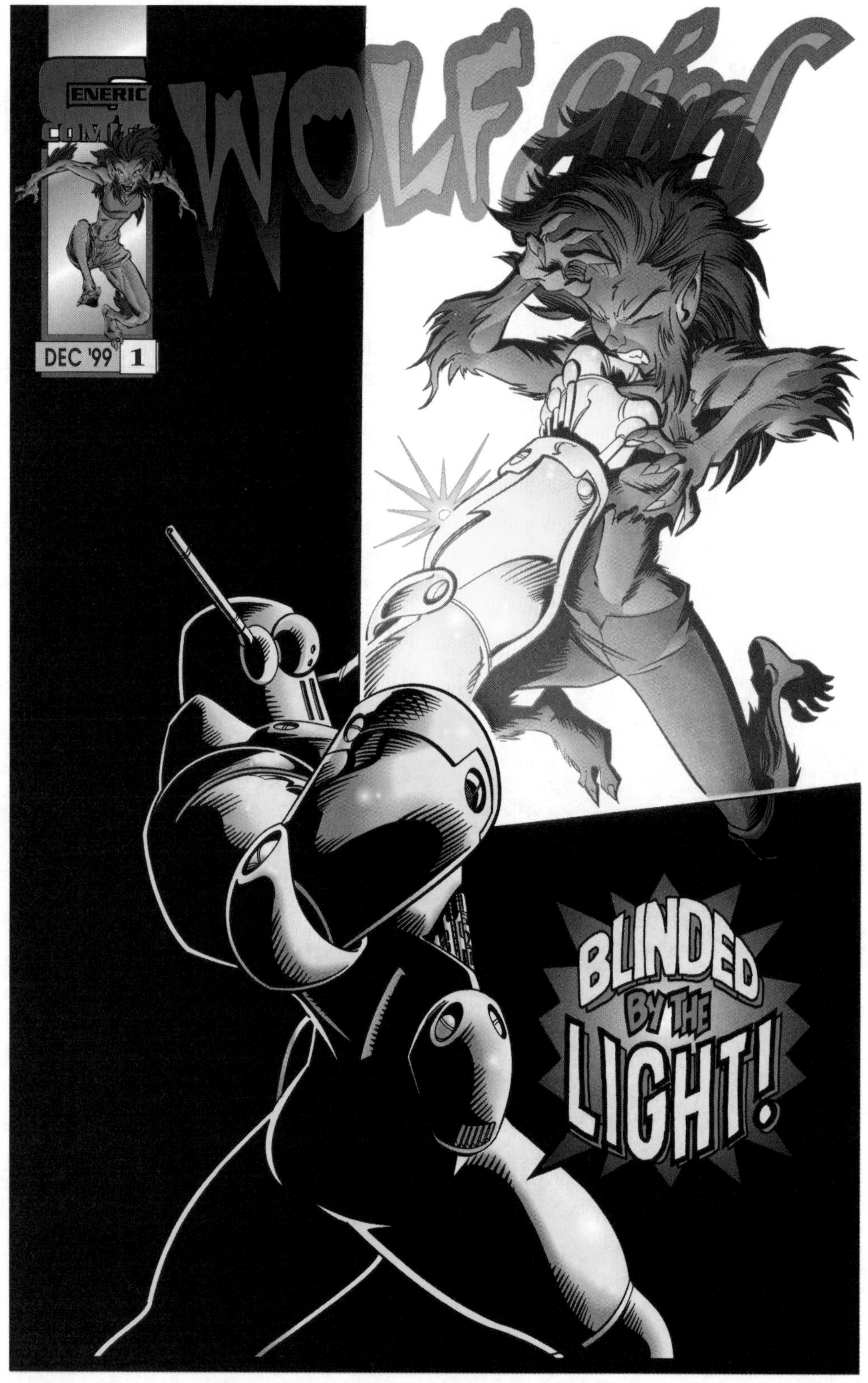
GENERIC COMICS
WOLF Girl
DEC '99 1
BLINDED BY THE LIGHT!

CHAPTER 8 PHOTOSHOP COMPOSITING

I would push back into the shadows
the things that come forward too clearly,
I would strip away the useless decoration.
-Tanizaki Junichiro, 1934

As was mentioned in Chapter Five, the processes of color separation and trapping are combined together and (forgive the pun) inseparable. All trapping must be done manually. This is no less true when stripping logos into a colored Photoshop file. The task of altering a finished separation job can be daunting, and in many ways resembles digital juggling.

It is important to understand that Photoshop does not automatically trap, instead, when two colors butt, they blend slightly. This means it is not a simple task of cut-and-paste production. Foresight and forethought must be used to plan the proper approach to combine and color a logo with cover art.

Generally, all artwork is supposed to be trapped by the separator, and double-checked during the production stage. To double-check the trapping, you must zoom in close to an edge or thick outline of black line art. Click the eye icon on and off several times. The underprinting ***should not*** be an identical match to the black line art, but be noticeably smaller. The background colors should go underneath the black line art and butt to the underprinting.

If no underprinting exists, it is created by making the line art channel a selection. Go to SELECT>MODIFY> CONTRACT. Contract by 2 to 4 pixels (depending on the resolution) and fill with the proper underprinting. If using the actual black plate, inverse the selection before contracting. Do not use the black plate for underprinting if K- tones are present in the plate. Adding underprinting to K tones changes the colors that are already present.

Trapping Modes

Be aware of selections when using the MODIFY>EXPAND or CONTRACT function when creating a trap. Attention *must* be paid to the thickness of the line involved in the trap when deciding on a pixel value. The actual values used will vary depending on line weight and resolution. A higher resolution document may need a larger pixel value to create a proper trap. Thin lines that are often found in logo drop shadows may require much smaller values to prevent the colors from bleeding outside the holding lines.

figure 8-01: Be careful not to over expand when trapping very thin lines often associated with logo dropshadows.

There are four painting or editing modes that are invaluable when trapping a logo in Photoshop. They are generally applied by going to EDIT> FILL and selecting the appropriate mode, or, if working with layers, an entire layer can be assigned a specific mode. Become familiar with these modes, and how they function in order to trap any variable that may arise. They are:

normal mode: This is the default mode for Photoshop. It simply replaces the colors inside a marquee selection with the color chosen in the palette. It blends the neighboring colors at the edge of the selection. Generally, use delete or option delete to achieve this effect. This serves the purpose of deleting art at the same time as you color. Usually, this mode will be used if the black plate is separate from the color plates.

multiply mode: This mode adds the values of the colors in the palette to the colors already present in a selection. Therefore, multiplying C20M40 Y50K15 into C50M40Y30K0 will result in the color C70M80Y80K15. Multiplying a color several times will make the color darker each time. Generally, this mode is used to increase the values of a single plate over multiple colors.

darken mode: This mode uses the higher value of each channel to create the end color. Therefore, darkening C20M40Y50K15 into C50M40Y30K0 will result in the color C50M40Y50K15. This mode should be considered the all-purpose trapping mode and is used when adding the black plate to the color channels. However, you need to be careful when using this mode with layers. The background layer should be deleted to white, except for the area to be trapped.

lighten mode: This mode uses the lower value of each channel to create the end color. Therefore, lightening C20M40Y50K15 into C50M40Y30K0 will result in the color C20M40Y30K0. This mode is very rarely used, and is generally restricted to certain special effects. Although it is of very limited use in trapping, it is a very valuable tool to know when coloring logos or creating certain ghosting effects.

Dropping in Illustrator Logos

Before bringing any logo from Illustrator into Photoshop, make sure that it is already the correct size/ proportion that will be needed. Re-sizing a logo in Photoshop may cause the lines to blur or stair step adversely. Also, the logo should be in black and white. Illustrator trapping will not necessarily make the proper transition into Photoshop, and it becomes much more difficult to attempt to trap a logo that has already been colored in Illustrator.

The easiest way to transfer a logo from one application to another is simply select and copy the logo in Illustrator, and paste (as pixels) into Photoshop.

Unfortunately this does not always work for some extremely complex logos. If this should occur, open the Illustrator file from inside the Photoshop application. This will create a separate Photoshop document from the Illustrator document. Make sure the resolution is equal to the resolution of the document you intend to paste it into, and make the mode grayscale. Select all, Copy, and Paste the logo into the document. Remember, when copying items from one Photoshop document to another, it is vitally important that they both have identical resolution. If they do not, the proportions of the pasted item will change size.

Placing logos in an exact spot can be tricky, since proper placement is determined by eye. It is possible to measure out the location in Quark, but remember to take the bleed into account, since Quark's rulers are zeroed on the trim line. Also, the art may have been shifted in the page layout for design purposes, making measurements difficult.

figure 8-02: Most logo placements in Photoshop must be done by eye, so it is a good idea to look for visual landmarks where the logo and art cross or connect. This particular example has several areas that can help in proper placement.

The best way to place an object by eye is to locate several 'landmarks' where the art and logo 'interact' in a distinct fashion. Near tangents and clearly positioned cuts are the best bet. The logo channel's options should be set for a distinct color, and an opacity that allows for clear visibility of both art and logo. Then use these landmarks when placing and moving the logo.

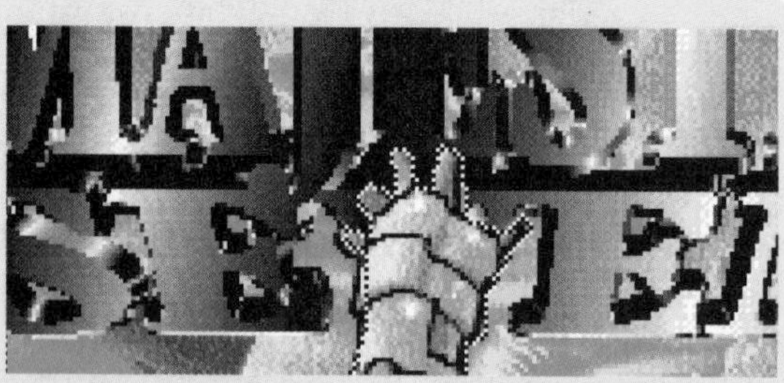

figure 8-03: It may be a good idea to have the Quark layout open on the computer screen to use as a visual reference while placing a logo in Photoshop

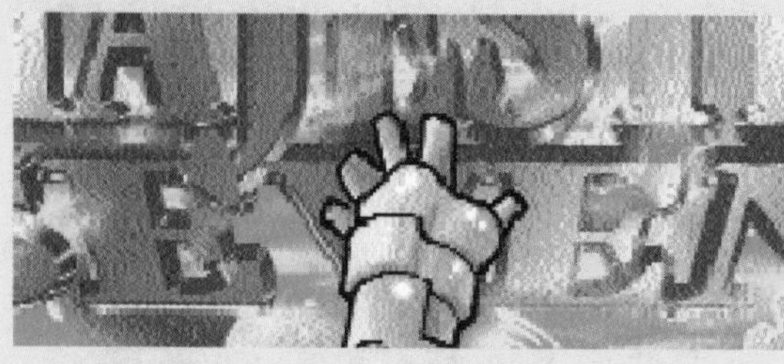

Paste-Up and Trapping Logos in Photoshop

Due to the nature of dropping logos into Photoshop, the procedure for pasting-up and trapping logos are inseparable. Therefore, the following instructions deal more with pasting up logos so that the end product is properly trapped ***and*** underprinted. The instructions deal with the following variables:

- logos with black outlines
- logos with color outlines
- art with a separate black plate
- art with the black plate merged with color plates

Remember, do not paste-up logos in Photoshop unless the art has already been separated. Otherwise, editing colors in either logo or art may become difficult. It is also easier to carry over certain special effects from the art to the logo if they are kept separate.

Black in Logos/Separate Black Plate

This combination is generally the most straightforward. The basic steps are: paste up the logo into the black plate, drop a copy of the black plate into a channel on the color document, and color logo accordingly. If the logo is in Illustrator, make sure it has the correct dimensions at print size, and that the logo is in black and white. Select the logo and copy.

Open the black plate and change the mode to grayscale. Paste logo into a separate layer. Place the logo, and cut art in front. Delete the art that lies behind the logo. Convert the logo layer to darken mode in order to eliminate any white 'fringe' that may be appearing around the outside of the logo art. Flatten image, and change mode back to bitmap. Save as a tiff.

Image size the black line art down to color document resolution (this plate will eventually be discarded, so do not worry about converting it back to grayscale). Copy and paste the line art into a channel in the color document. Do ***not*** save changes to the black plate.

In the line channel, select the face of the logo with the magic wand. Then go to

SELECT>MODIFY>EXPAND. Expand by 1 pixel for every 100 ppi in document resolution. Be careful, if trapping thin black lines, a smaller contraction amount will have to be used. The color should bleed under the black line, but not outside the line. In the color channels, drop in the appropriate colors.

After all the colors have been dropped in, make the line channel a selection by dragging the entire channel to the dotted circle icon at the bottom left corner of the channel menu. Go to SELECT>MODIFY>CONTRACT and contract by the appropriate amount. Go to the color channels and fill selection with the correct underprinting. Delete line channel and save the document.

Colored Outlines Logos/ Separate Black Plate

Combining a full-color logo, which contains no black, into separate black and color documents can be the most awkward of tasks to perform. This combination is generally the driving force behind merging the black plate with the color plates. Consider combining the documents in order to avoid some of the convoluted steps involved with this process.

If the logo is in Illustrator, make sure it is the correct dimensions at print size, and that the logo is in black and white. Select the logo and copy. Paste the logo as pixels into a new channel of the color document. Make a second channel, and create a mask for all art cutting in front

figure 8-04: An overview of stripping logos with black outlines into documents containing a separate black plate:(A) Convert the high res black plate to grayscale and place the logo into a layer, deleting any areas that should not cover the art; (B) Flatten the image, and place a copy of the new line art into a separate channel of the CMYK document; and (C) Color the logo using the channels as a guide for proper trapping.

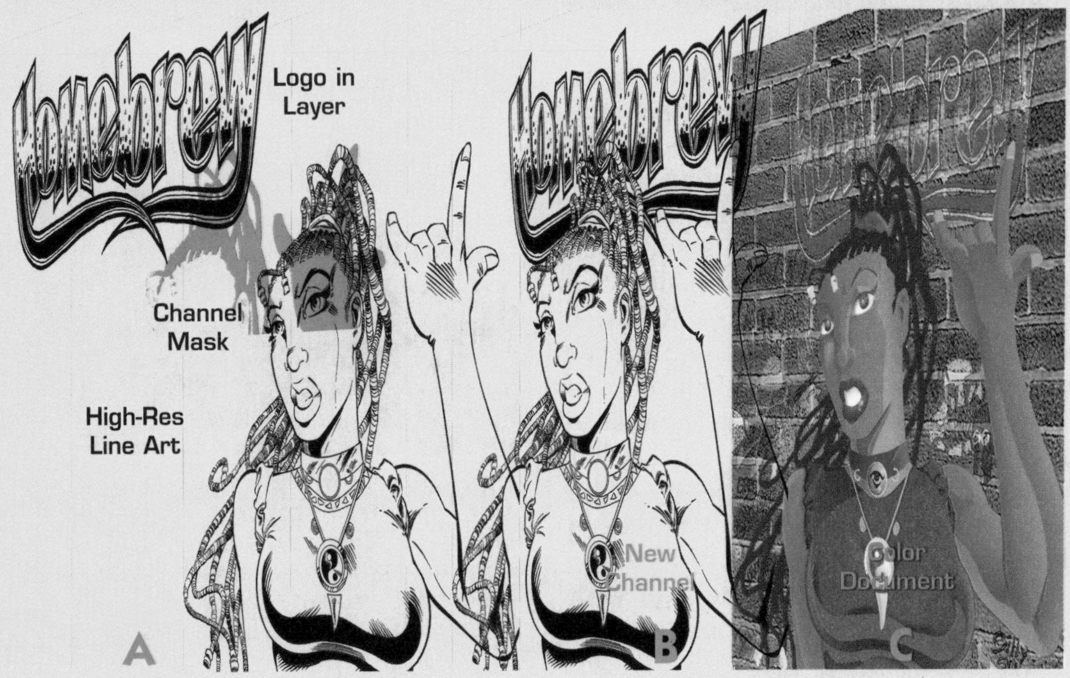

of the logo. Keep in mind that sections of the logo colors must trap underneath the black line artwork, so the mask will be made to create this trap.

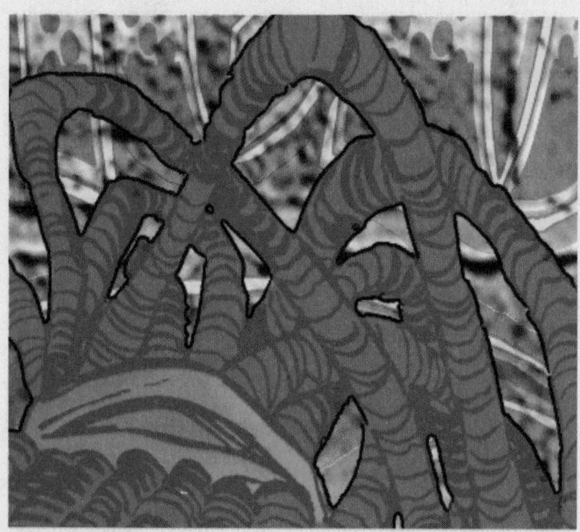

figure 8-05: This example shows a detail of a channel mask that will create a proper trap with the black plate. Deselect the black channel to avoid accidentally deleting any black when coloring the logo.

In the logo channel, select the entire logo by drawing a selection box around the logo, and deselect the white outside the logo outline by using the magic wand tool. Deselect any area inside the logo where any background art is supposed to show through (such as inside the letter 'O'). SELECT>MODIFY>CONTRACT the selection in order to create a proper trap (this is called a choke). Deselect the mask by dragging the entire channel to the dotted circle icon at the bottom left corner of the channel menu while holding down the option key. Delete to white in the color channels,.

Now, select the face of the logo with the magic wand, and deselect the mask. Go to SELECT>MODIFY>EXPAND to create a trap. Be careful, if trapping thin black lines, it may be necessary to use smaller expansion amounts. The color needs to spread under the black, but not outside the line. Drop the appropriate colors into the color channels.

After all the colors for the logos face and drop shadow have been created, make the logo channel a selection by dragging the entire channel to the dotted circle icon at the bottom left corner of the channel menu. Deselect the mask channel. Make your foreground color the correct color for the outline. Go to EDIT>FILL and set the foreground color to 'Darken.' This will drop the colored outline into the color plates while creating a choke for the surrounding colors.

Make a copy of the logo channel, and fill the face of the logo with solid black. To eliminate any white halos, expand the selection. This new channel

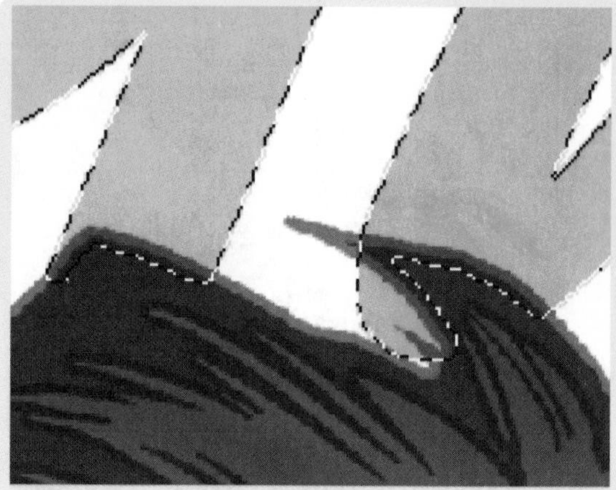

figure 8-06: When dropping logo colors into art it is important to trap these colors to the surrounding colors. The channel mask should be designed to create the proper trap, and the colors are dropped in using EDIT>FILL>DARKEN.

will be referred to as the logo mask.

Make the art mask channel a selection by dragging the entire channel to the dotted circle icon at the bottom left corner of the channel menu. Go to the logo mask and delete to white. Select all and copy the entire logo mask channel.

Go to FILE>NEW, make sure your new document is grayscale and not CMYK, then paste. Go to IMAGE>IMAGE SIZE and change the resolution to match the black line art. The resolutions must be the identical, otherwise the dimensions of the logo mask will change when pasted into the black line art. Select all and copy the entire channel once again. It is important to use the select all command so that the logo does not change position.

Open the black plate and change the mode to grayscale. Create a new channel and paste the logo mask into it. Make the logo mask channel a selection, and go to SELECT>MODIFY>CONTRACT. Contract to create a small trap, then delete to white. Be careful not to delete any line art that goes over the logo. The intention is to delete only background elements. Change mode back to bitmap, and save as a tiff.

Combined Plates

Generally, having combined plates on a cover is the best way to go, even if the interiors are done as separate plates. Usually, the cover is where all of the

figure 8-07: An overview of stripping colored logos into documents containing a separate black plate: (A) Convert the high-res black plate to grayscale and delete any art that should not cover the logo. (B) Place a copy of the new line art, logo, and any art masks into separate channels of the CMYK document; and (C) Color the logo using the channels as a guide for proper trapping.

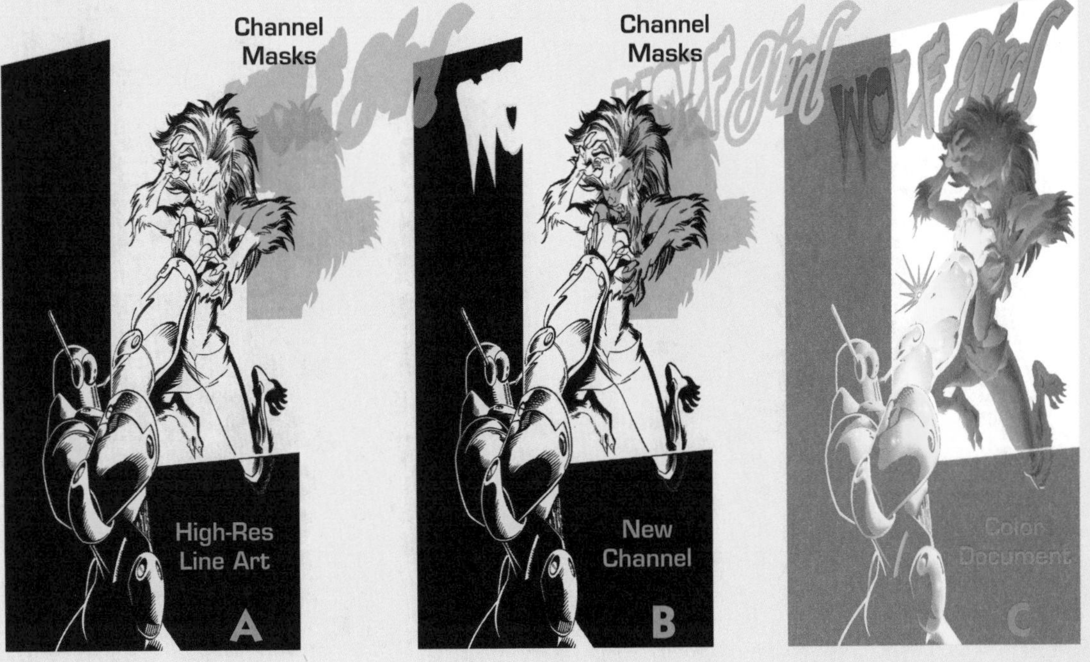

bells and whistles, and special effects will be pulled out in order to dazzle and entice the consumer. This often means special effects overlapping the logo itself. A feat that may be impossible if the plates are separate. The process for stripping in logos containing black and those logos with no black at all is almost identical (differences will be noted in the text). So, on with the show.

Paste the black and white logo (as pixels) into a channel in the color document. Make a second channel and create a mask for all art cutting in front of the logo. Keep in mind that sections of the logo colors must trap underneath the black line artwork. In the logo channel, select the entire logo by drawing a selection box around the logo, and deselect the white outside the logo outline by using the magic wand tool. Also, deselect any areas inside the logo where background art is supposed to show through. Contract the selection to create a choke. Deselect the mask channel by dragging the entire channel to the dotted circle icon at the bottom left corner of the channel menu while holding down the option key. With only the black channel selected, delete to white.

In the logo channel, select the face of the logo with the magic wand. Now the selection expansion and mask deselection come in different orders depending on whether or not there is any black in the logo. If black is present, expand the selection first, then deselect

figure 8-08: An overview of stripping colored logos into combined documents: (A)Place logo into position in a channel of the color document (note this logo example requires two separate channels); (B) Create a trapped mask for the art that cuts in front of logo; and (C) Color the logo using the channels as selections–by expanding/contracting the selections in order to create a proper trap with both the background and black plate.

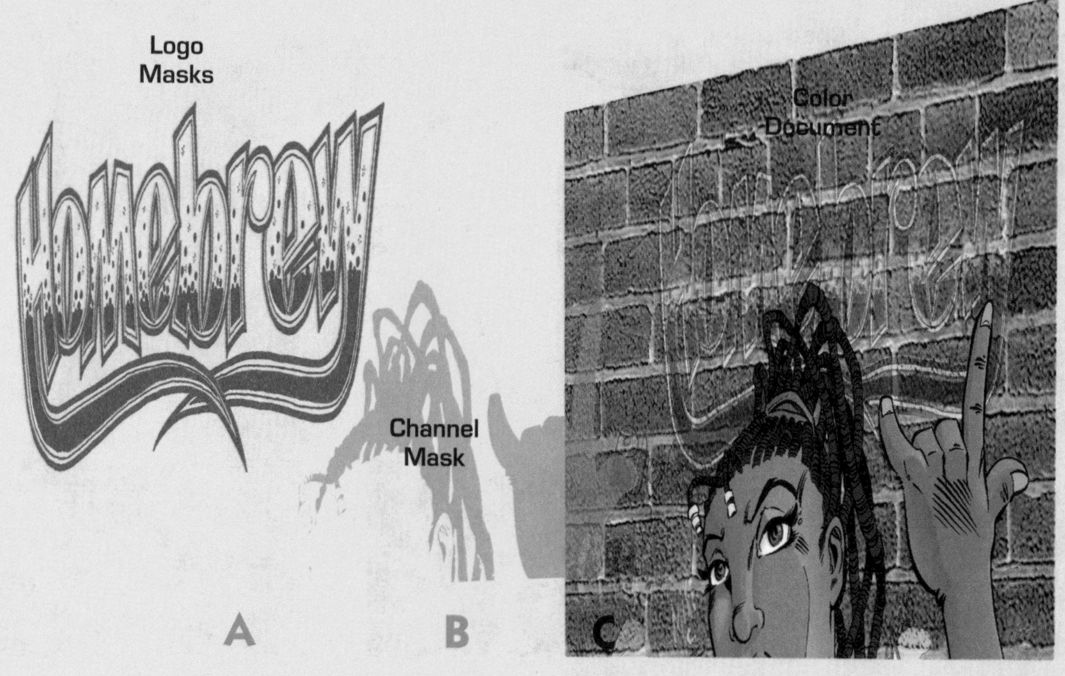

figure 8-09: An overview of stripping black logos into combined documents: (A) Place logo into position in a channel of the color document; (B) Create a trapped mask for the art that cuts in front of logo; (C) Color the logo using the channels as selections–by expanding/contracting the selections in order to create a proper trap with both the background and black plate. Remember to drop in underprinting for the black logo.

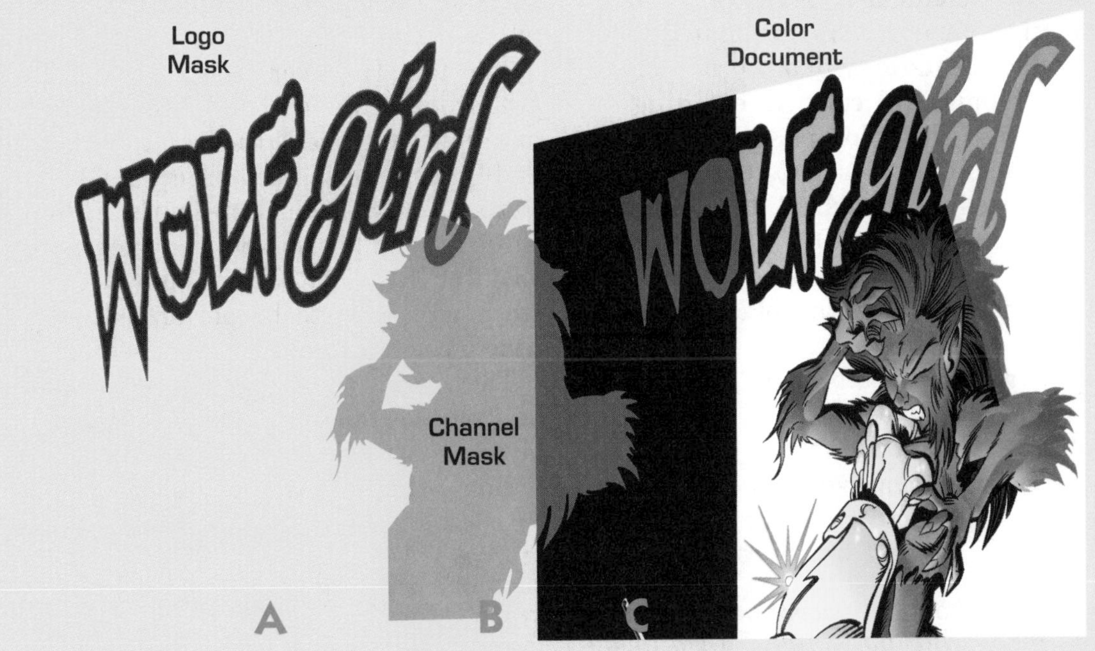

the mask. If there are only colors present in the logo, deselect the mask first, then expand the selection to create the trap.

Make sure that the black channel is *deselected* and that only the color channels (cyan, magenta, and yellow) are selected, then drop in the appropriate colors. If the color you are dropping in contains a K-tone it will have to be dropped in separately with darken mode.

After all the colors have been dropped in, create an underprinting color for any section of the logo that will remain black. Make the logo channel a selection and deselect the mask channel. If the outlines of the logo is black, make the foreground color 100%K with no other colors present. Otherwise, make the foreground color the appropriate color needed. Go to EDIT>FILL and select darken for the foreground color. This will drop the outline color on top of the pre-existing colors without deleting what is underneath.

K-Tones and Combined Plates

Every situation encountered will be slightly different. In order to successfully complete each new task requires the ability to learn and adapt. The instructions laid out above contain only the basic combination of elements that will be encountered. Unfortunately, they cannot account for every variable or special effect.

The most glaring omission from the above instructions is the use of K-tones in the color palette. This will make no difference if your black plate is a separate document. However, when working with combined plates the following paradoxes will be encountered:

a) dropping a color containing a K-tone into the color plates while the black channel is deselected will cause the K-tones to vanish (M100Y100K30 becomes M100Y100K0).

b) colors cannot be trapped properly to black line art while the black plate is selected without deleting the black lines in the area intended to trap.

There are two ways around this problem, one is tedious, the other uses more memory. However, either one will work effectively, so the choice is a personal preferences. We shall refer to these two methods as toggling and layers.

In the toggling method, follow the steps outlined above, including dropping in the colors while the black channel is deselected. However, as soon as colors are dropped in, without altering your marquee selection, deselect the C, M, and Y channels, and select the black channel only. Then drop in the K-tone value needed to complete the color using EDIT>FILL>DARKEN. These extra steps will have to be performed every time a color with a K-tone is used.

The layers method requires the logo be colored in a completely different layer, separate from the background art. Follow the steps outlined in the

figure 8-10: An overview of coloring logos in a layer: (A) Delete area occupied by logo from background layer; (B) Color a trapped logo in a separate layer, eliminating any areas that should not cover background art; and (C) Convert logo layer mode to darken to preserve trapping and flatten image.

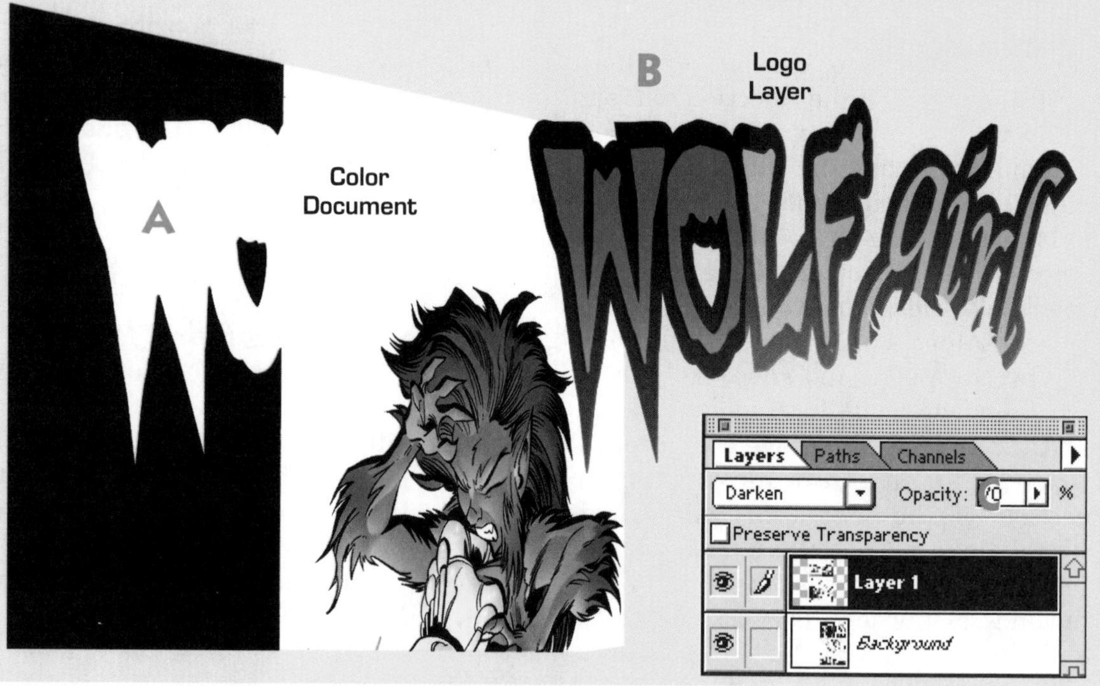

combined plates instructions above. However, delete *all* colors to white in the background layer, not just the black plate. This will prevent any adverse color changes in the logo later on. Create a new layer in the layers palette. This layer should be set to 'Darken'. Setting the entire layer to 'Darken' will ensure that the logo layer will be trapped to the background layer. Follow all instructions concerning coloring the logos, making sure to only work in the logo layer and not the background. Since the work is being done in a completely different layer, the black channel need not be deselected. After the logo is completely colored, flatten the image, and follow the last remaining steps normally.

Special Effects

The layers method should also be used when recreating any special effects that may cross over the logo from the background. This will allow for the luxury of making multiple changes without adversely affecting the background. The most common effect needed to be reproduced are ghosting effects. Sections of the logo layer can be ghosted using curves, without ghosting the background any further than it already may be.

figure 8-11: Recreating this ray of light effect involved making a selection of the affected areas and ghosting the logo by 50% using curves.

Another type of ghosting effect used in this fashion is to give artwork appearing over the logo a translucent look. In this case, the section of art needed is copied into a layer first, then the logo can be added directly to the background. Set the art layer to darken, and ghost the section of logo directly behind the layer to make the art more visible.

Figure 8-12 contains both a translucent ghost and glowing symbols that were colored in layers to affect the logo.

Energy effects are often ghosted, or colorized, in front of logos. These can be far easier to accomplish using layers. In figure 8-13 the outside color halo of the lightning was airbrushed directly on top of the logo layer. Then the internal details of the effect were brought out using the eraser tool set in airbrush option. This tool can be used to bring out small details–like the sparks–that may be difficult to select, or changing the opacity in the options palette can create a more transparent look.

figure 8-13: lightning effect

In figure 8-16, the logo was colorized using a channel mask and an adjustment layer set to hue saturation. The use of an adjustment layer for the colorization allows for later changes to the effect itself, leaving the background unchanged until the document is flattened.

These are but a few of many effects that can be created. Once satisfied with the effect, flatten and save the image. It may be wise to keep an unflattened image just in case, and it is always a good idea to keep a copy of the colored art with no logo attached.

Once the logo has been stripped into Photoshop, its Illustrator counterpart can be deleted from Quark, and the final art is updated. At this point, the cover is almost done. Nothing left but dotting i's and crossing t's. But before addressing the final minutia, a discussion of specialty covers is in order.

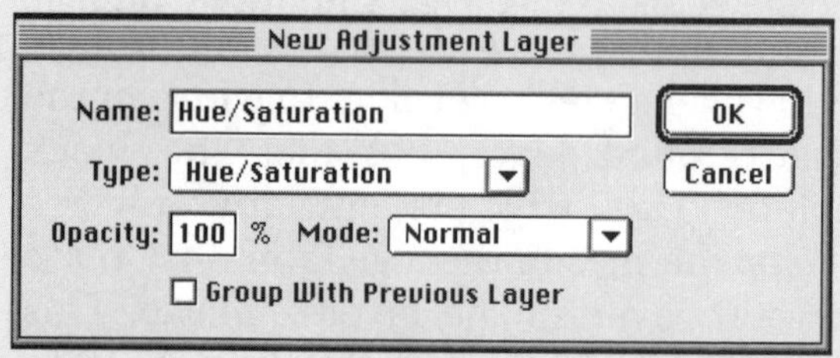

figure 8-14: To create an adjustment layer, select it from the layer palette options. A window appears where the specific adjustment can be selected. The adjustment can be edited at anytime prior to the flattening of the layers by double clicking on the adjustment layer.

figure 8-15: This multiple cover displays several examples of special effects. The first logo has been colorized behind the green energy bubble. The history brush was used to paint part of the fire in front of the second logo. The third logo is covered by lightning.

figure 8-16

CHAPTER 9
SPECIALTY COVERS & COLOR CORRECTION

To gild refined gold, to paint the lily,
To throw perfume on the violet,
To smooth the ice, or add another hue
Unto the rainbow, or with taper-light
To seek the beauteous eye of heaven to garnish,
Is wasteful and ridiculous excess.
King John, act IV, scene ii
William Shakespeare, 1596

There was a time when every comic book company in the business was pandering to a class of buyer called the speculator. This type of consumer only bought certain types of comics for the sole purpose of selling them at a future date at an enormous profit. These comics needed to be collectors' items. All of a sudden, it seemed every comic on the stand sported some fancy new foil, embossed, varnished, die cut, holographic, glow in the dark, acetate cover. Collect all five covers!

Unfortunately, most covers were turned into specialty covers after they were halfway through the production process. The result was confusion and chaos. In some cases, editors, having an unwanted enhancement thrust upon them at the last minute, would choose to use the effect on the smallest area they could get away with to "preserve the integrity of the art." Other editors, driven into a state of speculator frenzy, were looking for the newest gimmick in town, usually embarrassing or disappointing themselves in the process. One editor wanted to add a UV coating to his cover, not realizing this coating was totally invisible, its sole purpose was to keep foil from flaking off covers. And any serious discussion of flocking covers brought titters of disbelief from the production department. (*Flocking n.:* tiny, fine fibers of wool, rayon, or like substance, applied to a cover with glue to form a velvet like pattern. Fuzzy covers!)

Ultimately, the speculators deserted the market, but they left the impression on some marketing departments that specialty covers could increase the lagging sales of books. As a result, enhanced covers occasionally appear on the stands bringing up memories of a fad filled time of 'wasteful and ridiculous excess.' Granted, some of these covers can be quite attractive. This is especially true when the artwork is designed with a specific enhancement in mind. Therefore, if a specialty cover is really worth doing, it is worth doing right. Which is the very purpose of this chapter.

Fifth Colors

The least expensive type of enhancement is the addition of extra inks, usually referred to as fifth colors (but you can add as many as you like... for a price). Any printer with four color capability can print fifth colors, and most larger printing companies run most four color jobs on six color presses for just such an occasion.

Fifth colors can also be referred to as Pantone colors, after the Pantone Matching System used by the entire printing and publishing industry. The Pantone system contains thousands of colors, and is supported by all major publishing software, including Adobe and Quark products. Additional colors used on enhanced covers are usually some type of special Pantone ink, such as metallic or fluorescent colors.

A mistake often made during the specialty cover fad was the selection of a Pantone process color ink. Process colors have equivalent CMYK values, therefore, a process color will look no different than any other ink on the page. These process colors are generally used on printing jobs of less than four colors.

Another thing to remember is that process colors are mostly transparent, fluorescent colors are mostly translucent, and metallic colors are usually opaque. It is a good idea to trap these colors the same way as any CMYK

Choosing Pantone Colors

Quark: *To choose a Pantone color in Quark go to EDIT>COLORS>NEW, change the Model to a Pantone model, and select the new color. Make sure Spot Color is checked in version 4, or Process Color is unchecked in previous versions. The Pantone color will now appear in the Colors window, and can be trapped as any other color would be.*

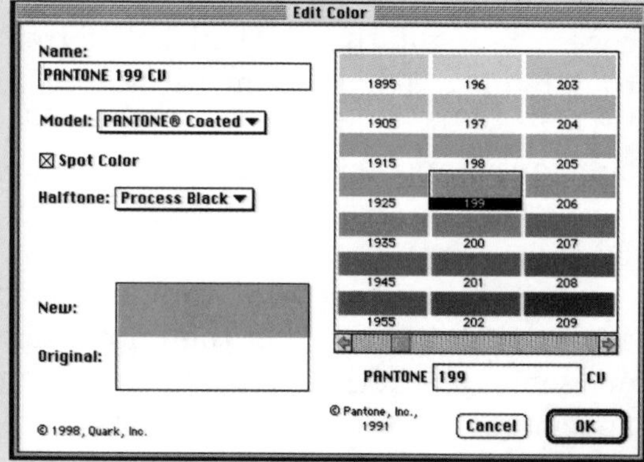

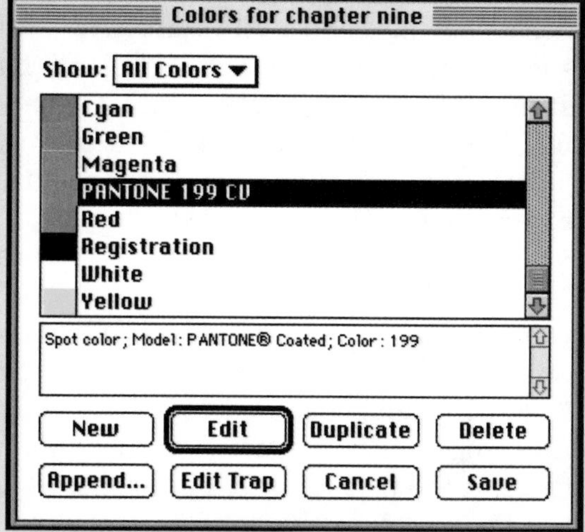

Photoshop: *To choose a Pantone color in Photoshop 5 go to New Spot Channel in the channel palette options. Double click on the color chip in the New Spot Channel window to bring up a second window where Pantone colors can be selected. The fifth color now appears in the channel palette.*

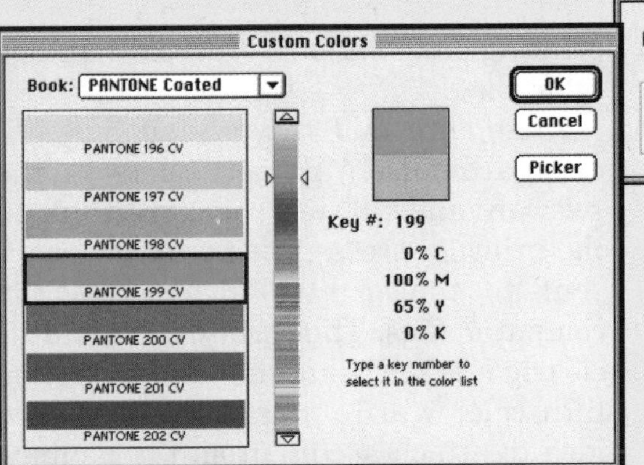

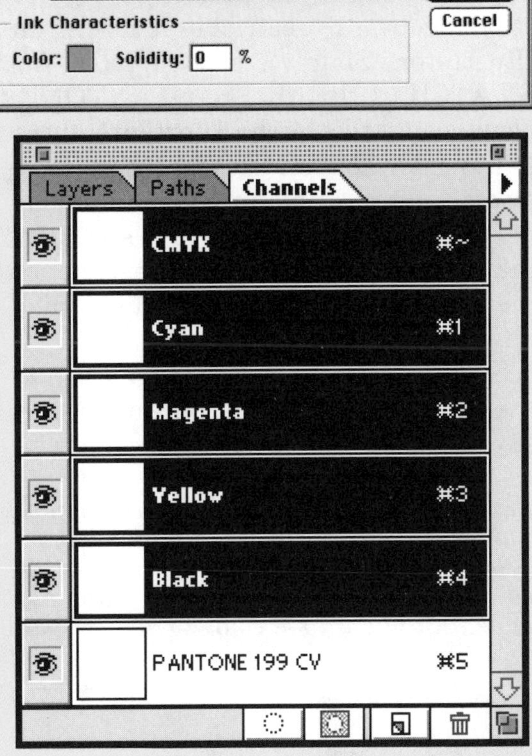

The Photoshop document must now be saved in EPS DCS 2 format (below) in order for the imagesetter to generate the additional plate.

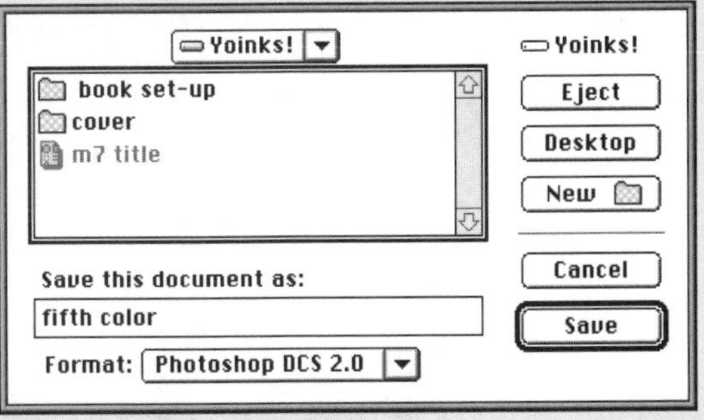

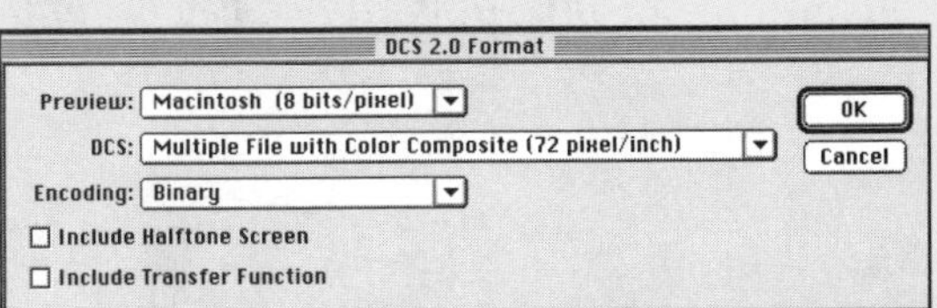

Illustrator: *To choose a Pantone color in Illustrator go to WINDOW> SWATCH LIBRARIES >PANTONE, and a Pantone color palette will appear on the desktop (right). When trapping be aware of the order in which inks will be printed.*

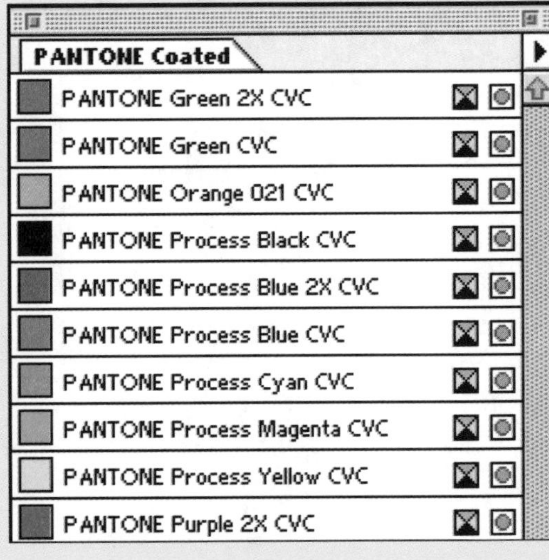

color. Also, varnishes are considered additional colors and can be put to good use.

Pantone colors are easy to work with in the supported software. If these colors are appearing in an Illustrator logo or cover copy, it can be chosen in Illustrator. Simply go to WINDOW> SWATCH LIBRARIES >PANTONE. Now comes the hitch! There are three Pantone swatch libraries to choose from (coated, process, and uncoated) and none of them may contain the specialty ink needed, such as fluorescent or metallics. No problem! Just pick any color.

Some people say pick a color close to the same hue as the ink needed, others say pick a truly obnoxious color that will stand out as being different. I recommend the latter. Just make sure to use the exact same Pantone color in all three programs (if necessary), because the imagesetter will generate a different printing plate for each different Pantone color used.

Make sure that the printer knows to disregard falsely named colors in the software and will use the correct ink on the printing press. A print out is always sent to the printer along with the computer files. This printout should be clearly marked as to what and where the fifth color will be located. It is a good idea to attach a 'chip' from the Pantone swatch book to the printout as well. The swatch book contains a half dozen labeled, perforated color chips for each

figure 9-02: Fifth-color inks are usually printed before the black ink for trapping purposes (below). However, Photoshop only allows the spot color to go on top of the four process colors, therefore the printer must be informed of the proper order. Trap the fifth color as if it were beneath the black plate and remove any of the process colors from beneath the Pantone color to avoid ink oversaturation.

individual Pantone color, and can be purchased from any major graphic art store.

In Photoshop 5, additional channels can be converted into printing plates. Open the channels options and choose 'spot color.' Changing the opacity will not change the color value on the screen as it does in a normal alpha channel. The opacity setting in a spot channel is intended to accurately reproduce the opacity of the ink. Double click on the color chip at bottom left, and click the 'custom' button in the color picker window to bring up custom colors window. From here, Pantone colors can be selected, but remember to use the same color used in other programs. To insure that the film is outputted properly, the document must be saved in DCS 2.0 format. Earlier versions of the DCS format do not support this feature.

Earlier versions of Photoshop also do not support this technique. Fifth colors were created as a separate color overlay saved as a bitmap TIFF (as discussed in chapter six). The color of the TIFF is then chosen in Quark in the EDIT>COLORS windows under color model. Be sure to have spot color checked in version 4 of Quark, and process color un-checked in earlier versions. This is necessary in order for the imagesetter to generate an additional piece of film for the fifth color. Trapping is the same as any four color value.

As long as the same Pantone color is used in all three programs only one additional piece of film should be generated. However, clarify with the printer in what order to print the extra ink. In most cases it is better to print the fifth color before the black to create a proper overprinting black trap. If it is not expressly requested to print the black plate last, the Pantone color will be printed last. This often will not make a difference, but certain opaque or translucent inks will look odd when overprinting black. Also remember that color saturation does not change, so do not overprint fifth colors over large areas of CMYK colors.

Foils and Die-Cuts

Foil stamping is the second most often used specialty effect used on covers. A heavier stock of paper is required for this process, and the cover is printed and

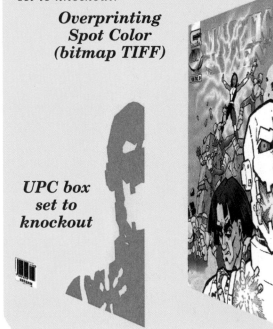

figure 9-03: Prior to version 5, fifth-colors had to be created as bitmap TIFFs and placed into Quark as a spot color. If the black plate were combined with the color plates, the fifth color had to be set to overprint, so as not to destroy its own trapping. In this example, the UPC box was placed on top of the spot color and set to knockout.

allowed to dry before the foil is applied. As the cover goes through the stamper, a sheet of foil covers the entire cover. A thick hot plate containing the foil image stamps the cover melting the foil onto the affected areas. Any foil in an unaffected area is discarded, so the use of only a small amount of foil is wasteful and just as expensive as using large amounts of foil. Often, a UV (ultraviolet) coating is applied to protect the foil. This also protects the cover (somewhat) from fading due to exposure to sunlight.

Creating a foil plate is identical to creating a fifth color plate–in fact using a Pantone color to indicate the foil is usually suggested. The additional piece of film will be used to create the foil-stamping plate. There is one major difference, however, and that is how the foil will be trapped.

Foil is most definitely opaque. Since it is stamped at a completely different time as the colors, more shifting may occur requiring larger traps. Foil indication colors should always be set to overprint; fills, strokes, frames –everything, no exception. Create an extra large trap to choke underneath the foil, but leave large areas under the foil white so that the foil adheres better to the paper.

Occasionally, small details in line art are printed on top of the foil after stamping. This is done by running the

figure 9-04: Foil plates are created in the same manner as fifth-color plates, however they must be stamped after the initial four-color run. Since the foil is applied at a completely separate time from the ink, an extra thick choke is applied when trapping to compensate for registration difficulty. It may not be possible to knockout thin black lines from the foil, making it necessary to create an additional black plate to be printed on top of the foil.

Additional black plate prints fine detail over foil

Foil Plate

Die-Cuts

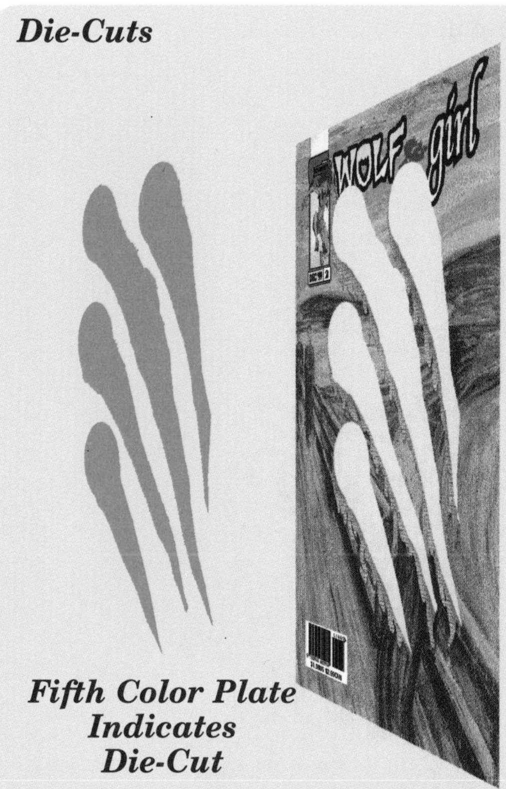

Fifth Color Plate Indicates Die-Cut

Die-cuts are created as bitmap TIFFS placed in Quark as a fifth-color set to overprint, so as not to delete any art from underneath the die-cut. The TIFF should be placed on top of all art boxes in the Quark document. It is usually a good idea to place this same TIFF on the inside covers as well, to be used as a visual guide for the art that is removed from the inside front cover, as well as to see what art will be visible through the die-cut (below).

cover through the printing press again, after the stamping process. This requires creating an additional color overlay containing just the line art in question. This is considered an additional fifth color, even if the normal process black is used.

There are some types of foil covers that simply use a foil stock instead of paper. This type of cover requires no special production work and is printed normally, with the possible exception of a fifth color opaque white that is required if using a UPC bar code.

Die-cuts are holes in the cover that are cut out in specific shapes to reveal areas of art on a secondary cover. The consideration here is not to create small slivers of paper, or angles that may get caught or torn on the display rack. Die-cuts are created in exactly the same manner as foils, including the extra large trap. The fifth piece of film is then used as a guide to create the cutting plate.

Foils and die-cuts do require more printing time. This requires that the cover be at the printers several weeks earlier than is required on normal covers. This additional time must be worked into the production schedule.

Embossing

Creating a raised or indented surface on a cover requires no additional computer production work, but still needs to be covered. In addition to the art, two embossing guides are required. These guides are usually done by hand, although it is conceivable to do them on the computer.

The first is a fully rendered pencil drawing to define the form and shape of the embossing. This drawing is usually done on a piece of tracing paper overlayed on top of the art. The black lines of the art should not be reproduced on this drawing, unless the lines themselves are intended to be embossed (which may be the case for logos).

figure 9-06: Example of a gray scale rendering used as an embossing guide.

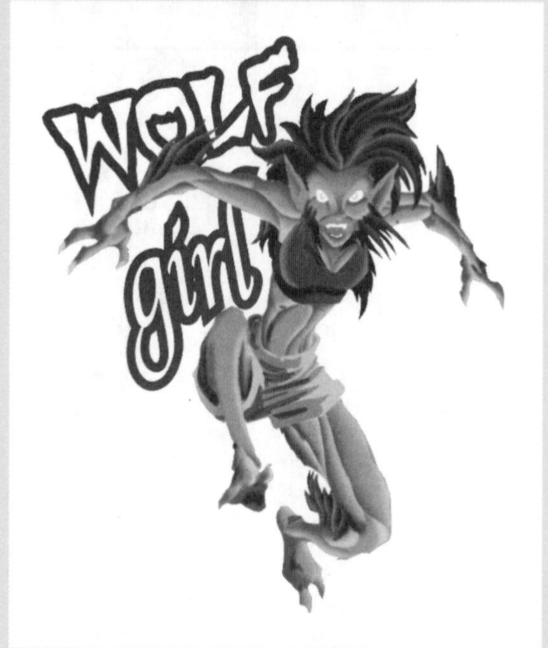

The second guide is an overlay placed over the first guide. It is a topographical guide indicating the different levels of the embossing. These levels are indicated in a combination of outlines and colors. A color key is included on the overlay. It is possible to indent (slightly) as well as emboss, as long as the levels do not drop sharply between high and low.

Again, it is certainly possible to recreate these guides on the computer, but ultimately a hard copy printout is required. Also, since the embossing plate

figure 9-07: Example of a topographical rendering used as an embossing guide. Each color represents a different level.

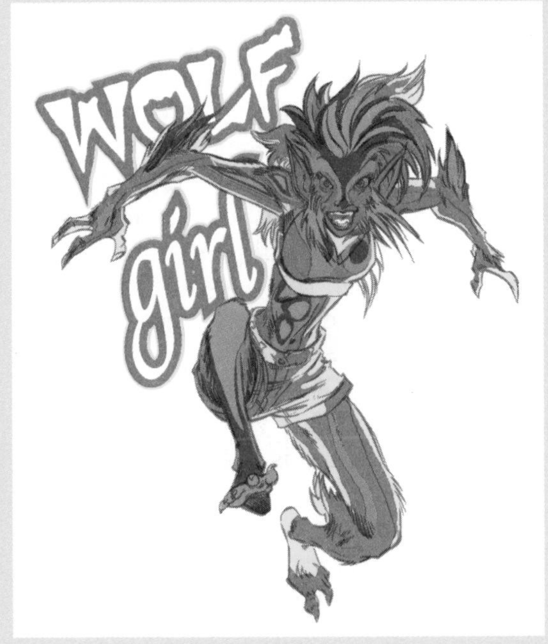

is created by hand, the engraver will probably want the guides at art size for easier viewing. The engravers may also require the guides be done on tracing paper so that the relationships can be seen together. All in all, it may easier to do this particular job by hand.

figure 9-08: It is possible to deboss at the same time as embossing, but avoid dramatic shifts in levels to prevent the paper from tearing.

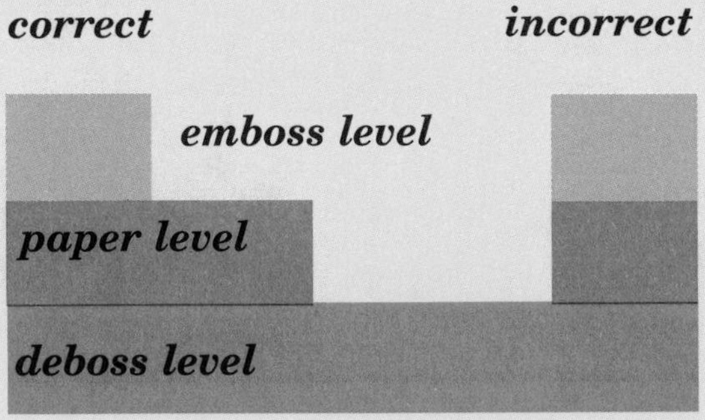

correct ***incorrect***

emboss level

paper level

deboss level

Color Corrections

Full color art, such as paintings, are not considered specialty covers, because no special cost or printing process is incurred. However, from a production standpoint, a great deal of extra time and work are required to make the job print well. Therefore we shall discuss this subject here.

Make no mistake, this type of work is a specialized skill that takes practice and experience. There are people whose sole occupation is color correcting scans of photographs and paintings. These individuals are well paid and highly sought after by major publishing, advertising, and printing companies. Professional color correctors usually have years of experience and training behind them. These people would probably be aghast at the instructions this book is about to give, pointing out that they are both too general and too narrow, and that each job is unique and requires an individualized approach.

I completely agree with them.

The instructions that will be discussed in this book are merely a starting point, and not intended to turn anyone into an overnight expert in the art of color correction. If full color art is absolutely required for a project, and there is not enough time or money to hire a professional, these guidelines should provide for an adequate print. But, there is no guarantee of that.

Scanning Color

The job of color correction is made a lot easier when starting out with a good scan. Due to the physical laws which

figure 9-09: This uncorrected scan is an RGB image printing in CMYK.

govern light, all scanners scan in RGB. There are some flat bed scanners which claim to scan in CMYK. These claims are misleading and suggest that the scanner is capable of breaking the laws of physics! In actuality, these scanners convert the RGB information to CMYK on the fly. It is better to ignore this feature, scan in RGB, and color correct the art properly. Mathematical algorithms cannot replace human aesthetic judgements.

On the other hand, many drum scanners do in fact scan CMYK images by utilizing the same technique used by stat camera operators in the pre scanner days of color separation. This involves using a colored filter to create each individual color plate. The drum scanner uses a different wavelength of light for each plate, and scans the image four times. A skilled drum scan operator can virtually eliminate the need for major color corrections, leaving only minor fine tuning or 'tweaking' of colors. I am not aware of any flat bed scanner that scans CMYK in this fashion.

Assuming a drum scan is out of the question, we will begin with an RGB scan made on a flatbed scanner. The threshold settings will be similar to that of a grayscale, in that a white and black point will be selected. Some scanners allow for additional information to be scanned in the form of a 48 bit RGB scan. This is of fairly little use, unless the entire image is heavily weighted towards one end of the value spectrum. The final printing resolution should probably range between 300 ppi and 400 ppi at print size. The higher resolution is necessary if logos need to be stripped into the art. If the art contains strong line work, such as black outlines, an even higher resolution may be required. But understand that the memory requirements for these documents will be large, and it will take a relatively long time to actually scan. Crop and set-up the art before color correcting, and always keep a copy of the uncorrected version in case of disasters.

CMYK Setup

CMYK Model: Built-in / ICC / Tables — OK — Cancel — Load... — Save... — Preview

Ink Options
Ink Colors: SWOP (Coated)
Dot Gain: Standard 20 %

Separation Options
Separation Type: GCR / UCR — Gray Ramp:
Black Generation: Light
Black Ink Limit: 85 %
Total Ink Limit: 265 %
UCA Amount: 0 %

Gamut Warning

Before color correction begins, certain preferences should be set. The first is the gamut warning, which highlights RGB colors falling outside of the printable range of CMYK. This setting is found in FILE>PREFERENCES> TRANSPARENCY & GAMUT. Select a gamut color that will stand out well from the colors of the art. Under FILE>COLOR SETTINGS>CMYK SETUP, use built in CMYK Model, SWOP coated ink colors, and GCR separations with light black generations. The other settings shown in the CMYK Setting window shown on the previous page, are good for general all purpose uses, but may not be appropriate for more sophisticated corrections. Note there are areas to enter ink limits and dot gains. Also alter the info palette options to display actual colors and CMYK values.

Establish and label key colors on the original art with CMYK percentage values using a color chart or Pantone process color guide. These are the values used to adjust the scan. Open the document, and the gamut warning should appear over several areas. Attempt to eliminate as much of the gamut as possible by manipulating the curves of each individual RGB channels.

figure 9-10: The bright green gamut warning shows RGB colors that fall outside the CMYK color space.

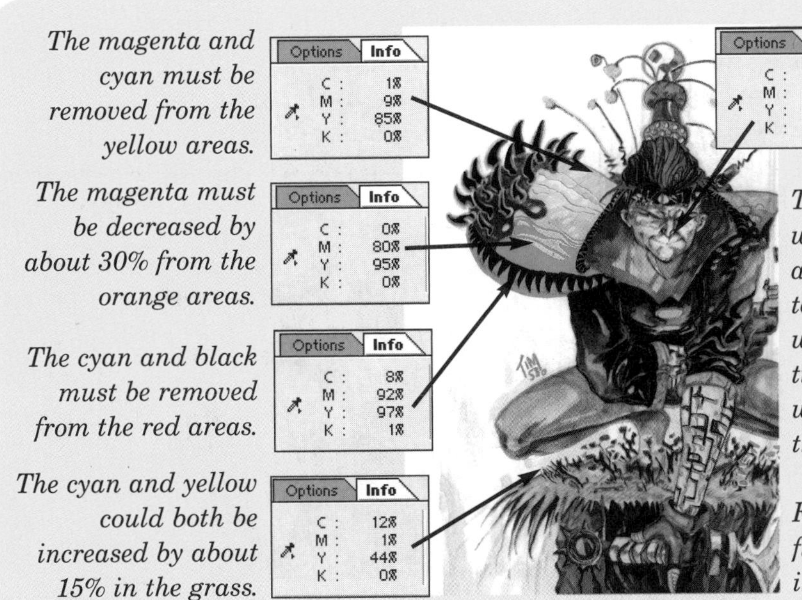

The cyan must be removed from the flesh areas, and yellow could be increased by 10%.

There is also some concerns with the gray areas. These areas need to be darkened to add contrast to the line work, while at the same time, maintaining the warm and cool castes of the different tones.

Furthermore, the pink flames at the bottom of the image virtually disappear.

figure 9-12: The following are the global curve corrections used on the image. Note the complexity of the magenta and yellow channels, needed to compensate for the different corrections at both the high and low end of the curves.

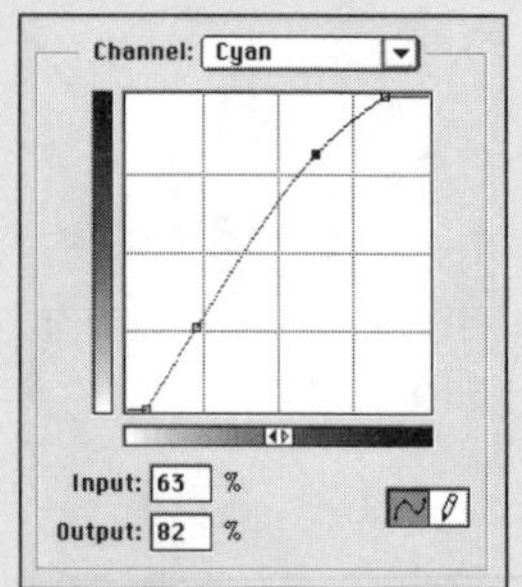

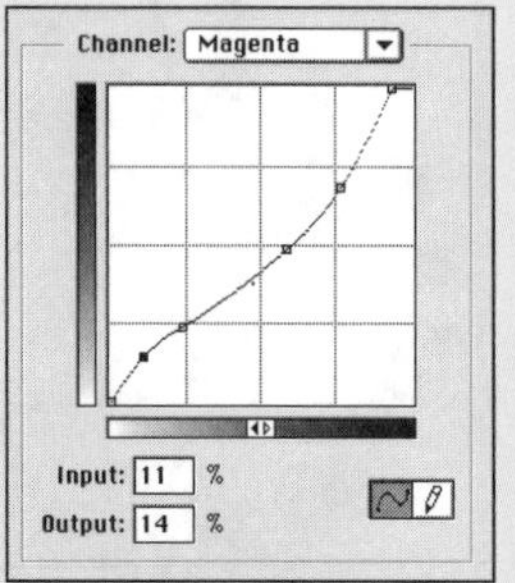

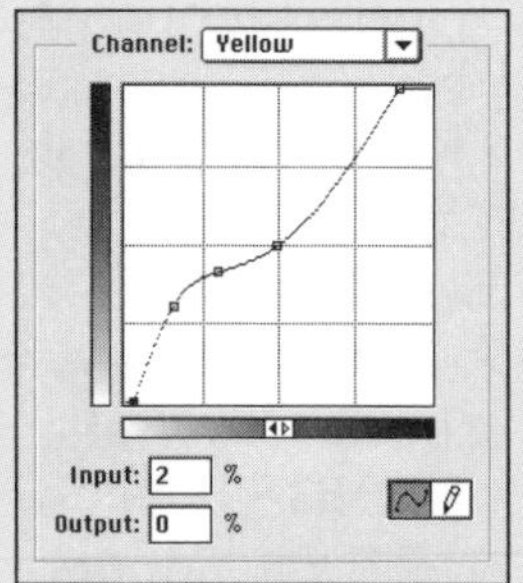

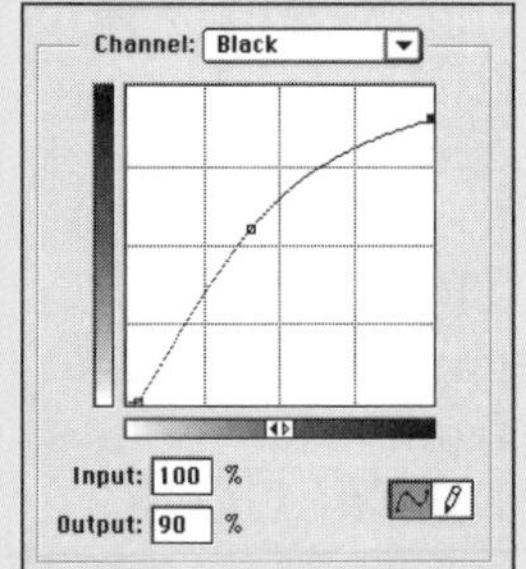

It may impossible to remove all of the gamut alarm color, so just remove as much as possible. Do not attempt to correct individual colors at this point.

Keep an eye on the CMYK values of the target areas, and try to avoid losing contrast or tonal range in the process. If the entire image has a particular color caste, manipulate its compliment. For instance, if a yellow caste is present manipulate the blue channel. Once this is achieved, convert the image mode to CMYK, but, if possible keep a copy of the RGB. Once an image is converted to CMYK the gamut warning will vanish from the screen, because the out of gamut colors are forced into the printable color range.

The conversion process will invariably add small amounts of each color into all other colors. Yellows will contain small amounts of cyan or black. Blues will contain some yellow and magenta. Now manipulate the curves of each individual CMYK channel with the goal of actually matching the codes of the key colors in the painting. These initial corrections should be done globally, in other words, affect the entire image without making individual selections. Try to get all the colors as close as possible using this global method first. Afterwards, if any single color remains unacceptable, make a selection and attempt a correction. Be sure to feather the selection to avoid creating a selection 'cut' in the art.

At this point, double-check the ink saturation by changing the info palette options to display 'total ink.' If possible

figure 9-13: After the global adjustments were made, the flames at the bottom of the image needed further corrections to prevent them from completely vanishing in the final version.

figure 9-14: The final corrected version of the image.

try to get a decent matchprint to determine if any additional corrections are required.

Heavy Blacks

The above process may not adequately handle oversaturation in art that uses a large quantity of black (including the use of black line art). The use of curves may not be enough to bring the oversaturation into acceptable limits without adversely affecting other colors in the art. In such a case the following additions should be added to the process.

Eliminate as much of the gamut warning as possible as described above, but do not convert to CMYK. Go to IMAGE>DUPLICATE to create an open copy of the document. Go to

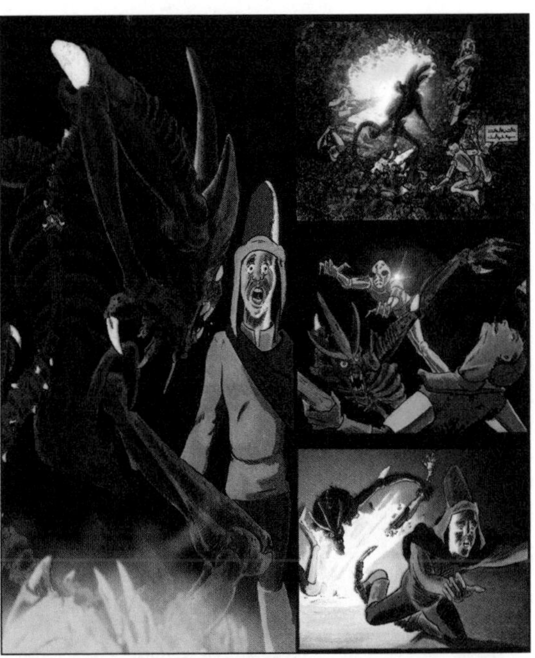

figure 9-15: This is the original scan.

FILE>COLOR SETTINGS>CMYK SET UP. Set the Separation options to UCR, 100% black ink limit, and the total ink limit to 400%. Now convert the duplicate document to CMYK.

CMYK Setup

CMYK Model: Built-in ICC Tables

Ink Options

Ink Colors: SWOP (Coated)

Dot Gain: Standard 20 %

Separation Options

Separation Type: GCR UCR

Gray Ramp:

Black Generation: Heavy

Black Ink Limit: 100 %

Total Ink Limit: 400 %

UCA Amount: %

OK

Cancel

Load...

Save...

Preview

The colors created in this conversion will probably look awful, but we are only interested in the black plate. Select only the black channel, and adjust the curves to wash out as much of the K tones as possible, while preserving only the strong blacks. Usually this involves moving the zero point all the way over to 70%-75%. The black point may have to be moved to a darker position if it was lightened by this drastic change. Select and copy the entire black channel.

figure 9-16: The black plate created using the UCR set-up (above) is converted into a mask (below) using curves.

Reset the CMYK Setup options to GCR, light black generation, and set the total ink limit to the proper ink saturation limit. Since there are heavy blacks in this image leave the black ink level at 100% (it is usually set at 85% for normal color corrections).

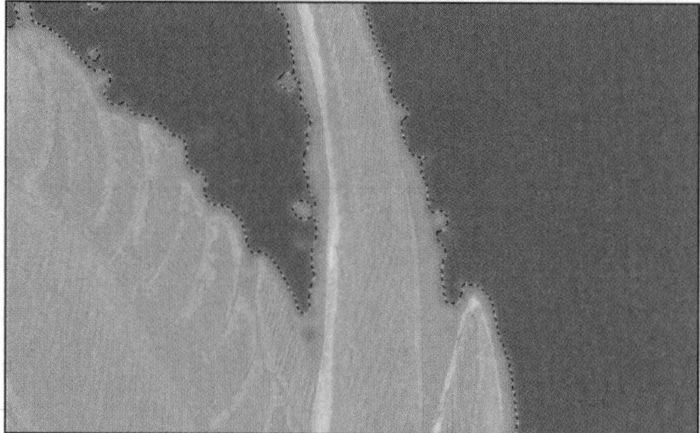

figure 9-17: The selection is feathered before the underprinting is added.

Now return to the original RGB document, and convert to CMYK. Create a new channel and paste in the duplicate black channel. Color correct as usual. Once the colors are correct, turn the channel mask into a selection and contract by four or five pixels. Feather the selection by two or three pixels (SELECT>FEATHER). Now use the curves to create an appropriate underprinting in the selected areas (or simply fill in the correct underprinting), and save the document.

This process allows more control over the saturation in the black areas, without adversely affecting other colors. But do not let the contraction process fool you into thinking the art is trapped. Paintings that contain little to no black need not be trapped (they usually trap naturally), and full color scans that contain heavy black areas are, by their very nature, impossible to trap.

figure 9-18: The final version has been color corrected, as well as having a proper underprinting which prevents the heavy use of black from becoming oversaturated. The feathered selection prevents any possible sharp edges from being visible beneath any light areas in the black plate.

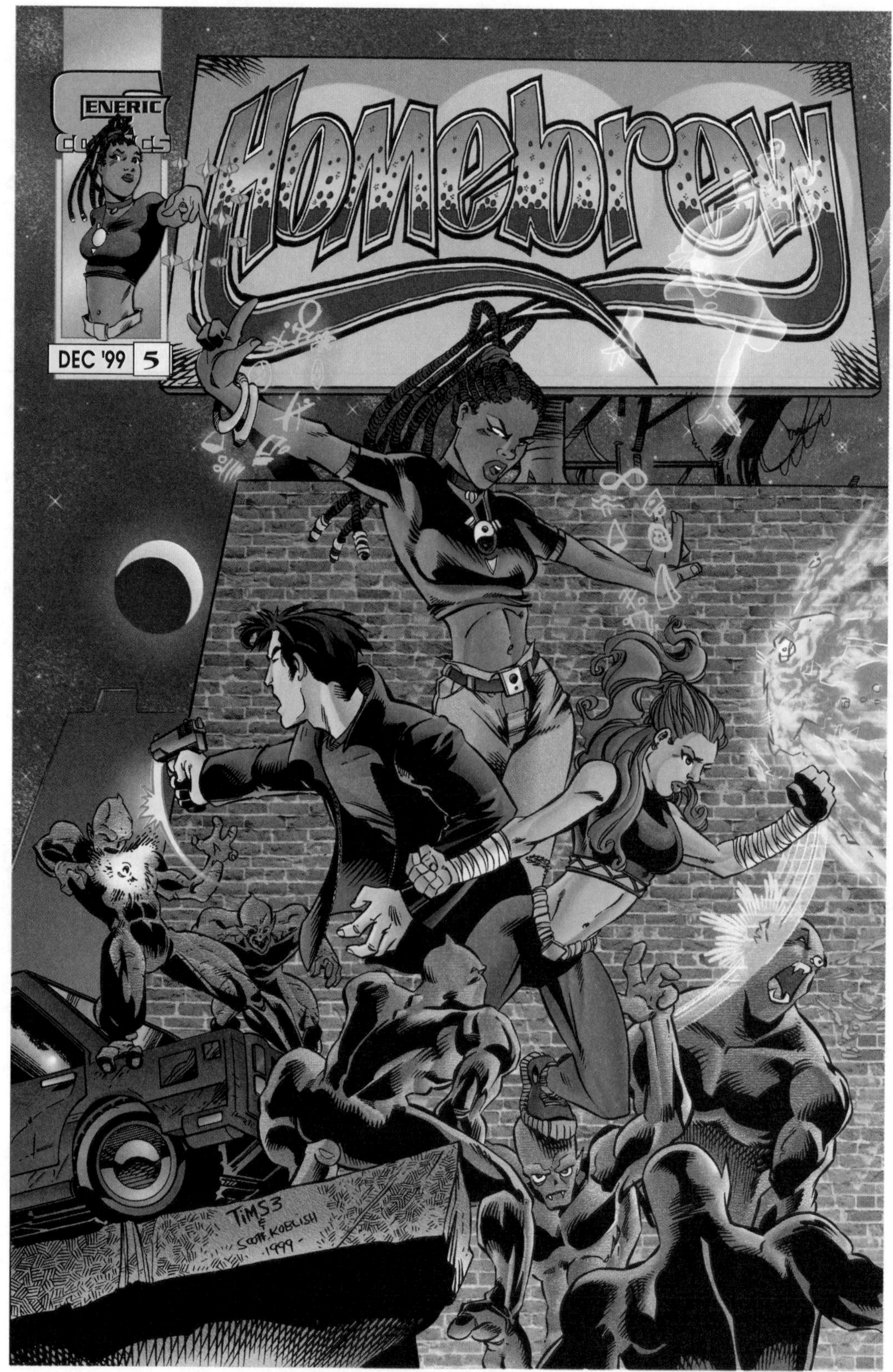

ENERIC comics
Homebrew
DEC '99
5
TIMS3 & SCOTT KOBLISH 1999

CHAPTER 10 FINAL WRAP-UP

Gather up the fragments that remain, that nothing be lost.
John, 6:12

The devil is in the details, my friends! This is the motto for pre-flighting all documents before sending it off to the printer. More headaches, mis prints, and foul-ups can be attributed to minor oversights or omissions than any other cause. That is why good organization and procedure is crucial to save time, and more importantly, money. There is nothing worse than paying for press time for an idle press.

Once the job is complete, a series of checks, double-checks, and safe guards must be run to insure a smooth transition between publisher and printer. A final pre-flight check should be run on all files. double-check all trapping and underprinting. All colors should be CMYK, no RGB allowed. Convert all Illustrator lettering to outlines. Make sure all files have been saved in the proper formats.

Organize all files into appropriate folders within a single project folder. There should be separate folders for the covers and interior pages. Within these folders should be a free floating Quark file, and two folders containing all material used in the page layout file. One folder will contain all Photoshop files, the other is for all Illustrator files. Remove all unused and unnecessary files from these folders.

Open the Quark files and check the font and picture usage. Use only true bold and italic fonts, and keep a list of all fonts used in the project. Make sure all pictures are updated, and double-check the Quark trapping. Group all elements on individual pages and covers together. This allows printers to grab the contents of an entire page, and place it imposition without fear of shifting elements.

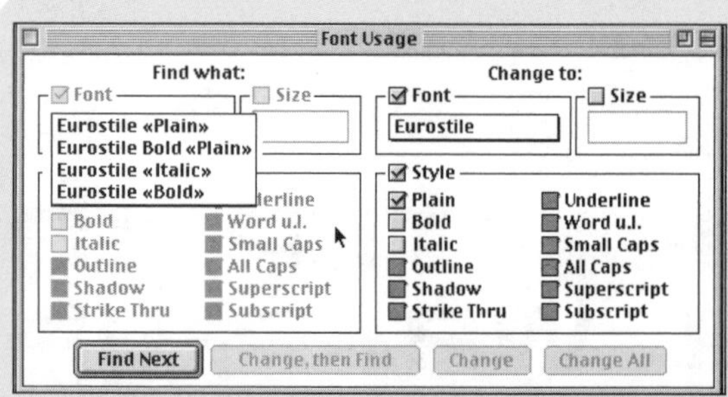

*Before sending any document to a printer, go to the UTILITIES>FONT USAGE window. ALL of the fonts used in the document should read **font name<<Plain>>**. If the font names read **<<Bold>>**, **<<Italic>>**, or anything other than **<<Plain>>**, it must be replaced by a true italic or bold font. Always send a copy of the fonts used in any document to the printer along with files.*

Legalese

This is also the point in time to check all legal marks and statements. Specifically: trademarks, copyright notices, and indicias. So perhaps now would be a good time to go over what's what and why. Trademarks are pieces of art or logos used in the promotion of trade. These include company logos, cover logos, and any piece of art used to identify a specific company or book title. These trademarks are indicated by one of two symbols (for publishing), they are ™ and ®. The ™ is usually placed to the lower right side of an image and indicates an unregistered trademark. This indicates that someone is publicly claiming to own and use this item in the course of doing business.

The ® indicates that this item has been officially registered with the government trademark offices. This is accomplished by submitting a trademark form, a copy of the art to be trademark, and a not so small fee to the trademark bureau. The office will do a search for conflicting trademarks, and send notification once registration is completed (or rejected). The symbol usually appears on the upper-right side of an image. The ® can only be used on officially registered trademarks, so when in doubt use a ™.

These symbols must appear on all covers and advertisements where the logo is used. They do not have to appear on interior art pages, or in body copy. Trademark ownership will be listed in the indicia.

figure 10-02: Both logos and artwork can be trademarked if it is used for trade purposes such as product identification or advertising. This particular example contains two trademarks; the Generic Comics logo is (hypothetically) a registered trademark, while the Homebrew corner box figure is unregistered.

The indicia contains all legal statements concerning a printed project. These will include the name of the magazine, volume and issue number, price, copyright and trademark notices, publisher's name and business address, subscription information (if any), and legal disclaimers. Indicias must appear on the inside front cover or the within the first four to six interior pages.

The importance of proper indicia and trademark use can not be stressed enough. There have been cases where logos and characters have become public domain because these items were not placed on a single issue of a comic book series. Make sure they are visible and legible when printed. Trademarks should only be knocked out or overprinted in a solid color as to avoid line screen vanishing. In other words, small trademarks held as tints of colors on top of multiple tints can disappear when converted to line screen dots.

figure 10-03: Now you see it, now you don't. The 100% cyan trademark is still clearly visible after a linescreen is applied, while the 50% cyan mark all but vanishes during the transition.

Another item that falls into the business category is the use of bar codes. If magazines are only being sold in comic specialty shops (the direct market), no bar code will be necessary. However, bar codes are absolutely necessary if these same magazines will be sold at newsstands or bookstores. These codes can be costly, running hundreds of dollars for each individual issue.

If bar codes are a necessary part of business they should be placed in a white box (cyan and black ink can interfere with scanner that reads the code) on the cover. Although there are computer programs that can generate them, most bar codes are purchased individually, and supplied as film. This film must be stripped in by the printer. Be sure to include the bar code film when sending the job to the print house. For more information on bar codes and ISSN numbers go to the following internet site – *www. bowkers.com/*.

Disk Copy

Once all files are in order and pre-flighted they must be copied to a disk that will be sent to the printer. If the magazine is black and white, all the files may fit on a Zip disk, which can store between 100 to 250 megabytes of information. Color magazines may require far more space.

The two main options for color documents are Jaz discs that can hold one or two gigabytes, or CD storage which holds roughly 650 megabytes. Jaz discs are excellent for back ups and temporary archives, but may be a bit too expensive to be sending cross country. Although very sturdy, they can still be accidentally erased or corrupted. CDs on the other hand are inexpensive, especially when purchased in bulk. CD-Rs will only suffer data loss if physically damaged, and re-writable disks (CD-RW) can only be erased on a CD burner. This makes CDs an excellent choice for permanent storage and archives.

No matter what media will be used, always make back up copies of any disk sent out of house. This will serve as an archive, as well as a reference if any questions should arise later on. Non-lossy compression programs, such as StuffIt, can be used to fit information onto a disk. However, use a program that creates self extracting files or the printer may not be able to de-compress the documents.

Copy all relevant files to the disk. Include all Photoshop and Illustrator files. The number one problem that arises for printers and service bureaus are customers who send a Quark file alone, with no copies of the images contained within. Page layout programs do not actually contain images, they merely direct the imagesetter to the appropriate files. Always update the picture usage of the Quark file to locate the images on the send out disk (this is not possible on CD).

Wolf-Girl#3.oct

41 items — 1.4 GB in disk — 528 MB available

Name	Size	Kind	Label	Last Modified
Wolf-Girl#3.covers	–	folder	–	Thu, Jul 15, 1999, 10:40 AM
Wolf-Girl#3.c1/4	448K	QuarkXPress™ 4.04 ...	–	Wed, Jun 30, 1999, 2:25 PM
Wolf-Girl#3.c2/3	448K	QuarkXPress™ 4.04 ...	–	Wed, Jun 30, 1999, 2:25 PM
illustrator	–	folder	–	Thu, Jul 15, 1999, 10:42 AM
Wolf-Girl logo.eps	480K	Adobe Illustrator® 7...	–	Wed, Jun 30, 1999, 1:07 PM
Wolf-Girl#3.cover copy	480K	Adobe Illustrator® 7...	–	Wed, Jun 30, 1999, 1:07 PM
tradedress	288K	Adobe Illustrator® 7...	–	Wed, Jun 30, 1999, 2:24 PM
photoshop	–	folder	–	Thu, Jul 15, 1999, 10:45 AM
Wolf-Girl#3.c1/4-450	25.3 MB	Photoshop® TIFF file	–	Thu, Jul 15, 1999, 10:44 AM
Wolf-Girl#3.c1/4-clip	1.3 MB	Photoshop® EPS file	–	Thu, Jul 15, 1999, 10:44 AM
Wolf-Girl#3.c2/3-600	576K	Photoshop® TIFF file	–	Thu, Jul 15, 1999, 10:45 AM
Wolf-Girl-Cbox.eps	1.3 MB	Photoshop® EPS file	–	Thu, Jul 15, 1999, 10:44 AM
Wolf-Girl#3.pgs01-32	–	folder	–	Thu, Jul 15, 1999, 10:47 AM
Wolf-Girl#3.p01-32	448K	QuarkXPress™ 4.04 ...	–	Wed, Jun 30, 1999, 2:25 PM
illustrator	–	folder	–	Thu, Jul 15, 1999, 10:42 AM
Wolf-Girl#3.01-LET	480K	Adobe Illustrator® 7...	–	Wed, Jun 30, 1999, 1:07 PM
Wolf-Girl#3.02-LET	480K	Adobe Illustrator® 7...	–	Wed, Jun 30, 1999, 1:07 PM
Wolf-Girl#3.03-LET	288K	Adobe Illustrator® 7...	–	Wed, Jun 30, 1999, 2:24 PM
photoshop	–	folder	–	Thu, Jul 15, 1999, 10:45 AM
Wolf-Girl#3.01-450	25.3 MB	Photoshop® TIFF file	–	Thu, Jul 15, 1999, 10:44 AM
Wolf-Girl#3.02-450	1.3 MB	Photoshop® EPS file	–	Thu, Jul 15, 1999, 10:44 AM
Wolf-Girl#3.03-450	576K	Photoshop® TIFF file	–	Thu, Jul 15, 1999, 10:45 AM
Wolf-Girl#3.04-450	1.3 MB	Photoshop® EPS file	–	Thu, Jul 15, 1999, 10:44 AM
•Fonts	–	folder	–	Tue, Jul 13, 1999, 10:15 AM
Anna	–	folder	–	Fri, Aug 25, 1995, 9:27 PM
Dolmen (3d) Letraset	–	folder	–	Sat, Mar 22, 1997, 5:26 PM
Eras	–	folder	–	Mon, May 2, 1994, 4:20 PM
Eurostile 1 044(A)	–	folder	–	Wed, Aug 23, 1995, 5:11 PM
Eurostile 2 130(A)	–	folder	–	Wed, Aug 23, 1995, 5:11 PM

A copy of all fonts used throughout the entire job must be included on the disk as well. Even standard fonts like

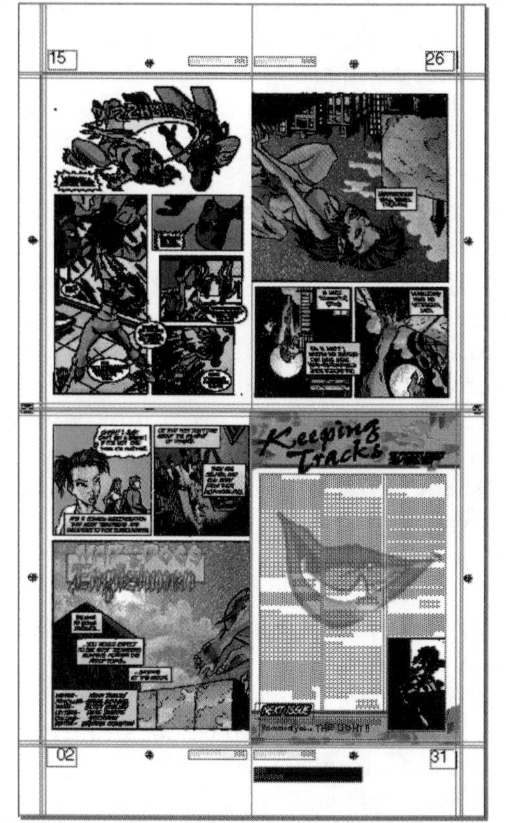

*figure 10-04: Imposition is the process of arranging pages for print, so that they will be in order **after** the publication is folded, bound, and cut. Most imposition files for comic books are 'four-up', which create four pages on each side (front and back) of the printed sheet. This makes an eight page signature, which is stacked and folded with other signatures before binding.*

Helvetica should be sent in an effort to prevent type from re-flowing on a page.

Once everything has been copied to disk, print out two copies of the disk contents or disk window. One copy will be sent to the printer, the other will be retained as a record of what was sent out.

Printouts

The printer will also require a printout of every page and cover that will be printed. These printouts should contain the name of the file and the page number. The printer will use these files to make sure every page is present and in the correct order. This is especially important when creating an imposition file where the pages do not read in order.

Most imposition files are best left for the printer to create. The main reason for this is to prevent the problem known as 'creep.' Creep occurs in saddle-stitched magazines due to the thickness of stacked and folded paper. The inner pages of a signature will stick out and trim, more than the outside signatures. This gives the illusion of the art moving closer to the trim as you approach the center of the magazine.

This problem is remedied by moving the art closer to the fold line on progressive signatures. The distance is determined by paper thickness, and may vary from job to job.

Color files require color printouts, however be aware that the printer may use these printouts to match color accuracy. This is an area that requires communication with the printer. If the color printouts are inaccurate, they should not be used as a match print, but as a general proofing guide. The printer must be made aware of these limitations or the job may be printed to match the inaccurate print outs.

That is why many printers provide color proofs (for an additional cost). If this is done additional time must be

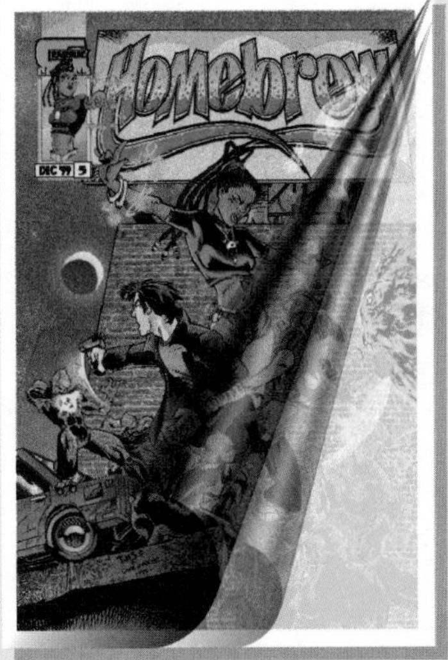

figure10-05: At left is an example of an overlay proof. It contains a color overlay for each color printing plate. At right is an example of a blueline proof used to check content.

built into the schedule. There are several types of color proofs used for different purposes. Overlay proofs print out each color on a separate sheet of acetate in overlay form. These can be used to check trapping, underprinting, and saturation. They are not necessarily reliable in matching colors perfectly. Digital proofs and laminate proofs provide a more accurate color representation, but will not show trapping errors and can be costly.

Color proofs may be bypassed to save time and money, however, bluelines should always be requested. This type of contact proof is made directly from the film separations, and are bound and folded in the same way as the final product. Use these proofs to make sure all pages are present and in order. Also check for scratches and smudges, as well as bleeds and spread alignments. This will be the last check before the job goes to press, so look carefully.

figure 10-06 Checking the content of blues includes looking for imperfections in the film such as scratches or specks of dirt. Make sure digital lettering is still in alignment, and hand lettering does not become illegible by closing up or getting too thin. This is the last time corrections can be made before the project goes to the printing press.

Reports

Always include a report when sending files and printouts to the printer. This report will include most of the items discussed with the printer, such as price quotes and publication specifications –like binding and trim proportions. It should also include special file preferences if necessary, and delivery instructions. Most importantly, include a contact name and both day and night telephone numbers. The last thing in the world anyone needs is to have the printer unable to contact a customer with an emergency on a job sitting on the press.

Afterword

Now the book has left house, and there is nothing left to do but hope and pray. And of course, be distributed. Distributors are only a phone call away, but that is a subject for other books I'm afraid. As I have often said, this book is about production. Limited to that often overlooked area of getting your hard work and effort off the art table and onto the printing press.

Just remember, this is a learning process, continually open to change and modification. It is far better to know why something must be done, just in case the how has to be modified. I hope that this book has been useful and informative. Best of luck on all of your endeavors, and always remember:

Ignorance may be bliss, but knowledge will set you free.

APPENDIX A IMAGESETTING AND HALFTONES

Understanding how an imagesetter translates digital files into film for printing plates can explain many misconceptions held by graphic artists. But first, one must understand the definitions involved.

A **pixel** (or picture element) is a square section of a grid pattern that make up a raster image. The dimensions of a pixel can be altered without changing data, thereby changing only the dimensions of an image. Therefore, if an image is scanned at 300 ppi and the height and width of the image is 900 pixels, the image will be three inches square. Change the resolution to 150 ppi and the height and width remains 900 pixels, however, the image is now six inches square. The same number of pixels, only this time, each pixel is four times bigger.

PPI (pixels per inch) is the number of pixels per linear inch. Our 300 ppi image above has 90,000 pixels per square inch, for a grand total of 810,000 pixels in the entire image (900 pixels wide x 900 pixels high).

An imagesetter has to convert all these pixels into **halftone spots**, which are made up of **printer dots** (don't worry this will become clear in a moment). The halftone is also made up

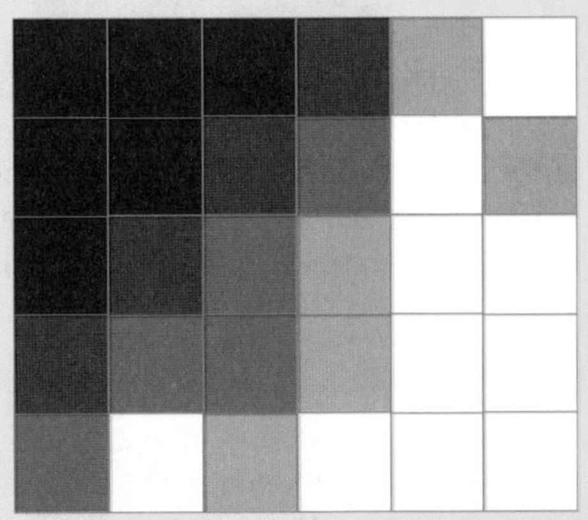

figure A-01 A raster image is made up of a grid pattern called a bitmap. Each individual square in the grid is an individual picture element, or pixel.

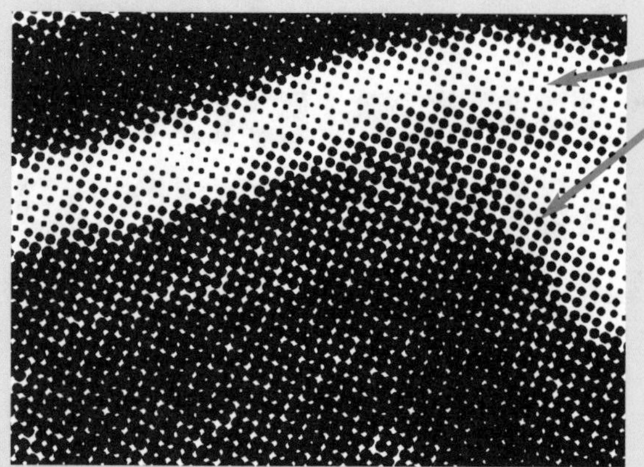

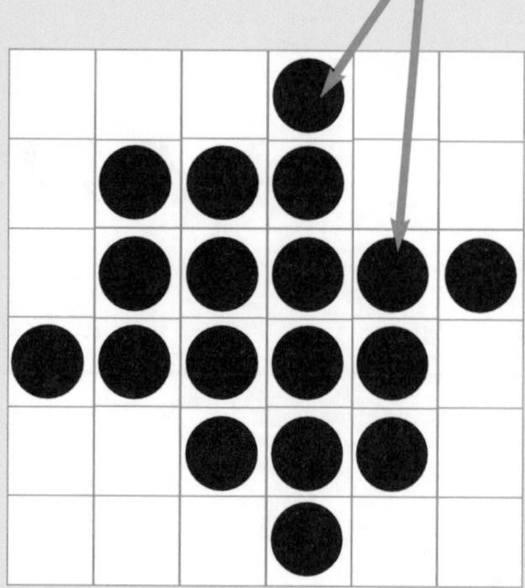

figure A-02 A screened image is created using halftone spots which change size and shape (above). Halftone spots are created by laying printer dots which cannot change shape, into a pattern within a grid called a halftone cell (right).

of an imaginary grid pattern with the center of the spot's spaced equidistant from each other. **DPI** (dots per inch) refers to the number of halftone spots per linear inch. The screen ruling is referred to as **LPI** (lines per inch), which is the number of rows of dots per linear inch.

Each spot is a solid color, namely black. However, the size and shape of a spot can change. The size of the spots in combination with the space surrounding them give the illusion of continuous tone when viewed from a distance. The spots are so small that the viewing distance is only arms length for magazines. The smaller the spot, the lighter the color.

Halftone Cells

But how are pixels converted into spots? And how do spots change size? The answer to both of these questions lies in a really, *really* small dot. The imagesetter can, in actuality, print one size of dots. An imagesetter with a resolution of 2400 dpi can only print dots that are 1/2400th of an inch in size. No bigger. No smaller. No lie.

To create a halftone spot that can change size, we have to create yet another grid pattern. This grid pattern is called a **halftone cell**. The number of dots available in a halftone cell will determine how many shades of grey will be available. The fewer grays, the more noticeable the jump between values become, which is referred to as **posterization**. Since the postscript language can only describe 256 shades of grey, this is generally the goal we shoot for.

A halftone cell that is three dots square can only produce 10 shades of grey (including white and black). With 25 dots in a square, there are only 26 shades of grey. We need 256 dots to create 257 shades of grey (including white). That translates to 16 dots high by 16 dots wide to create circular spots. To create elliptical spots we could have a

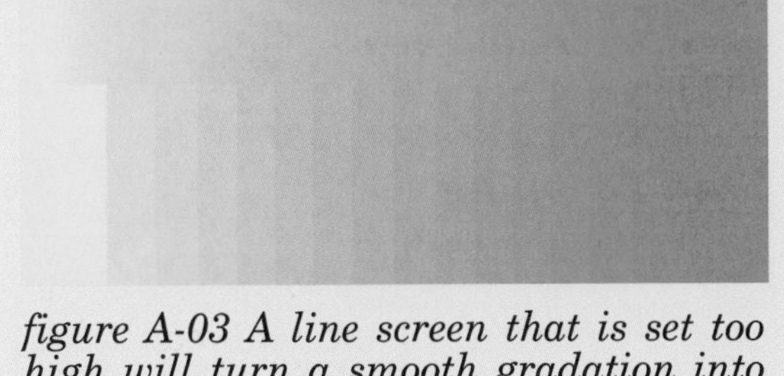

figure A-03 A line screen that is set too high will turn a smooth gradation into visible bands of color. This banding effect is called posterization.

rectangular grid 8 dots wide by 32 dots high, as long as the total number of dots equals 256.

The higher the line screen the smaller the halftone cell. The smaller the halftone cell, the fewer number of grays. So how do we get 256 shades of grey out of a 2400 dpi imagesetter? With the following formula:

$$(\text{output resolution} \div \text{screen ruling})^2 + 1 = \text{shades of grey}$$

Therefore a 2400 dpi imagesetter can only have a maximum of 150 lpi to create 257 shades of grey (including white and black).

Pixel Conversion

Now that we have a halftone cell capable of creating a wide variety of grays, it is time to convert pixels to spots. Based on the concept of a pixel resolution two times the line screen, we arrive at four pixels equal one halftone spot. Overlaying the raster grid pattern with the halftone grid (NOT the smaller halftone cell grid), the point at which the corners of the four pixels meet will be the location of the center of the halftone spot.

The grey values of the pixels are averaged together to determine the grey value of the halftone spot. But remember, the spot itself is a solid color. Its value is determined by its size and the negative space surrounding it. Therefore, if the pixels are a 50% value, the imagesetter will create a halftone spot that occupies 50% of the area inside of a halftone cell by filling in 128 out of 256 printing dots.

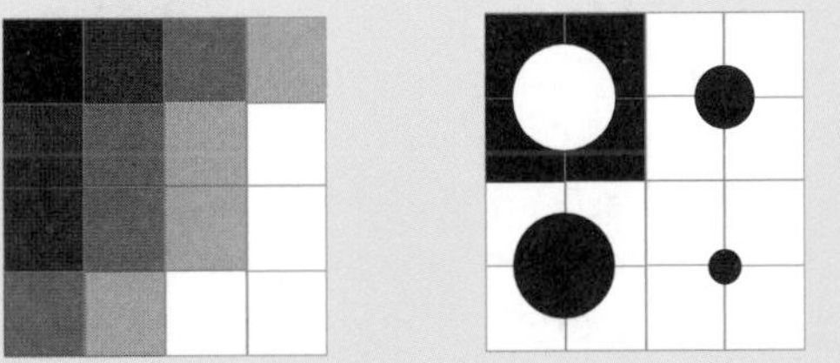

figure A-04 Given a resolution of twice the line screen, the value of four pixels will be averaged together to determine the size of one spot.

Quality in Balance

There is a relationship that exists between ppi, dpi, and lpi that must be balanced to create the best possible image. The relationship between dpi and lpi must balance the fineness and coarseness of an image with the number of grey tones available, both of which are determined by the line screen. The higher the line screen the finer the image detail, but with fewer available grey values.

This explains why line art is usually generated at a higher resolution than color art. Line art only needs two shades of 'grey,' which are black and white. Therefore, all grey tones are sacrificed for maximum image detail. On the other hand, the objective of quality color reproduction is reliant on the maximum values available and the smooth transitions between these values within a gradation. This means a maximum number of 257 values (including white) as defined by the postscript language, which translates as a lower line screen, a lower dpi (because the halftone spots are bigger), and a smaller ppi.

Why a smaller ppi? Remember that pixel resolution at twice the line screen means that four pixels make up one halftone spot. If the resolution is doubled, 16 pixels now make up one spot, but the file now takes up *four times* more computer memory. If we take this to the extreme, and have a resolution of 2400 ppi, one pixel will equal one printing dot. Printing dots are either black or white and do not change size. Halftone spots are also a single color whose 'value' is determined by its size. Therefore the value of the 256 pixels in a halftone cell are averaged together to create a single halftone spot of a fixed size. At a certain point, increasing pixel resolution does not increase print quality.

All of this must be taken into account when looking at the big picture. A high resolution is a good idea when only printing black and white bitmap images. When reproducing a grayscale or color image, resolution must be sacrificed to create smoother transitions.

Colored pages with a separate black plate can have the best of both worlds: high image detail in the high-res bitmap black plate, with smooth transitions in the lower resolution color plates. But you sacrifice the types of special effects available. Combining the plates means sacrificing line quality for better looking special effects. Sure you can save your documents at 2400 ppi, but the final printing resolution remains at 150 lpi.

Stair Stepping

When and where does stair stepping occur? Stair stepping is a result of the scale at which pixels are viewed. It can be seen on high resolution images under great magnification. The problem that arises is when individual pixels can be seen at normal magnification.

This usually occurs due to errors in resampling an image. These errors include resampling an image in bitmap mode as opposed to grayscale. Grayscale produces a softer edge made up of grey values. The bitmap edges will become jagged since only black and white squares can be created. When imagesetting at a high line screen these jags can become apparent.

Stair steps can also occur when resing an image up. In such cases, one pixel can become four pixels, or even 16 pixels. In either case, the square shape of the

figure A-05 Above is a visual example of stair stepping, but is it a result of low resolution or over magnification?

original pixel is maintained.

Most stair stepping is *perceived* as being a result of a file whose resolution is too low. This is not necessarily the case. Stair stepping may be seen on a Photoshop file when viewed on a computer monitor. That same stair stepping may be reproduced on a color proof made on a continuous tone printer that reproduces pixels faithfully.

Imagesetters, however, do NOT reproduce pixels faithfully, they translate them into halftone spots. Four square pixels become one round spot, and stair stepping disappears. Jagged Photoshop images become smooth when printed. This will not be the case if the resolution is too low to support the line screen.

figure A-06 The example above shows how an imagesetter turns pixels into spots, and eliminates the square shape.

Stair stepping appears in print when the line screen is high enough to create halftone spots that are small enough to maintain the square shape of a pixel. This happens when pixel resolution is incredibly low, or the line screen is so high it reproduces every detail and flaw in the image.

Again, we return to the balancing act. The pixel resolution has to be high enough for individual pixels to be turned into spots, while the line screen is low enough to smooth out 'jags.'

figure A-07 In this example, the resolution of the raster image was too low, therefore the linescreen faithfully reproduced the square shapes of the individual pixels.

Dot Gain

Another drawback to higher line screens is an increase in **dot gain**. The higher the line screen, the smaller the halftone spots. The smaller the spots, the more spots in a given area (higher DPI). Increased number of spots means increased susceptibility to dot gain. The higher the dot gain the muddier the image prints.

Why are smaller spots more prone to dot gain? Technically, they are not. Given a 20% dot gain, each individual (50% value) dot increases by 20% along its outside edge, no matter what size the dot. However, the size of the dot in combination with the space surrounding it gives the illusion of value. A single spot that spreads 20% will not 'devour' as much white space as the dot gain on a hundred spots occupying the same area.

Remember, not only are the spots smaller, but so is the space between them. The more of this negative space that disappears, the darker the values appear.

Screen Angles

Another aspect of the line screen that needs to be addressed is the angle at which a halftone is printed. The whole idea behind a halftone is to give the illusion of grey (or color) values. When a line screen is printed perpendicular to the edges of a page (0^0), the pattern of spots is visible. Rotate the angle, and the pattern *appears* to disappear. An angle of 45^0 is the least noticeable to the human eye. Therefore, black plates are almost always printed at this angle.

Halftone at 0⁰

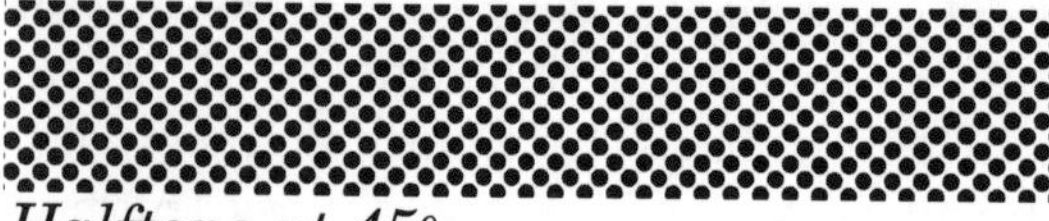

Halftone at 45⁰

Once color is added, things start to get complicated. Colors cannot be printed at the same angle, otherwise each colored dot would print one on top of the other. The colors need to be close together, but not superimposed. However, laying screens on top of each other will create a new pattern that is not only noticeable to the human eye, but distracting as well. These distracting patterns are called moire´s.

The least noticeable pattern created is called a rosette. It is created by placing the screens at 30^0 intervals. Since 45^0 creates the least noticeable spot pattern it is reserved for the darkest color: black. Cyan and magenta are then placed at 15^0 and 75^0 respectively. Yellow is placed at 0^0, because the light value of the ink makes the obvious patterns created at this angle less noticeable.

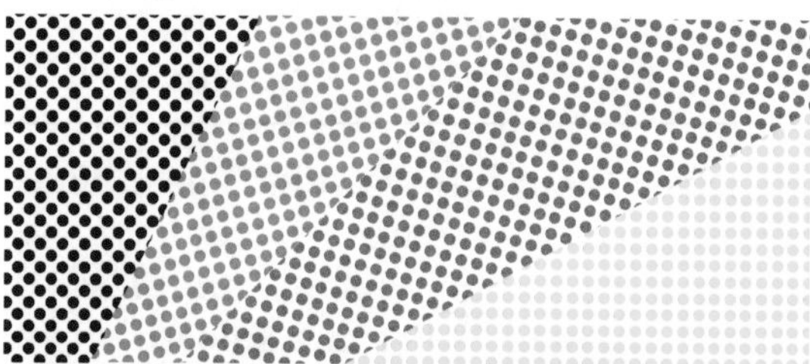

CMYK Screen Angles

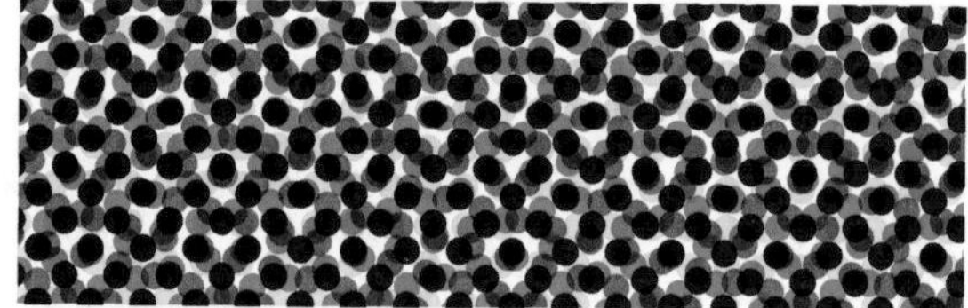

Rosette Pattern

It's All An Illusion

It is interesting to note that the entire four color printing process is an elaborate illusion created to trick the human eye. The halftone printing plates and screen angles create the appearance of millions of different colors and values. It simply isn't true.

There are only four colors: cyan, magenta, yellow, and black. And each color prints at only one value: 100%. A 20% cyan is actually a spot of 100% cyan ink that occupies 20% of a defined area. When printed next to a 100% magenta ink spot that occupies 50% of its defined area, the human brain will blend the colors and perceive a pale violet.

Talk about magic!

APPENDIX B TRAPPING

This appendix collects all sections covering the subject of trapping that were covered elsewhere in this book.

One of the most important issues that needs to be worked out with the printer before a project begins is: *who will be responsible for trapping color files*. This should be a key issue in discussions with ALL contractors, and who will be responsible for the trapping what, should be clearly resolved beforehand. The printer should be able to tell you what the trap tolerance is for the project beforehand. This number will be used in both Illustrator and Quark Express during the trapping process and is based on dot gain and ink saturation.

Ink saturation is the amount of ink that the paper will be able to absorb before the inks start to pick up or smear. It will be a percent value in the range of 230% to 300%. This number will play a part in determining the values of ink used to underprint the black plate in order to create a rich black color.

The saturation level needs to be passed along to the separators to insure that they do not accidentally over saturate the coloring. Keep in mind that if a different stock of paper is used for the covers, there may be a different set of values for both ink saturation and screen frequency.

The basic idea here is to open lines of communication between yourself and the contractors early in the process. Treat these people as partners in this project and listen to their advice. Understand that this job cannot be complete without them,so iron out who is responsible for what, and what to expect from each other. If this simple advice is followed, you will avoid many unforeseen problems.

Trapping

Trapping is the intentional overlapping of colors along common boundaries to prevent unprinted paper from showing in the event of misregistration during the printing process. As paper runs through a printing press at high speed, a certain amount of shifting occurs from page to page. Slivers of white paper sandwiched between two colored inks are particularly distracting to the human eye. Therefore trapping strives to prevent this from occurring.

The following terms are used in relation to trapping:

choke: creating a trap using the background color.

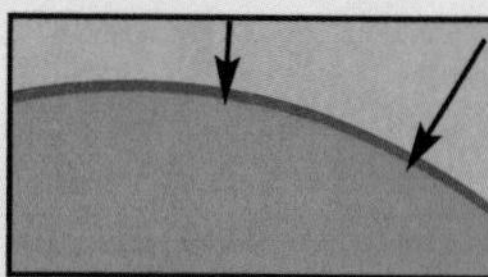

spread: creating a trap using the color of the object in the foreground.

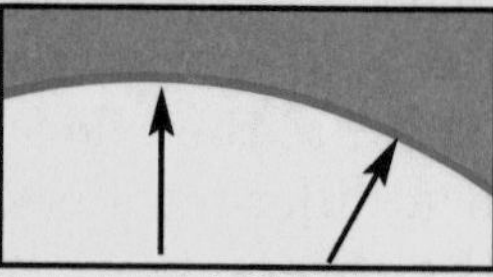

overprint: When colors or inks are printed one on top of another. For instance magenta overprints blue to create purple.

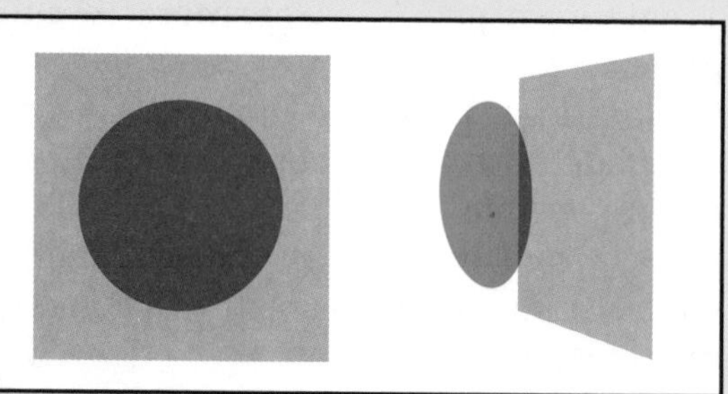

knockout: The opposite of overprint, knockouts create a hole in background colors to accommodate objects or colors in the foreground. Unless properly trapped, knockouts will create a 'kiss-fit' where two colors butt together without overlapping.

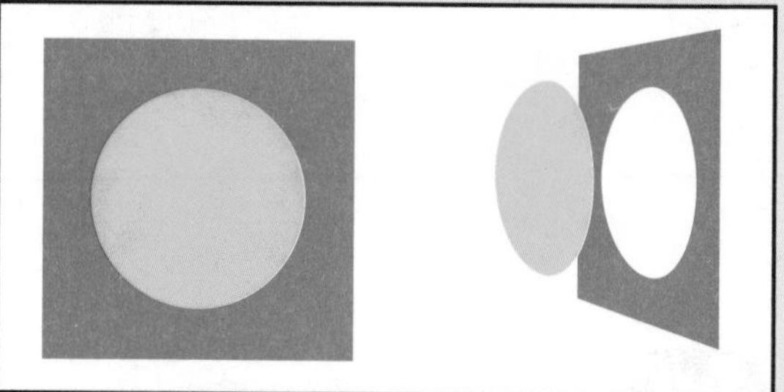

path: In Adobe Illustrator, it is the vector lines that defines the shape of an entire object and falls exactly in the center of a stroke.

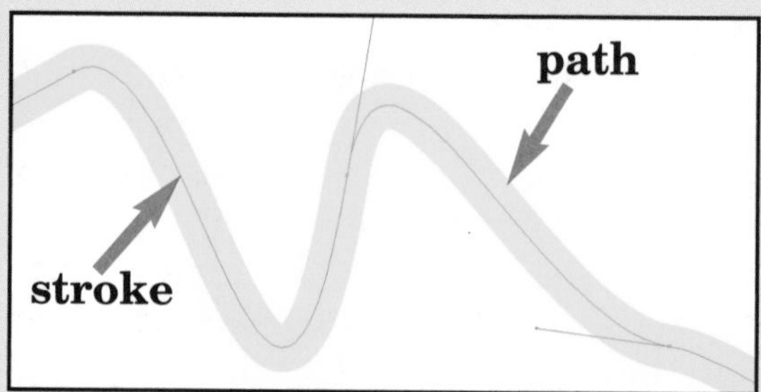

stroke: In Illustrator, it is a colored line that can be created on top of a path that can be used to trap an object.

General Guidelines to trapping colors:

Rule #1: In general always use the lighter of two colors as a trap. If there is a question as to which color is lighter use the following steps:

1) Determine the RGB values of the colors in question.

2) Use the following formula: (30% x R)+(59% x G)+(11% x B)

3) The higher the outcome the lighter the color.

If the colors in question are both dark or the combination of both colors will create a noticeable third color or a distracting trap, then you may wish to trap with tints of one or both colors. However, never set any CMYK values in a trap color to less than 15%, the Postscript language will knockout any value less than 15%.

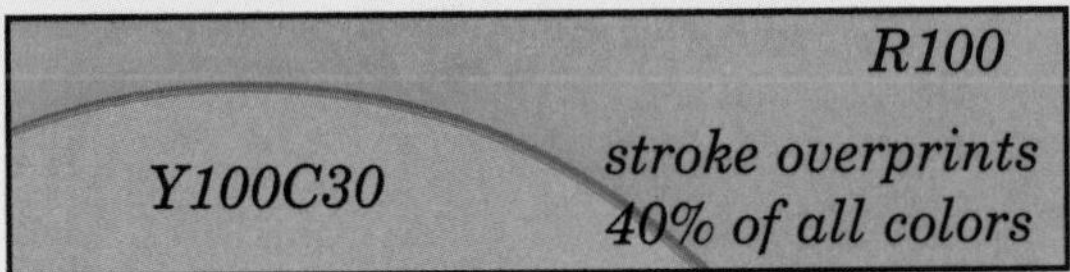

Rule #2: You do not have to trap colors that trap naturally. Objects that have at least one color in common will not leave any paper unprinted if the plates are misregistered. Examples are: green object on yellow background or yellow on red.

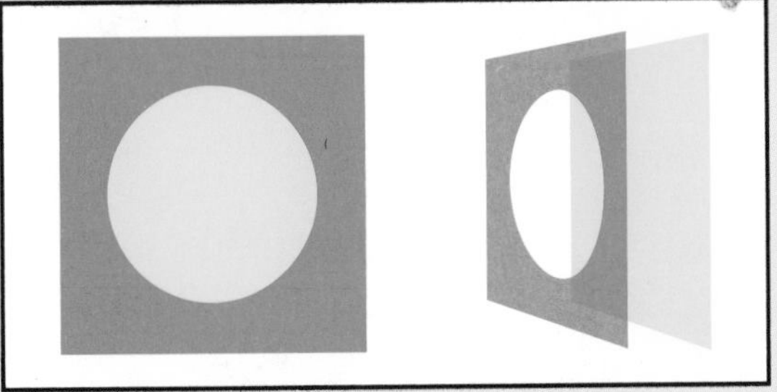

Rule #3: Illustrator documents must be trapped to the Photoshop and Quark documents that they are placed upon. This is done with the use of an overprinting stroke.

Rule #4: All Illustrator documents must be brought into Quark at 100%. Scaling Illustrator documents in Quark will scale the size of the trap as well, and this is incorrect.

	X%:100%	X+: -2.321"
	Y%:100%	Y+: -3.318"

Rule #5: A Quark document can be corrupted or damaged if trapped wrong. If Quark tells you that a document is damaged when you try to open or save it, this is what you should look for in the trapping palette (in order of likely cause):

a) Items labeled MULTIPLE: change them to a single setting where applicable.

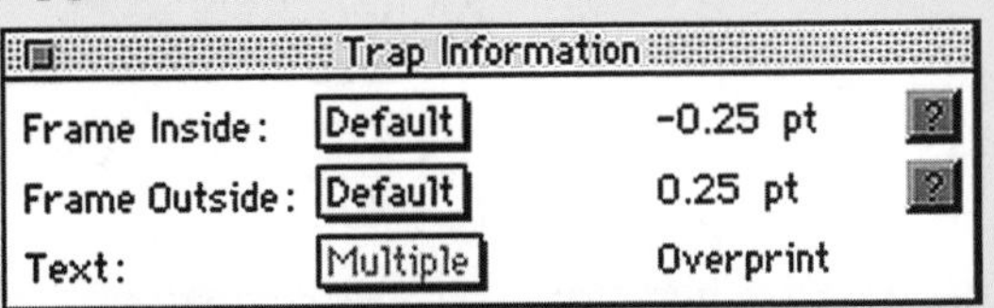

b) Items labeled DEFAULT: change them to an applicable single setting. Default settings can vary from computer to computer, therefore it is incorrect to leave an item at default.

Color files must be trapped in their program of origan, where as, bitmap files will be trapped in Quark. As a result trapping a job containing multiple files may appear more difficult than it actually is in reality. Since each software program traps differently, more specific instructions will be covered in later chapters.

An example of an untrapped misregistered Photoshop file.

Trapping in Illustrator:

General Guidelines:

1) Generally the stroke is set to overprint and the fill is set to knockout. An x in the box indicates overprint. No x means the color will knockout.

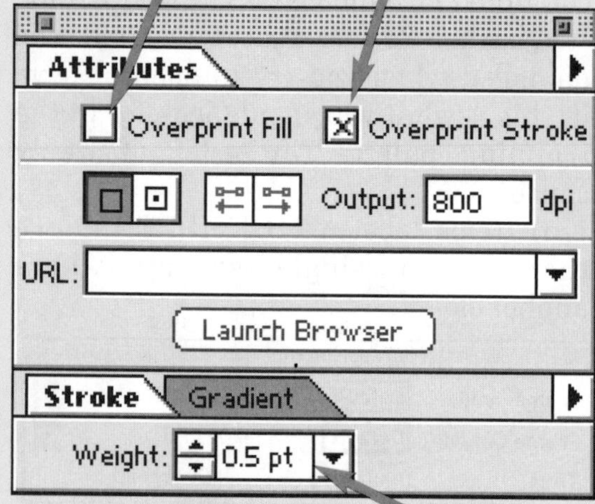

2) To create a .25 pt trap in Illustrator you must set the stroke at .5 pt, because the stroke is centered along the path.

3) Trap Illustrator documents to the Photoshop and Quark documents that they will be placed on. Be aware that Illustrator knocks out all colors by default; you must tell the computer when to overprint.

4) Don't forget to create blacks with underprintings in Illustrator.

Simple sound effects should have a fill that knocks out and a half-point stroke (.5 pt) that overprints. The stroke and print are the same color.

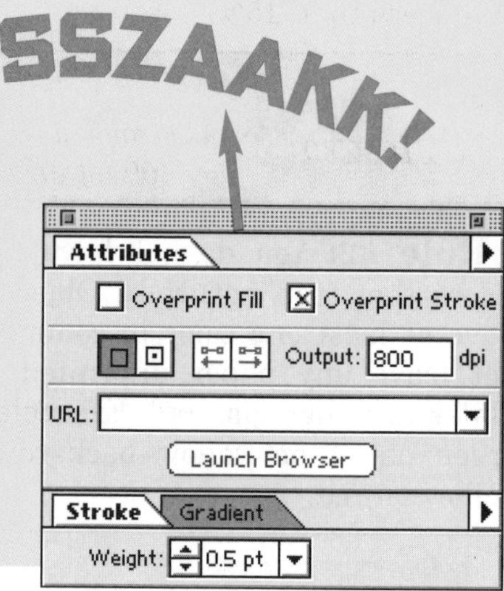

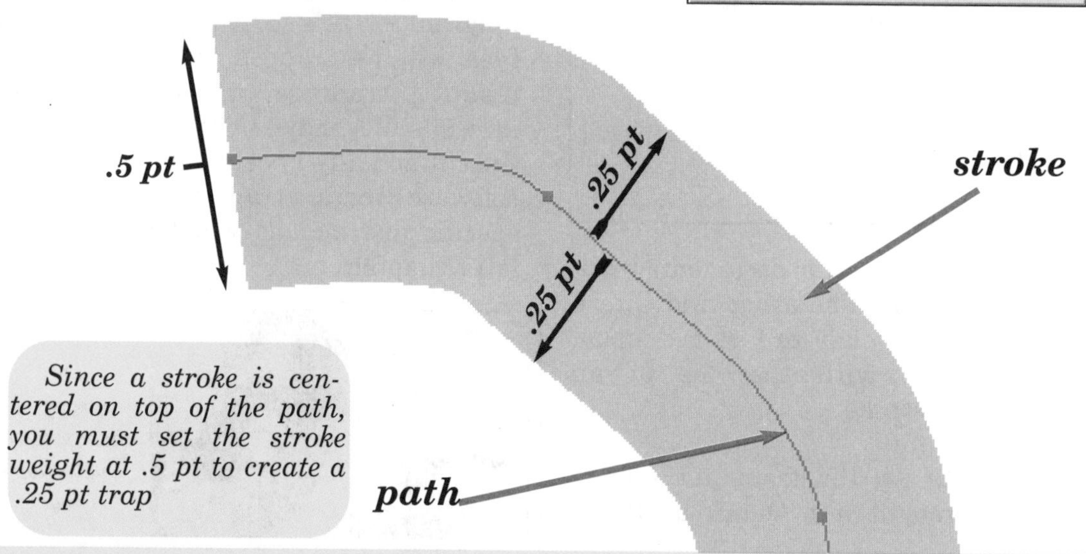

Since a stroke is centered on top of the path, you must set the stroke weight at .5 pt to create a .25 pt trap

Word balloons and caption boxes should have a fill (any color) that knocks out plus a stroke (100K) that overprints. Colored strokes 1 pt or less should knockout.

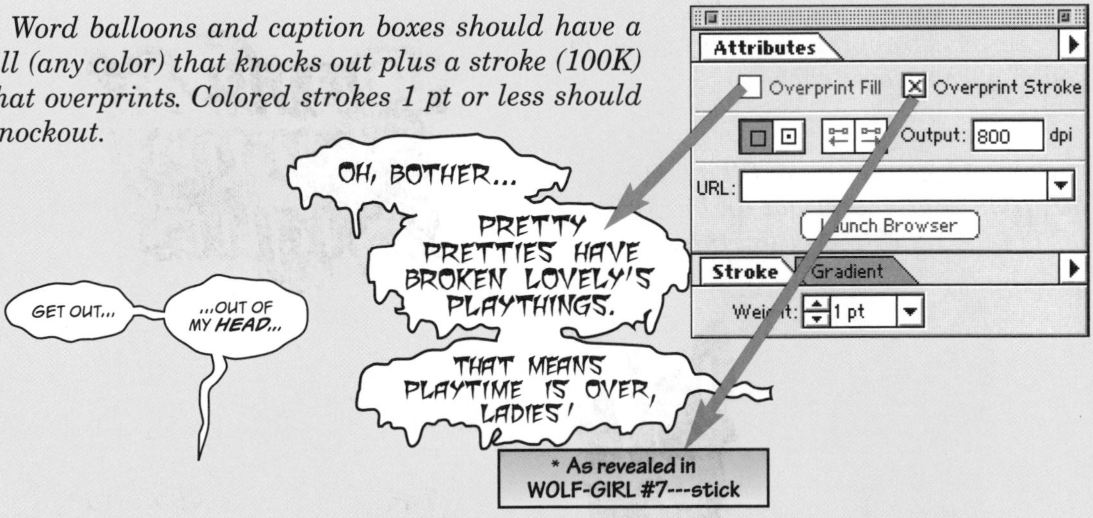

Attributes
Overprint Fill
Overprint Stroke
Output: 800 dpi
URL:
Launch Browser
Stroke
Gradient
Weight: 1 pt

GET OUT...
...OUT OF MY *HEAD*...

OH, BOTHER...
PRETTY PRETTIES HAVE BROKEN LOVELY'S PLAYTHINGS.
THAT MEANS PLAYTIME IS OVER, LADIES!

* As revealed in WOLF-GIRL #7---stick

"FLAMES FLICKER AT MIDNIGHT...
...MELTED WAX DRIPS DOWN DRY...
...ASHES STANDING FROM WOOD TO COAL...
...CURRENTS DANCE AND SWAY...
...JASMINE SMOKE SWIMS IN NOCTURNAL AIR...
...RISING, FLOWING, TWIRLING, CASTING SHADOWS...
...REFLECTIONS THROUGH THE GLASS--

Attributes
Overprint Fill
Overprint Stroke
Output: dpi
URL:
Launch Browser
Stroke
Gradient
Weight: 0 pt

Do not trap small fonts with strokes. Lettering inside balloons and captions have fills that overprint, or knockout in cases of light lettering on dark backgrounds.

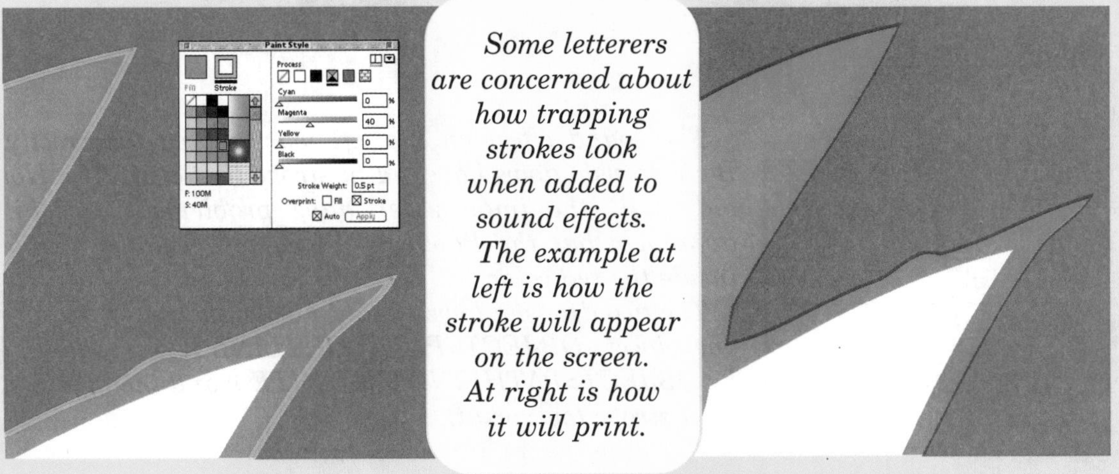

Some letterers are concerned about how trapping strokes look when added to sound effects. The example at left is how the stroke will appear on the screen. At right is how it will print.

The examples at right and below show the correct trapping and layering for sound effects / cover copy.

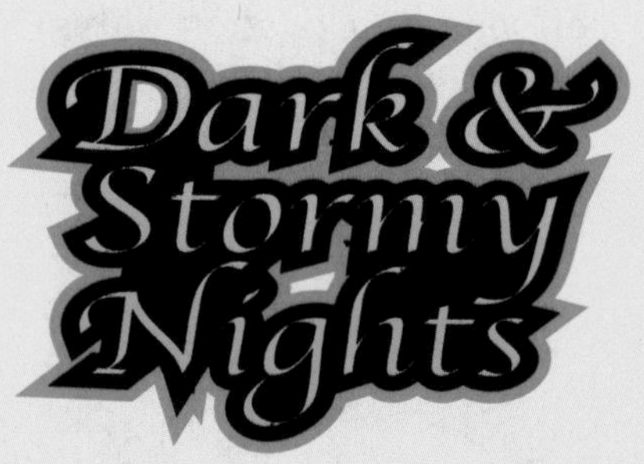

Black objects have a fill of 60C40M 40Y100K that knocks-out and a stroke of 0C 0M 0Y 100K that overprints.

Gradation fill knockouts, 0B0R0Y100K .5 pt stroke (overprint)

100Y100R fill (knockout) 100Y100R .5 pt stroke (overprint)

Although this gradation knocks-out, it does not require a stroke because it traps naturally to the red color underneath.

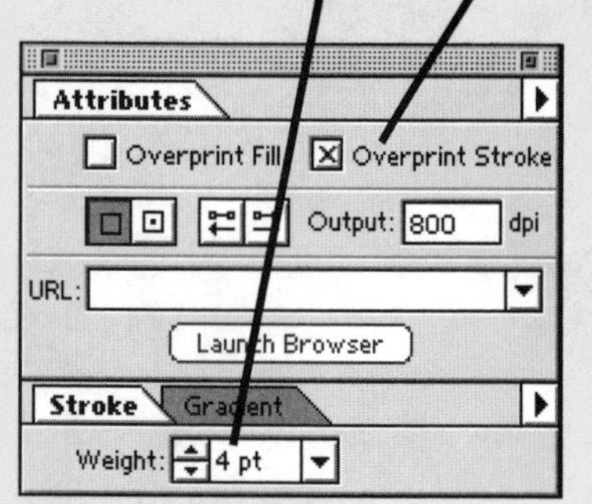

The sound effect on the left was created incorrectly. Both dropshadows have a 4 pt stroke that overprint. Not only will the imagesetter have problems with this approach, but the Photoshop document will be visible inside the red color.

The two dropshadows should have been combined into one object (OBJECT>PATH>OUTLINE PATH followed by OBJECT>PATHFINDER>UNITE); and then given a .5 pt stroke (overprint).

Avoid cover copy, sound effects, or logos that have overly complex layers.
Below is an example of a logo that can cause an imagesetter to mis-print due to complexity.The unnecessary layers were created in an attempt to trap.

The original logo had over ten layers, where as the final logo only needs four.

The example at left was created by using strokes as large as 10 pt on multiple layered objects. There is an incredibly large number of points used to create the letterforms.

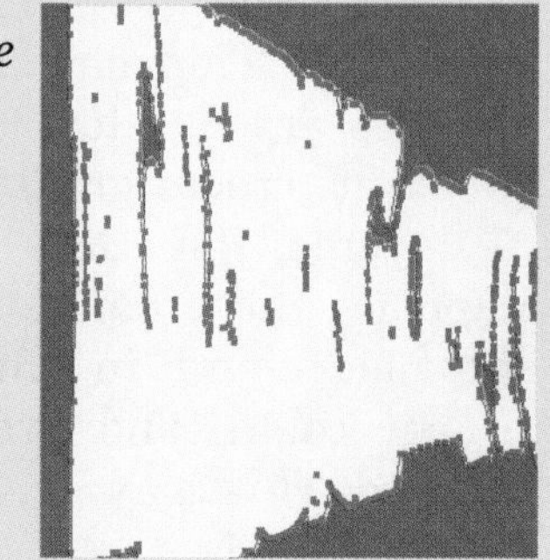

The two green layers should have been combined into one layer (at right), and converted into a single object by: (1) going to OBJECT>PATH>OUTLINE PATH followed by (2) going to OBJECT>PATHFINDER>UNITE; the object is then given a .5 pt stroke that overprints.

Digital Logos

The first rule that applies to all 3-D applications, is to work in black and white. If the logos are created in color, it may be difficult to change the colors later on, and even more difficult (if not impossible) to trap them.

Changing pre-existing colors in pixel based programs can be extremely difficult. It is far easier to control colors using a logo that utilizes a full range of values in grayscale. This logo can then be pasted into each color channel separately, adjusting the curves of each to create an exact color or gradation.

The logo above was created in gray scale using a vector based plug in for Illustrator. It was then imported into Photoshop (below) where it is more easily colored and trapped.

When working in vector based systems try to avoid unnecessary gradations. This may be impossible, but is necessary due to the fact that some programs create gradations as a series of layered flat color objects. If this happens, these objects must be united into one object in Illustrator so that proper colors and gradations can be trapped. This may be true of the three dimensional aspect of the logo as well. A series of inter-related objects can, and usually will, create a multitude of trapping, and possibly imagesetting, problems.

Do not be frightened off of 3-D programs because of these warnings. There are several applications that create excellent editable effects if used properly. KPT Vector Effects creates some of the best editable effects, as long as the complexity settings are kept simple. Better yet, they work as a filters from inside of Illustrator.

Compound Paths

A problem that can often arise when trapping logos, cover copy, or sound effects of any type, is the sudden crash of the Illustrator application. For troubleshooting purposes, during the 'outline path' function of the trapping

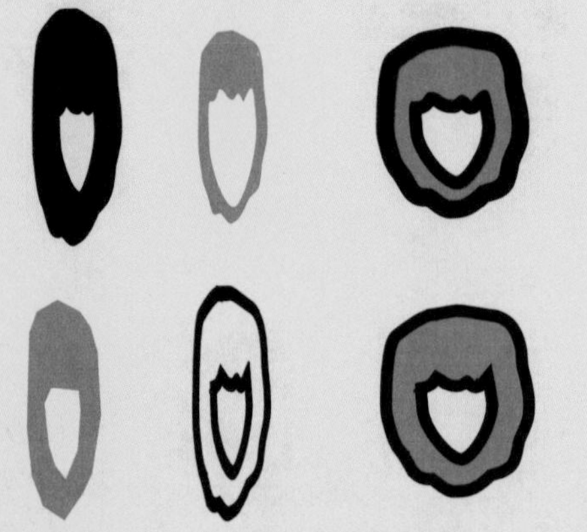

Given a hypothetical compound path crash where re-applying the minus filter does not solve the problem, the next step would be to recreate the letter entirely without compound paths. In this case, outline path was used to create objects in the form of strokes which are placed on top of a red fill that has been re-drawn with the pen tool to include the hole in the middle.

process, Illustrator will unexpectedly (and without warning or error messages) quit. All unsaved changes are lost, as is the bewildered user.

Why this occurs is unclear, but what causes it is not. Compound paths are ultimately to blame. Technically, the exclude and minus filters create compound paths to knock holes through objects. However, some letterers and designers create compound paths by 'hand' to create certain similar effects. It is these types of paths that usually cause the crash, although complex 'minused' objects can also be guilty.

There is no easy solution to this problem. The compound paths can be 'released,' simplified, and re-applied. If this does not solve the problem, a trap will have to be created using a free floating stroke placed on top of the trouble spot

Gradation Traps

Sometimes it is necessary to trap an Illustrator gradation to a Photoshop document. The best way to create a gradating trap in Illustrator is to create a duplicate object in a separate layer in exactly the same position as the original by option dragging a copy between layers. Give the bottom object an appropriate sized trapping stroke. Then outline the path, and unite the path with the object. This object is now the appropriate size for the trap. Set its fill to overprint in the attributes palette. The top object should be set to knockout. Select both objects and apply the gradation. As the extreme enlargement at right shows, the bottom gradation creates the trap.

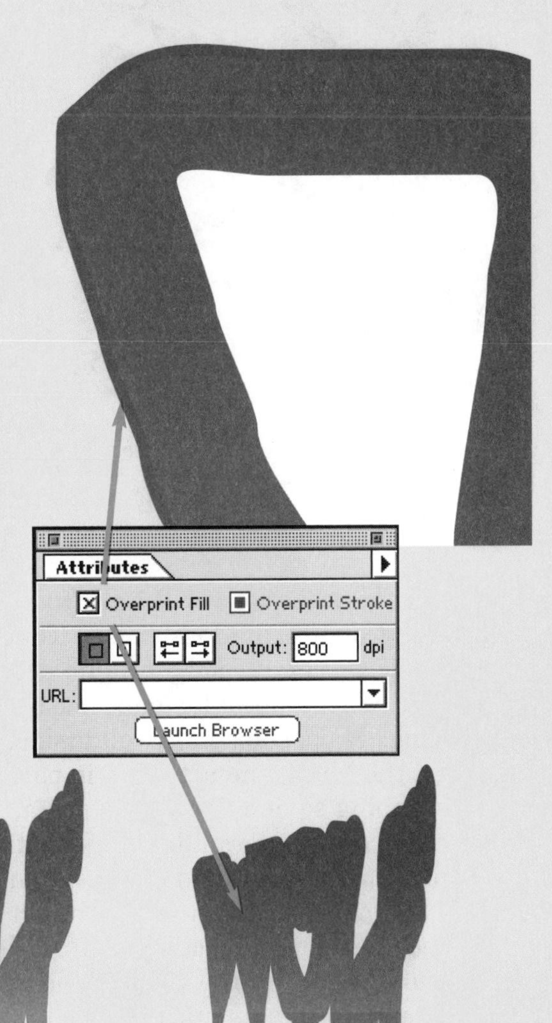

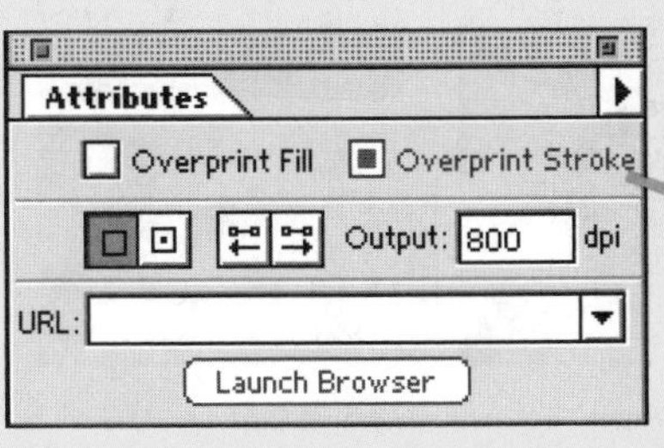

Trapping in Photoshop

All processes begin with ***flats***. This requires making each selection a flat color with no gradations or modeling, until the entire page is filled. Flats allow for swifter magic-wand selections when adding modeling and gradations at a later stage.

An example of flats. Note how the colors butt together leaving no white spaces where the black line art will eventually fall. This is part of the trapping process.

Initially, all selections will have to be made using one of the lasso tools. This job is made easier if using a light pen and tablet which allows for more natural 'drawing.' Make selections well inside, or under, the black line art. This is part of the trapping so don't be timid, put as much color as you can under the black; and since this area is hidden, precision is not a major concern. Since the line art is located in a separate channel it will remain unaffected by the color (as long as the channel remains inactive).

A good way to work is to color from the background and move forward. This allows for large imprecise selections to begin with, by simply ignoring the foreground images entirely. Objects closer to the foreground require more and more precise selections. Intricate or overly complicated selections may be saved in additional channels if there is a possibility of a later color changes or special effects.

Usually, the magic wand can not be effectively used at this point, due to hatching techniques and broken or open line work. If the line work does accommodate the magic wand, the selection must be expanded considerably. Good judgement is necessary when expanding or contracting wand selections for trapping purposes. Again, you want as much color underneath the black as possible, without going 'outside' the lines. If the underprinting will be contracted by four

Working from background elements to foreground objects is a time-efficient way to separate. It allows for fast selections at first, and creates better traps.

pixels (this will be covered later) then expend the initial color selection by six or eight pixels if possible.

CMYK vs. RGB

The biggest production problem that accompanies RGB coloring: trapping and ink saturation. Where is the black plate? In RGB, black is the absence of all color, which translates as equal amounts of all inks in CMYK. This conversion of black results in untrapped line art, with an ink saturation between 320% to 400%. This is well above the limit of the majority of paper made these days. A magazine would look like it was run through the rinse cycle of a washing machine at these limits.

The trapping filter in Photoshop will not help, because its functions only allow for spreading colors, making them larger. The type of trapping required here is to choke, make smaller, the colors underneath the black. Furthermore, some of the undercolor may actually spread outside of the black because cyan and magenta spread equally into each other when butting. This filter was never intended to be used on line art or continuous tone images.

If coloring in RGB is done, the color space ***must*** be converted and color corrected before the black plate is added. This is the only way to insure proper trapping and prevent oversaturation.

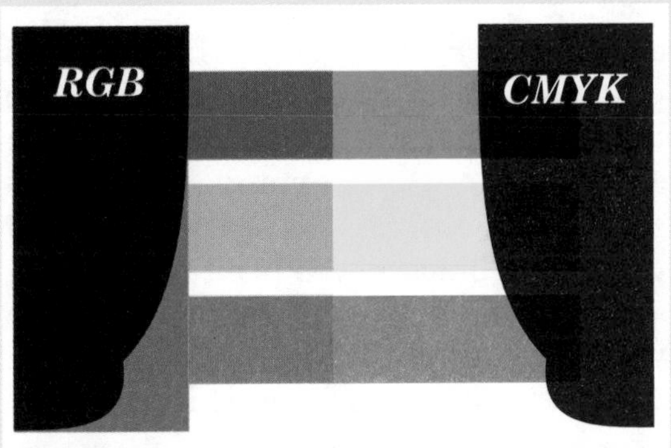

*To test how RGB colors change during conversion create strips of pure ink colors in CMYK, and add an overprint of 100%K (EDIT>FILL> DARKEN) over a section of the colors as shown above. Convert the file to RGB, then back to CMYK. Check to see how the colors have changed. Also note if the black section is oversaturated, and how it has eliminated the colored blocks underneath. To complicate matters further, the CMYK setup under **Color Settings** will alter the conversion process. Change the settings, and repeat these steps to see the difference.*

Conversions and Underprinting

Once all of the modeling has been done, it is time to make all of the necessary conversions relating to the production techniques that will follow. Increase the resolution if necessary, and replace the line channel with art that has not been resampled. If working in RGB, it is time to convert to CMYK and correct the colors. It would also be wise to double-check the saturation levels of the colors at this point (the info palette can be set up to read both CMYK values as well as ink saturations). And finally, (barring any color holds or texture effects) add the underprinting and check the trapping.

It is important to create the proper trap when adding the underprinting. The correctly trapped underprinting is created by making the black line art a selection. Go to SELECT>MODIFY> CONTRACT. Contract by 1 pixel for every 100 ppi of resolution, therefore a 500 ppi file would be contracted 5 pixels. Failure to contract properly may result in the destruction of the trap.

Fill with the appropriate underprint color. This color will be 110 to 120 points less than ink saturation limits, and will contain equal portions of magenta and yellow, and slightly more cyan ink. A good undercolor for a 250% saturation book would be 60C40M40Y. Make the black line art a selection for a second time (***do not contract***), and fill with 100%K only by going to EDIT> FILL>DARKEN. This will add the black plate to the art without deleting any colors underneath.

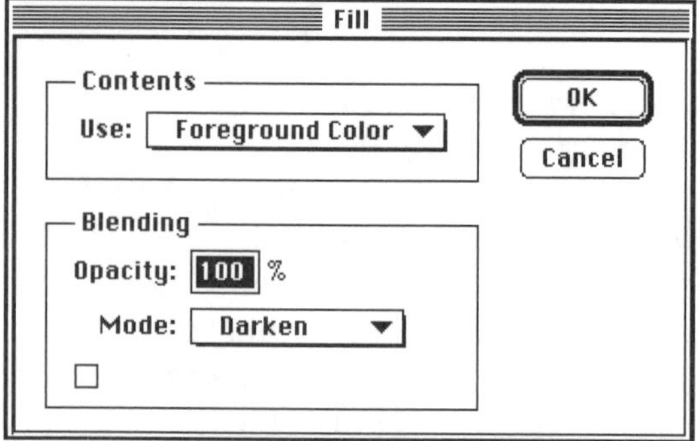

Now double-check the trapping, you must zoom in close to an edge or thick outline of black line art. Click the eye icon on and off several times. The underprinting ***SHOULD NOT*** identically match the black line art, but be noticeably smaller. The background colors should go underneath the black line art and butt to the underprinting. There should be no noticeably large areas of white beneath the black line art.

Technically, underprinting is not utilized for any trapping purpose. It serves two important functions in the printing process. The first function is to

The underprinting should be contracted from the black plate to create a proper trap. The trap is the area of color beneath the black plate which butts to the underprint color.

create a rich, even black. If 100%K is printed on white paper with no underprinting, it will appear less dense (or washed out) than many of the colors surrounding it. On the other hand, if that same black ink is printed on top of several colors of varying values, the value of the black itself will vary with the colors it overprints. This will give

Note how a color-hold gradation to black added after the underprinting is applied. The under print color may be visible behind the gradation on the computer monitor, but will not be seen in the final print.

the noticeable appearance of an uneven black tone.

However, the primary function of underprinting is to prevent oversaturation of the paper with ink. If black ink were to overprint a large area of YR, the saturation would be 300% (small trap areas have no real impact). This would be unacceptable if the saturation level is 250%. Therefore, we avoid this problem by creating an underprinting for black that is equal to 240% (60C40M40Y100K).

Note that you can see the color bars behind the overprinting black on the left. The underprinting on the center bar is 30C70M40Y. On the right bar it is 60C40M40Y. Is there a difference?

It should now be clear how proper trapping is incorporated into the actual process of coloring. As special effects are added, careful attention must be paid so as not to destroy the trapping already established.

Trapping Modes

Be aware of selections when using the MODIFY>EXPAND or CONTRACT function when creating a trap. Attention *must* be paid to the thickness of the line involved in the trap when deciding on a pixel value. The actual values used will vary depending on line weight and resolution. A higher resolution document may need a larger pixel value to create a proper trap. Thin lines that are often found in logo drop shadows may require much smaller values to prevent the colors from bleeding outside the holding lines.

Be careful not to over expand when trapping very thin lines often associated with logo dropshadows..

There are four painting or editing modes that are invaluable when trapping a logo in Photoshop. They are generally applied by going to EDIT> FILL and selecting the appropriate mode, or, if working with layers, an entire layer can be assigned a specific mode. Become familiar with these modes, and how they function in order to trap any variable that may arise.

They are:

normal mode: this is the default mode for photoshop. It simply replaces the colors inside a marquee selection with the color chosen in the palette. It blends the neighboring colors at the edge of the selection. Generally, use delete or option delete to achieve this effect. This serves the purpose of deleting art at the same time as you color. Usually, this mode will be used if the black plate is separate from the color plates.

multiply mode: this mode adds the values of the colors in the palette to the colors already present in a selection. Therefore, multiplying C20M40 Y50K15 into C50M40Y30K0 will result in the color C70M80Y80K15. Multiplying a color several times will make the color darker each time. Generally, this mode is used to increase the values of a single plate over multiple colors.

darken mode: this mode uses the higher value of each channel to create the end color. Therefore, darkening C20M40Y50K15 into C50M40Y30K0 will result in the color C50M40Y50K15. This mode should be considered the 'all purpose trapping mode' and is used when adding the black plate to the color channels. However, you need to be careful when using this mode with layers. The background layer should be deleted to white, except for the area to be trapped.

lighten mode: this mode uses the lower value of each channel to create the end color. Therefore, lightening C20M40Y50K15 into C50M40Y30K0 will result in the color C20M40Y30K0. This mode is very rarely used, and is generally restricted to certain special effects. Although it is of very limited use in trapping, it is a very valuable tool to know when coloring logos or creating certain ghosting effects.

Dropping in Illustrator Logos

Before bringing any logo from Illustrator into Photoshop, make sure that it is already the correct size/ proportion that will be needed. Re-sizing a logo in Photoshop may cause the lines to blur or stair step adversely. Also, the logo should be in black and white. Illustrator trapping will not necessarily make the proper transition into Photoshop, and it becomes much more difficult to attempt to trap a logo that has already been colored in Illustrator.

Paste-Up and Trapping Logos in Photoshop

Due to the nature of dropping logos into Photoshop, all of Chapter Eight should be reviewed in full.

This example shows a detail of a channel mask that will create a proper trap with the black plate. Deselect the black channel to avoid accidentally deleting any black when coloring the logo.

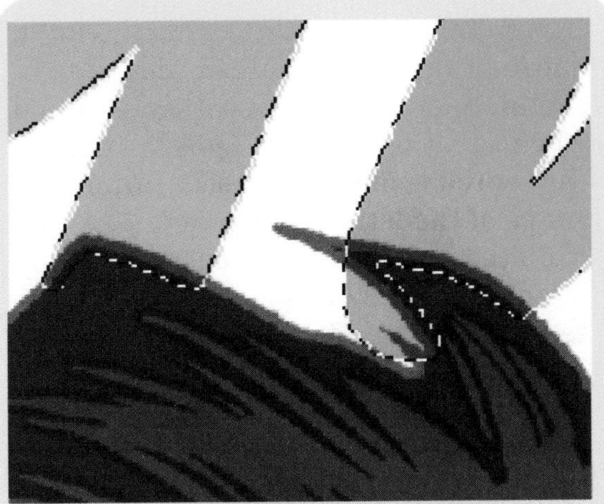

When dropping logo colors into art it is important to trap these colors to the surrounding colors. The channel mask should be designed to create the proper trap, and the colors are dropped in using EDIT>FILL>DARKEN.

Trapping in Quark

Trapping in Quark is actually quite easy, because the program does all the actual work. However, double-checking the document to make sure that the end product is trapped correctly is essential. At worst, this is tedious and, on occasion, actually requires some thought.

Before doing ANY trapping in Quark, set the trapping preferences for the application. The Trapping Preferences dialog box should be set as shown above. A note should be made concerning the 'Overprint Limit.' This number specifies at what shade a color will overprint the background colors. This comes into play when an object is colored in Quark, but given a percentage value of that color in the 'colors' window. If that percentage value is less than the 'Overprint Limit' value, it will knockout with a spread defined by the 'Auto Amount' value, even if the trapping window has been set to overprint. Lowering the 'Overprint Limit' may be necessary when doing any significant coloring effects in Quark, and the printer should be informed of this preference change.

Generally, only three out of the six

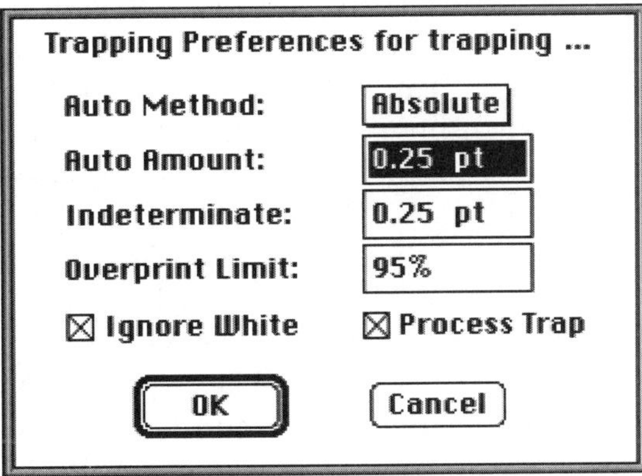

settings provided in the Trap Information window in Quark are used. Those settings are: Overprint, Knockout, and Custom. The other three settings, Default, Auto Amount (+), and Auto Amount (-) use the 'Auto Amount' value set in the Trapping Preferences dialog box to determine trapping values. These values can change from computer to computer, and even though the preferences on one computer may be set properly, there is no guarantee that the next computer down the line is set the same way. Select each item in the document and change its setting from Default to its appropriate setting.

To create chokes and spreads, your

Trap Information

Frame Inside:	Default	Overprint	?
Frame Outside:	Auto Amount (+)	0.144 pt	
Text:	Auto Amount (-)	-0.144 pt	

Trap Information

Frame Inside:	Custom	0.25 pt
Frame Outside:	Knockout	Knockout
Text:	Overprint	Overprint

setting will be Custom. A choke will have a negative value (e.g. -.25 pt); a spread will have a positive value (e.g. .25 pt). Knockouts should be used for small colored type or when the objects in question trap naturally (yellow knocks-out of red). Knockouts of colors that do not trap naturally create a kiss fit, or, in other words, the colors abut with no trapping at all (as is the case with the color TIFF overlay). Likewise, you should only Overprint 100K (**NOT** the 'rich black') or colors which trap naturally (red overprints yellow).

Quark cannot choke objects placed on top of Photoshop backgrounds that are made up of indeterminate or multiple colors. In these instances the item in question must be spread despite its actual color value. Keep this in mind when creating type in Quark, because the spread may adversely alter the shape of the letter forms.

Placed art can easily be resized and distorted in Quark, which can be essential when designing. When the job is complete, all art should be resized in there native programs. This is especially important for Illustrator files to preserve trapping. If a stroke of .5 pt is set in Illustrator, and is then resized to 25% in Quark, the resulting trap is virtually non-existent at .125 pt.

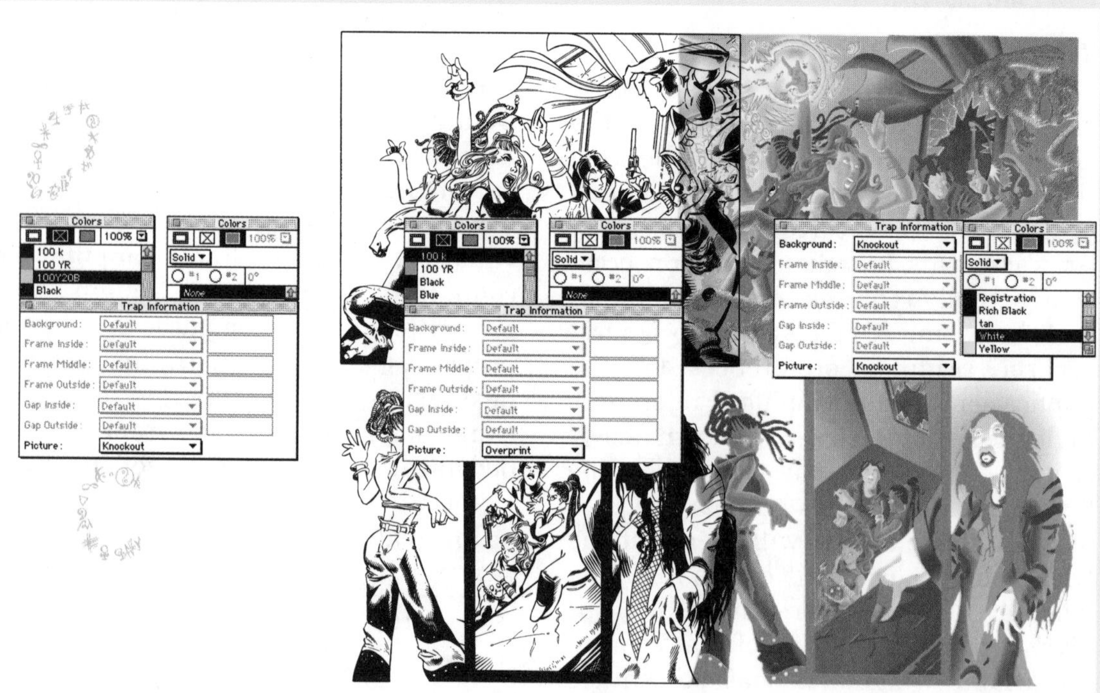

This example shows how three separate TIFF files are combined in Quark Express. The bottom-most art box has a background color of white and contains the CMYK file. Both are set to knockout in the trap info window. The middle layer contains the high resolution black line art set to overprint 100K, with a background color of none. The top layer contains bitmap line art which is set to knockout C20Y100, also with no background color.

GLOSSARY

anchor point–the graphic element that is used to define a vector and to edit that vector's curve in illustration programs.

art board–correctly proportioned paper that has pre-printed guides for trim, bleeds, and safe copy area. These boards are usually distributed by comic book companies in order to maintain their proportion constant.

art size–the size and dimensions of the original hand drawn artwork.

banding–a term used to describe visible 'jumps' between values within a gradation. Banding occurs there are too few gray levels to support a smooth transition from one value to the next. This can occur when the LPI of an imagesetter is set too high.

balloon–the graphic element that displays speech or thought in comics.

balloon placement–a photocopy of artwork on which the location of balloons and captions are laid out and numbered with a magic marker. The letterer uses the balloon placement as a guide when lettering a page.

baseline-The imaginary line on which the majority of characters in a typeface rest.

Bézier curve–the mathematical curve described by two anchor points used by most graphic art programs. The curve is edited by manipulating handles located on each anchor point associated with the curve. Removing the handles entirely creates a straight line. This interactive design tool was named after its developer, Pierre Bézier.

binding–the process used to assemble the pages and signatures of a magazine or book.

bit depth–the number of binary digits associated with individual pixels in an image. The number of 'bits' defines how much information a pixel contains. An image with a bit depth of one can only be black and white. An 8-bit image contains 256 (or 2^8) shades of gray. Color images usually contain 24 or 32-bits.

bitmap–a grid upon which the location of individual pixels are mapped. However, the term bitmap usually refers to an image that contains one bit of information per pixel. The pixels in such an image are either black (1) or white (0), with no possible shades of gray.

bleed–the area on the outside of a page that will be cut off when the final comic book is cut down to size. In a bleed comic, art is drawn into this area and 'lost' so that the printed art will extend beyond the trim. Non-bleed art also has a bleed, but no art is allowed to be drawn in this area so that pages can be butted closer together on the printing plates.

blueline–a printing proof made directly from the film separations used to check pagination, page count, layout, and positioning. Bluelines are the last stage at which corrections can be made. They are named for their blue color and are made in a similar fashion to architectural blueprints.

bounding box–a graphic element associated with the digital lettering files of comic book. The bounding box uses the dimensions of the magazines proportion constant to insure proper alignment when placing lettering files over artwork in a page layout program.

butt-two areas of color that meet edge to edge without overlapping. Also called a kiss fit.

caption–the graphic element that displays non-dialog narration in comics. The shape of captions are usually rectangular, but can be made ornate in any number of ways.

channel–an 8-bit section of an image in Photoshop. They are used to create the printing plates during color separation, and this may include spot colors for additional ink plates. Additional channels can be created to form editable masks, the digital equivalent of airbrush frisket. These masks are also used to save selections for key areas of art that may need repeated editing.

choke–Creating a trap using the background color.

clipping path–an embedded path used in raster images to define transparent and opaque areas in page layout programs. Photoshop clipping path documents must be saved as EPS's to be imported into Quark.

CMYK–the acronym for the four-color ink process or the 32-bit color space associated with it. The colors are cyan, magenta, yellow, and black. Black is given the letter K to distinguish it from blue.

collate-to gather pages together in a particular order for binding

color chart–a printing guide supplied to colorists displaying printed color combinations labeled with the ink percentages used to identify each individual color. Color charts are usually printed using 10% or 25% increments of ink values.

color codes–the codes used to identify colors by percentages of printing ink.

color correction–the term used to describe the adjustments made to a color image or scan to insure the most faithful printed reproduction when converting from RGB to CMYK. Color corrections are most often associated with scans made of color photographs or paintings.

color guide–a hand-painted guide created and coded by a colorist to be used by the separator to create printing film.

color hold–when line art is held as a color other than black.

color-matching system–Systems based on numbered color samples used by designers and printers to specify individual colors and inks.

color overlay–a piece of line art created to be held as a color or special effect. It is usually It is usually drawn and inked separately from the line art that is to remain black, usually on a piece of vellum overlay.

color separation–separating a multicolor image into monochrome elements used to create printing plates.

color sequence–the order in which inks are printed on press. The color sequence for process colors is usually yellow, magenta, cyan, and black.

color space–a system used to identify the range and limitations of comparative color models. The RGB 24-bit color space is based on the wavelengths of light, and contains millions of colors. The CMYK color space, although being 32-bit, is much smaller in comparison because it is based on printing inks.

color value–the tonal value of a color on a scale from light to dark in comparison to the colors equivalent value in grayscale.

compositing–a digital production process that involves combining two or more raster images together. In comic book production, it is the digital equivalent of 'pasting up' word balloons to artwork. Combining digital lettering with artwork in a page layout program is sometimes mistakenly referred to as *compositing*, when '*placement*' is a more accurate term. Transferring digital logos or sound effects from an illustration format into artwork is referred to as '*stripping*.'

continuous-tone -artwork or printouts that show gray scales or colors as uninterrupted solid values, such as photographs.

cover stock–the grade of paper used for printing covers on magazines or books. Cover stock is usually a thicker, with a slick look or feel.

crossover–artwork that is printed to carryover from one page, across the fold, onto the facing page, is said to crossover.

curves–in Photoshop it is one of several editable representations of tonal range. Curves are arguably the most versatile, and are most closely associated with color corrections.

darken mode–this blending mode uses

the higher value of each channel to create the end color. Therefore, darkening C20M40Y50K15 into C50 M40Y30K0 will result in the color C50 M40Y50K15. This mode should be considered the 'all purpose trapping mode' and is used when adding the black plate to the color channels. However, you need to be careful when using this mode with layers. The background layer should be deleted to white, except for the area to be trapped.

DCS(*Desktop Color Separations*)–an EPS file format that converts color images into its component color separation files. A 72 ppi image preview is also created that can be imported into page layout programs. This format can spool extremely quickly through an imagesetter, but can be somewhat fragile and prone to corruption. Once a file is saved in this format it no longer exists as a single document. The files would have to be reassembled if any editing were required. Also, proofing printers may only print out the 72 ppi preview.

die cut–holes in the cover that are cut out in specific shapes to reveal areas of art on a secondary cover. The term die refers to the tool used to make the cut.

dot gain–the enlargement of halftone spots that can occur at various stages in the printing process. Dot gain is measured by its effect on the midtone values. Therefore if a 50% value increases to 70%, dot gain is said to be 20%.

dpi(*dots per inch*)–usually refers to the number of halftone spots per linear inch. This acronym is mistakenly used for every form of resolution.

embossing–creating a raised or indented surface on a cover.

EPS(*Encapsulated PostScript*)–A file format that was created specifically to describe curves and angles associated with fonts and artwork Most imagesetters use the postscript language to translate art into film, therefore this is usually the better format for saving color files.

feathering–the blending of a selection with its surrounding areas in Photoshop. Feathering set at zero creates a hard edge line. Increasing the feathering softens, or blurs, the edge.

fifth-color–the addition of extra inks to the four color process. Two additional inks would be referred to as a six-color job.

film output–the process of creating color separations on an imagesetter. The acetate film is then used to create printing plates.

filter–an image editing tool used in Photoshop used to create specific effects, such as motion blurs, or textures.

flats–*in computer coloring or separations*, the idea of using a 'flat' value of color for each object in an entire image that can later be easily selected using the magic wand tool for editing and modeling.

In printing, a flat is a term applied to the assembled composite of film imposition used to make printing plates.

flocking–tiny, fine fibers of wool, rayon, or like substance, applied to a cover with glue to form a velvet like pattern.

foil–a specialty effect used on covers involving hot stamping a piece of metallic foil to the cover after the four color inks have been applied. There are some types of foil covers that simply use a foil paper stock.

font–a complete set of characters or symbols which share the same size and style.

font family–a complete character set of a font, that shares a common style and includes all sizes, weights, and postures (such as oblique or italic).

gamut–the range of colors capable of being reproduced by a color model. In CMYK, colors that fall out of gamut are considered unprintable. Photoshop provides a gamut warning view that highlight RGB colors that fall outside of the printable CMYK gamut.

gatefold–additional paper added to a page (usually a cover) which folds out from the book.

GCR(*gray-component replacement*)–substitutes black ink for areas where CMY inks produce gray when converting from some other color space. Unlike UCR, gray-component replacement effects the entire image.

ghost–to reduce the tonal values in a section of an image to make them appear lighter and insubstantial.

gradation–a transition from one color to another. A visible tonal jump within a gradation is called banding.

gutter–the space left between panel boarders, which, in non bleed books includes the margin area.

halftone–the process or image that reproduces the illusion gray tones by creating spots of solid ink of varying size. Each color plate in the printing process is created as a halftone.

halftone cell–a grid pattern of printing dots used to create halftone spots. The number of printing dots available to a halftone cell affects the number of gray tones that can be reproduced.

halftone spot–a spot whose size and shape can be varied within a halftone. Spots are made up of printer dots which are a fixed size.

highlight–The lightest part of an image or object that is the result of receiving the greatest amount of illumination.

imagesetting–*see film output*

imposition–the process of arranging pages for print, so that they will be in order AFTER the publication is folded, bound, and cut. These arranged pages are referred to as signatures.

ink saturation–the maximum amount of ink a paper stock can absorb safely. Exceeding the ink saturation limit can cause printing errors.

interpolation–the mathematical

process of estimating intermediate values during resampling.

italic–a font style in which letters slant to the right.

JPEG(*Joint Photographic Experts Group*)–A compressed file format that is considered 'lossy' because it discards image data and sacrifices quality. Files in this format can be imported into Quark and will display properly on the screen, however they will turn into grayscale when imageset. The EPS formats can be saved with a JPEG preview, but this too should be avoided.

kerning–improving the legibility of certain pairs of letters that do not work well together with normal letterspacing. These characters are referred to as kerning pairs.

kerning pairs–pairs of letters that do not work well together with normal letterspacing, and need to be edited to improve legibility. Kerning pairs for all capital comic lettering include: *AV, AT, AY, AW, CO*. In a font that includes both upper and lower case, there are many more troublesome pairs.

kiss fit–two areas of color that meet edge to edge without overlapping. Also called a *butt*.

knockout–The opposite of overprint. Knockouts create a hole in background colors to accommodate objects or colors in the foreground. Unless properly trapped, knockouts will create a kiss-fit where two colors butt together without overlapping.

K-tones–the term used for gray values in color separations and comic coloring.

layer–a part of the printing Photoshop art that contains information for all four printing plates, therefore, requiring more memory than individual channels. However, they are separate from the background, similar to an overlay. Individual layers can be edited without affecting the whole of the art. They can also be used to create editable special effects over specified areas of art.

leading (pronounced *'ledding'*)–is the space between rows of type stacked on top of each other. The measurements for leading is taken from baseline to baseline.

letterspacing–the space that falls in between letters. Too much or too little spacing can make words difficult to read.

lighten mode–this blending mode uses the lower value of each channel to create the end color. Therefore, lightening C20M40Y50K15 into C50M40Y30K0 will result in the color C20M40Y30K0. This mode is very rarely used, and is generally restricted to certain special effects. Although it is of very limited use in trapping, it is a very valuable tool to know when coloring logos or creating certain ghosting effects.

line art–artwork that is reproduced as a single color with no midtone values.

logo–the trademarked artwork used for the name of a magazine or company that appears on the cover or in advertising.

lpi(*lines per inch*)–is the number of rows of halftone spots per linear inch used during imagesetting or when creating halftones. The lpi plays a key role in determining the proper resolution needed to reproduce color and gray scale images.

LZW(*Lemple-Zif-Welch*)–a file format that uses a non-lossy image compression system that looks for long strings of repeating binary code or pixels and replaces them with a code that defines this repetition. Some imagesetters and application programs can not open (or decompress) this format. It is best to check with the printer before saving any files in this format.

makeready–all work done to set up a press for printing. Within the publishing industry, a makeready is an uncut signature that is used to view the finished job.

margin–the white area located between the art and the trim on non-bleed pages.

mask–a saved selection or channel that is used to edit an image.

match print–a digital printout of final pages that is used to match colors as closely as possible on the press. Printers will try to match colors as closely as possible to a match print.

mechanical–a term used for an analog paste-up of artwork and type on to a single art board that is reproduced photographically, thereby referred to as camera-ready.

mechanical pen–a pen designed to create straight lines of a consistent width using india ink. This type of pen is used to rule out mechanical boards.

metallic ink–an ink with a metallic sheen, that is created using metal powder suspended in a printing medium.

minus–the function of subtracting the shape of one object from the shape of a second object in Illustrator.

modeling–the addition of highlight and shadow colors in an image to define form and lighting conditions.

multiply mode–this blending mode adds the values of colors in the palette to the colors already present in a selection. Therefore, multiplying C20M40 Y50K15 into C50M40Y30K0 will result in the color C70M80Y80K15. Multiplying a color several times will make the color darker each time. Generally, this mode is used to increase the values of a single plate over multiple colors.

normal mode–the blending mode in Photoshop that replaces the colors inside a marquee selection with the color chosen in the palette. It blends the neighboring colors at the edge of the selection.

overprint–when colors or inks are printed one on top of another. For instance yellow overprints blue to create green.

overlay–any piece of art or lettering that is created separately from the line art, usually on a piece of vellum or acetate that is placed on top of the art.

page line-up–a form or guide that lists the order and page number on which articles, illustrations, advertisements, and the like, are to be printed. Printers use this page line-up when creating an imposition file.

Pantone Matching System–the registered trade name of a color system applied to a series of inks, paper, and other related design tools that is considered to be an industry standard.

Pantone inks–a series of 17 printer inks that are mixed in specific formulas to create all colors listed in the Pantone matching system. There are also a series of specialty inks for metallic and fluorescent colors.

paste-up–the production process of creating camera-ready mechanicals by hand using razor blades, glue, wax, overlays and photostats.

path–the vector line that defines the shape of an object in Illustrator. The path falls exactly in the center of a stroke.

perfect binding–involves gathering signatures together in a stack. The back of the signatures are ground to create a rough surface end then glued to the spine of the cover. This is also referred to as a square-bound book.

photostat–a method of reproducing images photographically. Prior to the advent of computer technology, this was the only way to create film, color separate full color art, and ultimately create printing plates.

pica–printer's unit of measurement used principally in typesetting or typography. One pica equals approximately 1/6 of an inch.

pixel(*picture element*)–is the smallest square section of a grid pattern that makes up a raster image. The dimensions of a pixel can be altered without changing data, thereby changing only the dimensions of an image.

point–printer's unit of measurement used principally for designating type sizes. There are 12 points to a pica; approximately 72 points to an inch.

ppi(*pixels per inch*)–is the number of pixels per linear inch used in calculating digital resolutions.

pre-flight–the process of checking the accuracy and formats of all components of a completed job before imagesetting.

prepress–the term used to describe any process used to prepare any work to be printed on a printing press.

press proof–a proof printed on a press prior to an actual print run that is rarely done due to cost.

press run–the number of copies in one printing.

print size–the size and dimensions of a printed magazine.

proportion constant–documents created by different software applications must be created with identical dimensions in order to properly align when printed. This size is determined by the trim for non bleed books, and the bleed for bleed books and covers. This proportion constant is used to create all templates, and to set-up all Photoshop documents.

raster image–a pixel based image. This type of image is created using a grid, called a raster, on which the location of square pixels are mapped (a *bitmap*). The term bitmap image usually refers to a 1 bit black and white raster image.

ream–five hundred sheets of paper

register mark–the symbol used to indicate a trademark; either a ® or ™ are used in publishing.

registration–the correct alignment of colors during printing

registration mark–a cross and circle mark defining the correct alignment of overlays and color during printing.

resampling–the alteration of pixel resolution. This is done by changing pixel resolution without changing image dimensions, or vice versa.

resolution–the term used to quantify the size of picture elements (such as *pixels, dots, or spots*) of any given device or output. The term resolution may have different unequivocable attributes depending on the device in question, leading to a great deal of confusion and miscommunication within the industry.

resolution free *or* **resolution independent**–the term applied to vector images, whose resolution is determined during printing. When an illustration is being outputted, the imagesetter uses the mathematical definitions to calculate the line being set at the optimum quality of the imagesetter. The illustration will be the maximum resolution of the printing device used.

reverse out–a term used when line art is held as a lighter color and knocks out of a darker background, such as white type reversing out of a colored background.

RGB–the acronym for the three colors within the 24 bit color space associated with light wavelengths. The colors are red, green, and blue. The absence of all three colors creates black, the presence of 100% of each color produces white.

rule–a solid or dashed line

ruling pen–a pen designed to create straight lines of a consistent width using india ink, gauche, or paint. Prior to the creation of mechanical pens, this type of pen is used to rule out mechanical boards. These pens are still used in painting and illustration.

saddle-stitched–a binding process that involves inserting folded impositions, or signatures, inside one another to form a common spine. They are then 'stitched' together with metal staples.

safe area–also called copy area. Since there is a certain amount of movement on the printing press, binders, and cutters; the exact location were each individual comic will trim varies slightly. The area of the page in which the cutter will never intrude upon is called the safe area. It is important that you keep all copy and word balloons inside this area so that they don't accidentally trim off.

scratch disk–free hard drive space which is utilized by pixel based programs to 'remember' changes in images in order to accommodate multiple undo's.

selection–the area of art that has been cordoned off for editing purposes. Only the art within this selected area can be affected.

set up–the process of preparing raw scans for the various forms of production and prepress work that need to be performed before imagesetting.

shade *or* **shading**–The darkest part of an image or object that is the result of receiving the least amount of illumination.

signature–a folded imposition

sound effect–the graphic elements that display noise other than speech in comics.

special effects–in coloring and separations; any manipulation of the line art to produce a specific look or effect, such as blurs, ghosts, or lens flares.

specialty covers–any cover that requires additional press work or printing processes, such as embossing, foil stamping, and the addition of additional inks. Covers that use an unusual paper stock may not require additional press work, but are still considered specialty covers.

spine–the back of a bound book connecting the two covers.

spread–*in trapping*: creating a trap using the color of the object in the foreground.

in production: two facing pages. Art that is drawn to cross from one page over to its facing page is usually referred to as a *double-page spread*.

stair step–the problem that arises when individual pixels can be seen at normal magnification.

stripping–*in printing*: the positioning (or editing) of film separations on a flat to compose a page or layout for platemaking.

In digital production: transferring digital logos or sound effects from an illustration format into pixel based artwork is referred to as stripping.

stroke–the colored line that can be created on top of a path in Illustrator, which can be used to trap an object.

thermography–a specialty effect that creates raised ink by applying a resin to the wet image and applying heat.

threshold–the point at which a gray value becomes either black or white.

TIFF(*Tagged-Image File Format*)–a file format commonly used to save images. All black line bitmap art to be imported into Quark must be saved as TIFF's so that they can be trapped properly. Also, any bitmap line art that will be used as a color hold in Quark must be saved in this format. Color files may be smaller when saved as TIFF's as opposed to EPS format.

tradedress–art that appears on a cover that displays necessary publishing and purchasing information. It prominently contains the name or logo of the publishing company, as well as: the publication month, the issue number, and (usually) the price.

trademark–pieces of art or logos used in the promotion of trade. These include company logos, cover logos, and any piece of art used to identify a specific company or book title. These trademarks are indicated by one of two symbols (for publishing), they are ™ and ®.

trapping–the intentional overlapping of colors to hide misregistration problems that occur during printing.

trim–the 'line' where a comic will be cut when printed. Any art that goes outside this line will 'bleed' off the page.

typeface–the interpretation, design, or appearance of a character set or font.

UCR(*undercolor removal*)–substitutes black ink only in areas where RGB colors produce black when converting to the CMYK color space. Unlike GCR, undercolor removal does not add K-tones to the entire image, but can create an unusual color cast.

undercolor–the actual underprinting color used to create a rich black during printing.

underprint–the addition of CMY inks to 100% black areas of an image to produce a rich black during printing.

vector–the section of line between two anchor points, multiple vectors form a path.

vector graphics–objects created in vector based illustration programs that are defined by mathematical lines and curves.

word spacing–the amount of space between each word in a line text. Unlike letterspacing, it can be varied to adjust line length without affecting readability.

wrapping *or* **wrap up**–the process of preparing a file to be sent to a printer, that involves preflight, copying files to disk, printing reports, etc.

RESOURCES

Here is a list of books which I highly recommend.

Scanning

Real World Scanning and Halftones
by David Blatner and Steve Roth
Peachpit Press, Inc
ISBN#1-56609-093-8

An Introduction to Digital Scanning
part of the *Digital Colour Prepress* series
Agfa Prepress Education Resources
P.O. Box 7917, Mt. Prospect, IL
60056-7917 tel:1-800-395-7007

Prepress/Production

Pocket Pal
A Graphic Arts Production Handbook
International Paper
No ISBN#, but is usually available in art stores. *This is a must have item.*

The Official Adobe Print Publishing Guide
Adobe Press
ISBN#1-56830-468-4
Highly recommended!

Digital Prepress Complete
by Donnie O'Quinn and Matt LeClair with Steve Kurth and Tim Plumer
Hayden Books
ISBN#1-56830-328-9
For advanced users, this 762 page tome is not light reading and is used as an encyclopedia of knowledge.

Makeready: A Prepress Resource
by Dan Margulis
MIS:Press, Inc
ISBN#1-55828-508-3
A series of educational article on the subject. *Highly recommended!*

The following are good introductory level books on prepress work, but essentially cover the same material:

Introducing Desktop Prepress
by Tim Meehan
MIS:Press, Inc
ISBN#1-55828-364-1

Color Publishing on the Macintosh
by Kim and Sunny Baker
Random House
ISBN#0-679-73977-7

Trapping

The Complete Guide to Trapping
by Brian P. Lawler
Hayden Books
ISBN#1-56830-098-0
A must have item. Highly recommended!

Color Correction

Professional Photoshop 5
by Dan Margulis
John Wiley & Sons, Inc
ISBN#0-471-32308-X
Don't let the name mislead you, the entire book is dedicated to the art of color correcting color photographs and artwork Highly recommended!

Computer Programs

Dozens of books on Quark Express, Adobe Illustrator, and Adobe Photoshop come out whenever the programs are upgraded, making it difficult to recommend specific books. However, I can recommend three imprints that put out good guides for these programs aimed at the new user.

... For Dummies
IDG Books
www.dummies.com
This is a good series for learning how to use a program for the first time.

Adobe ... Classroom in a Book
Adobe Press
A complete training manual with CDs.

Visual Quickstart Guide
Peachpit Press
www.peachpit.com
These are good reference books to keep close by for looking up specific solutions quickly. They are handy for every level of user, particularly after a program is upgraded. Fondly referred to as the Bunnie Books around our office.

Drawing

Drawing on the Right Side of the Brain
by Betty Edwards
J.P. Tarcher
ISBN#0-87477-088-2

Dynamic Drawing
by Burnie Hogarth
Watson-Guptoll
ISBN#0-87477-088-2
I highly recommend any and all of the Dynamic Drawing series by Burnie Hogart. There are about six of these books on specific topics such as hands, shading, etc.

How to Draw the Human Figure: An Anatomical Approach
by Louise Gordon
Penguin Books
ISBN#0-14046-477-8

Bridgeman's Complete Guide to Drawing from Life
by George Bridgeman
Sterling
Out of Print! But most chapters of this book are currently available separately as Dover Paperbacks.

How to Draw Animals
by Jack Hamm
Grosset & Dunlad
ISBN#0-448-01908-6

Inking

The Art of Comic Book Inking
by Gary Martin with Steve Rude
Dark Horse Comics
ISBN#1-56971-258-1
Highly recommended

Sequential Storytelling

Comics and Sequential Art
by Will Eisner
Eclipse Books
ISBN#0-9614728-0-2
Highly recommended!

Understanding Comics – The Invisible Art
by Scott McCloud
Tundra
ISBN#1-56862-019-5
Highly recommended!

Shot by Shot
by Stephen D Katz
Michael Wise Productions
ISBN#0-941188-10-8
This book is actual on film directing.

INDEX

art board, 15, 21, 24, 25, 30, 53, 54, 95

art size, 14, 21–24, 26, 31, 39

banding, 165

balloon placement, 53, 60, 62, 63, 70

balloon shape, 61, 64–66

binding, 16, 162

bit depth, 27, 33

bitmap, 19, 29, 31–34, 36, 40, 42–44, 46, 48, 55, 79, 96, 104, 105, 130, 131, 145, 147, 163, 166, 177

bleed, 17, 20–25, 30, 39–42, 50, 558, 70, 71, 99–103, 109, 118, 119, 124, 125, 129, 131, 162, 191

bounding box, 42, 56, 58–60, 70, 71, 102

channel, 33, 36, 45, 46, 90–97, 109, 115, 128–139, 143, 145, 151–154, 176–181

clipping path, 21, 51, 96, 117, 122, 123

CMYK, 19, 33, 36, 45, 66, 71, 80–85, 90–97, 104, 105, 131, 133, 142, 145, 150–154, 157, 168, 171, 179

color correction, 149–155

color guide, 79, 151

color hold, 79, 85, 90, 92, 94–96, 104, 105, 179, 180

color overlay, 45, 46, 85, 95, 145, 148, 161

compositing, 49
 in Quark, 99–109
 in Photoshop, 127–139

compound paths, 116, 176, 177

curves (Photoshop adjustment), 35, 37, 85, 92, 93, 115, 120, 137, 151–154, 176

DCS, 96, 143, 144

die cut, 141, 145–148

dot gain, 20, 29, 34, 35, 151, 167–169

double-page spreads, 23–25, 31, 49, 50, 70, 71, 101–104, 106, 162

dpi, 28, 29, 34, 43, 121, 164–167

embossing, 148–149

EPS, 21, 71, 96, 100, 101, 104, 117, 143

fifth color, 104, 142–148

film output, *also see imagesetting*, 20, 21, 27, 28, 55, 68, 102, 145,165

filter, *Illustrator*, 64, 65, 68–70, 115, 116, 176, 177
filter, *Photoshop*, 80, 81, 91–93, 179

flats, 85, 88, 178

foil, 141, 146, 148

gamut, 90, 151–153

gatefold, 21, 23, 25, 119, 120

GCR, 151, 154

ghost, 95, 108, 129, 137, 182

gradation, 33, 64, 74, 79, 92–99, 106, 115, 116, 165, 167, 174–178, 180

gutter, 17, 21, 23, 99, 118, 119

halftone, 28, 34–37, 179, 163–168

imagesetting, *also see film output*, 21, 27, 28, 30, 34, 37, 42, 54, 55, 68, 71, 74, 75, 85, 96, 104, 105, 108, 116, 117, 122, 123, 143–145, 160, 163–166, 174–176

imposition, 16, 70, 102, 104, 108, 157, 160, 161

ink saturation, *also see oversaturation*, 20, 80, 81, 90, 91, 94, 95, 145, 152, 154, 162, 169, 179–181

JPEG, 96

kerning, 57

kiss fit, 105, 107, 122, 184

knockout, 18, 19, 61, 64, 72–74, 100, 105, 107, 109, 117, 145, 146, 170–174, 177, 183
layer, *Illustrator*, 56, 58, 60, 61, 64–69, 74, 75, 114, 115, 174–177
Photoshop, 33, 46, 48–50, 92–97, 128–131, 136–138, 181, 182
Quark, 101, 105

line art, 21, 27, 29, 30–36, 42, 44–48, 60, 69, 71, 78, 81, 84–86, 90–96, 105, 106, 117, 120–126, 130–136, 146, 148, 153, 165, 178–180

logo, 11, 53, 54, 66, 68, 75, 82, 111–116, 118–123, 127–138, 144, 149, 150, 158, 175, 176, 181–183

lpi, 20, 28, 165, 166

LZW, 96

margin, 99, 100, 102, 109, 118, 119

mask, 33, 69, 70, 78, 82, 92, 93, 131–136, 154, 182, 183

minus, 64, 69, 70, 115, 116, 176, 177

modeling, 83, 85–90, 178, 179

overprint, 18, 19, 55, 60, 64–68, 72–75, 85, 91, 96, 100, 105–107, 109, 121, 145–147, 159, 170–175, 179–184

oversaturation, *also see ink saturation*, 80, 95, 144, 153, 154, 181

Pantone, 142–146, 151

path, 18, 55, 64–67, 69, 72, 113, 116, 168, 172, 176, 177

perfect binding, 16

ppi, 28–31, 43, 44, 90, 96, 101, 131, 150, 163, 165, 166, 180

pre-flight, 71, 157, 159

print size, 21, 23, 28, 30, 34, 39, 130, 131, 150

proportion constant, 22, 40–43, 46, 58–60, 99, 102, 103, 106, 122

resampling, 44, 43, 85, 166

resolution, 20, 23, 27–31, 34, 36, 39, 42–46, 51, 55, 69, 79, 85, 90, 102, 105, 106, 113, 117, 128–133, 150, 163–167, 179–181

resolution free vectors, 55, 56, 121

RGB, 18, 33, 66, 80–82, 90–93, 97, 150–154, 157, 168, 171, 179

saddle-stitched, 16, 103, 161

safe copy area, 20–25, 41, 58, 70, 99, 102, 109, 118

scratch disk, 97

signature, 16, 160, 161

sound effect, 47, 48, 53–58, 66–75, 115, 116, 172–176

specialty covers, 138, 141–149

spine, 16, 118, 119

stair step, 32, 43, 85, 101, 105, 106, 129, 166, 167, 182

stroke, 18, 19, 55, 58, 60, 61, 64–69, 72–75, 107, 116, 146, 170–177, 184

threshold, 31–36, 40, 44, 49, 150

TIFF, 21, 41, 44, 46, 49, 96, 100–105, 145, 147, 184

tradedress, 111–113, 117, 120

trademark, 158–159

trapping, 18–20, 44, 61, 64, 66, 68–75, 81, 82, 85, 86, 90–93, 96, 100, 101, 104–109, 115–117, 121, 122, 127–137, 142–146, 148, 154, 157, 162, 169–184

trim, 17, 21–25, 39, 41, 42, 58, 59, 70, 99–103, 109, 118, 119, 124, 125, 129, 161, 162

UCR, 153, 154

undercolor, 81, 90, 117, 179, 180

underprint, 72, 83, 86, 90–94, 104, 105, 125, 126, 130, 131, 135, 154, 155, 157, 162, 169, 172, 178–181

vector, 18, 55, 115, 116, 170, 176

wrap around, 25, 118–120

About the Author

Kevin 'Stickman' Tinsley has been working as a graphic artist for over 15 years. He works as a consultant, and is considered by many to be the leading expert on digital prepress and production for the comic book industry.

Stickman graduated from Virginia Commonwealth University in 1986 with a BFA in Painting and Printmaking, with minors in Art History, and Philosophy. In 1989, he graduated from the Joe Kubert School of Cartoon and Graphic Arts, and began working at Marvel Comics shortly thereafter.

At Marvel, Stick has worked as a colorist, separator, inker, and in art corrections. He rose through the ranks of the production department until 1995, when, as senior cover coordinator, he was assigned the task of assisting in the production department's transition from analog paste-up to digital compositing.

"Make sure it works," they said.

"Or else!"

And so it went until the job was complete in 1997, and Mr. Stickman took his leave from the staff position and entered the freelance community.

After over half a decade of dashing the dreams and aspirations of bright, highly skilled computer artists who had never been taught the requirements of publishing and basic production values, Stickman decided to write this book.

Deborah S. Creighton
editor

Deborah S. Creighton is a writer and editor. She was going to draw her picture, but was told she would be sued for trademark infringement for drawing a stick figure.

Timothy Smith III
penciler

Every road has its stops along the way to whatever it is that you want to reach in life. It's not the distance that you travel but the things you do along the way that can easily become the most important experience of your career. I've done illustrations for Off Broadway shows, and newspapers. Also, graphic design work in **Computering Japan**, and for Marvel Comics cover department. But in the wonderful arena of comic art, I've done work for Caliber and Marvel. I love the life I have chosen, this twisty path of illustration and computer craziness. Nonstop action and learning from here to Japan and back. This project was fun and I really love what I have contributed here, but it's time to move on and hope the next thing I do is as much fun as this was!!

Scott Koblish
inker

Scott Koblish's current incarnation has neither long nor blue hair on top of his head. He resides above the floor planes of the South Village in New York. While seemingly harmless, he is a barely contained whirlwind of rage, love and fear. His only outlet is his work, over which he obsessively spends every waking hour of every day pouring out onto two ply Bristol board. He works freelance for such companies as Marvel Comics, DC Comics, Scholastic and Disney. Some of his credits include: **Captain America, Doom 2099**, **Elektra**, **Excalibur**, **Mr. Myxzptlyk**, **Punisher:Year One**, **Superman One Million**, **X-Factor**, and countless licensed products from Marvel. He is working on his own comic book, **SK8**, which he hopes to have in stores sometime in the year 2000.

Fred Haynes
penciler

I've been in this business for over seven years. I've penciled books from **Marvel Comics Presents** to **What If**. I'm the most pleased with **Green Lantern #49**, a career high for me. Over the years, however, this has become a job for me and jobs stink. So I've been away for awhile to help me remember why I was doing this in the first place. It's never been to work for a big company like Marvel or DC. It has been and always will be to bring my characters and stories to life. Be on the lookout for **The F...** coming in 2000.

Gregg Schigiel
penciler

Gregg Schigiel was born and rasied in South Florida. He now lives in New York City, working for Marvel Comics as an assistant editor and comic book penciler. He plans on reading this book, or at least a good portion of it, to possibly glean even a fraction of the knowledge possessed by Kevin "Stick" Tinsley, the zen-master of production.

Keith Williams
inker

Keith Williams graduated from the School of Visual Arts in 1980. He started working for Marvel in 1982 as a background artist; about a year later he became the first Romita Raider. The following year, Keith became the assistant editor of the **Spider-Man** line of books for about nine months. The rest is a blur, working as a background assistant for John Byrne on **Alpha Flight**, **The Hulk** and **Action Comics**, and inking **Web of Spider-Man** for four years. **Quasar**, **Silver Surfer**, **Warlock Chronicles**, and **The Mask** for Dark Horse were other inking assignments. For the past five years he has worked on **The Phantom** comicstrip, which was created by Lee Falk, for King Features Syndicate.

Pondscum
inker

'Nuff said.

Dave Sharpe
letterer

WENT TO THE KUBERT SCHOOL...
LETTERED HUNDREDS OF BOOKS...
HAPPILY MARRIED...
HAS REPRODUCED... (TWICE!)
CURRENTLY RUNS THE MARVEL
IN-HOUSE LETTERING DEPARTMENT...
GOES TO A BAPTIST CHURCH (REGULARLY!)
TRIES TO AVOID STICK...

Order Form

☎ Fax orders: (718) 788-8858

☛Online orders: stickmangraphics.com

✉ Postal Orders: Stickman Graphics
141 16th Street
Brooklyn, NY 11215

Please send a copy of *Digital Prepress for Comic Books* to:

Name: ______________________________

Address: ______________________________

City: ____________ State: ________ Zip: ____________

Telephone: (____) ________________

Sales Tax: Please add 8.25% for books shipped to New York addresses.

Shipping:

Payment:

❑Check

❑Credit Card ❑VISA ❑Mastercard ❑Optima ❑AMEX ❑Discover

Card Number: ______________________________

Name on card: ____________________ Exp. date: /

I understand that I may return this book for a full refund– for any reason, no questions asked.

Order Form

☎ Fax orders: (718) 788-8858

☛Online orders: stickmangraphics.com

✉ Postal Orders: Stickman Graphics
141 16th Street
Brooklyn, NY 11215

Please send a copy of *Digital Prepress for Comic Books* to:

Name: ______________________________

Address: ______________________________

City: ______________ State: __________ Zip: ______________

Telephone: (____) ______________________

Sales Tax: Please add 8.25% for books shipped to New York addresses.

Shipping:

Payment:

❑Check

❑Credit Card ❑VISA ❑Mastercard ❑Optima ❑AMEX ❑Discover

Card Number: ______________________________

Name on card: ______________________ Exp. date: /

I understand that I may return this book for a full refund– for any reason, no questions asked.